M

Rekindling Desire

Rekindling Desire

A STEP-BY-STEP PROGRAM TO HELP
LOW-SEX AND NO-SEX MARRIAGES

Barry McCarthy, Ph.D.,
and Emily McCarthy

Brunner-Routledge
New York and Hove

Published in 2003 by
Brunner-Routledge
29 West 35th Street
New York, NY 10001
www.brunner-routledge.com

Published in Great Britain by
Brunner-Routledge
27 Church Road
Hove, East Sussex
BN3 2FA
www.brunner-routledge.co.uk

10 9 8 7 6 5 4 3 2 1

Library of Congress Cataloging-in-Publication Data

McCarthy, Barry, W., 1943–
        Rekindling desire : a step-by-step program to help low-sex and no-sex marriages /
Barry McCarthy and Emily McCarthy
        p. cm.
Includes bibliographical references and index.
        ISBN 0–415–93551–2 (pbk.)
        1. Sex instruction. 2. Sex in marriage. 3. Women—Sexual behavior. 4. Men—
Sexual behavior. 5. Sexual excitement. 6. Sexual abstinence. 7. Sexual desire
disorders. I. McCarthy, Emily J. II. Title.

HQ31 .M38 2003
306.7—dc21   2002014094

CONTENTS

Part 1
Understanding—The First Step

Part 2
Changing

Part 3
Preventing Relapse

PART 1

Understanding— The First Step

CHAPTER 1

Why Do Couples Experience
a Dead End to Desire?

THE NUMBER ONE sexual problem facing American couples is inhibited sexual desire. The second most common problem is discrepancies in sexual desire. Pundits laugh and say, What do you expect from people married 20 years? In truth, these are not the couples in trouble. Desire problems plague newly married couples, as well as unmarried couples. Contrary to cultural myths, neither boredom nor age are the main factors in inhibited sexual desire. Desire problems occur among all age groups and types of couples.

This book will explore the complex phenomena of inhibited sexual desire—specifically, low-sex and no-sex marriages. The cultural sexual revolution of the 1960s and the scientific sexual revolution of the 1970s, inaugurated by the work of Masters and Johnson, were expected to dramatically increase sexual satisfaction. Why did that not happen? What went wrong? Most important, what does this mean for your marriage? How can you understand and confront inhibited sexual desire? Are there really no-sex marriages, or are you a freak?

Take this true–false test:

the test

1. Sex is more work than play.
2. Touching always leads to intercourse.
3. Touching takes place only in the bedroom.
4. You no longer look forward to making love.
5. Sex does not give you feelings of connection and sharing.
6. You never have sexual thoughts or fantasies about your spouse.
7. Sex is limited to a fixed time, such as Saturday night or Sunday morning.
8. One of you is always the initiator and the other feels pressure.
9. You look back on premarital sex as the best time.
10. Sex has become mechanical and routine.
11. You have sex once or twice a month at most.

If you answered true to five or more statements, true to item 11, or both, you are among the more than 40 million Americans stuck in a low-sex or no-sex marriage.

The adage in sex therapy is that when sexuality goes well, it is a positive, integral but not major component—adding 15 to 20 percent to marital vitality and satisfaction. However, when sexuality is dysfunctional or nonexistent, it assumes an inordinately powerful role, 50 to 70 percent, robbing the marriage of intimacy and vitality.

The most disruptive sexual problem is inhibited desire. If this degenerates into a no-sex or low-sex marriage, it puts tremendous pressure on the couple, especially if affection and sensuality also cease. Desire is the core of sexuality. No-sex and low-sex marriages become devitalized, especially when this occurs in the first 3 years of marriage. Unless something is done to reverse this process, divorce is a likely outcome.

The functions of marital sexuality are to create a shared pleasure, to reinforce and deepen intimacy, and to use as a tension-reducer to deal with the stresses of life and marriage. An optional function is to conceive a planned, wanted baby. No-sex and low-sex marriages negate these benefits. In addition, lack of sexuality robs the couple of special feelings and intimate connection.

the stigma of desire problems

The initial focus of sex therapy was orgasm problems—premature ejaculation in men and nonorgasmic response (especially during intercourse) in women. The naive assumption was that if both partners had orgasms, everything would be fine. The simplistic concept was "orgasm = satisfaction."

Sexuality is complex, with many causes and many dimensions. The four components of sexual function are desire, arousal, orgasm, and satisfaction. When therapists refer to a primary sexual dysfunction, it means the problem has always plagued the couple. Secondary dysfunction means sexuality was once fine and then became problematic. Secondary inhibited sexual desire is the most common sexual problem facing married couples.

Desire and satisfaction are the core of sexuality. It is more socially acceptable to say you have a specific dysfunction—nonorgasmic response, female arousal dysfunction, vaginismus, painful intercourse, erectile dysfunction, premature ejaculation, or ejaculatory inhibition. It is hard to admit, "I am not interested in sex," "I do not like sex," or "I do not find sex enjoyable." In our sex-satiated culture, everyone is supposed to love sex.

Research studies (the most important being the *Sex in America* study) find that 1 in 3 women and 1 in 7 men report inhibited sexual desire. Sometime in marriage more than 50 percent of couples experience inhibited desire or a desire discrepancy. You are not alone. Feeling stigmatized and deficient is of no value. Desire problems are the most frequent complaint of couples seeking sex therapy. Inhibited sexual desire stresses a marriage more than any other sexual dysfunction does.

The extreme of desire problems is a no-sex marriage. The couple falls into the cycle of anticipatory anxiety, negative experiences, and, eventually, sexual avoidance. Sex is more of a pain than a pleasure. The partners did not plan to have a no-sex marriage; it is a pattern they fell into. A no-sex marriage does not mean total abstinence, but that sex occurs less than 10 times a year. A low-sex marriage means being sexual less than every other week (i.e., less than 25 times a year). Approximately 20 percent (one in five) of married couples have a no-sex relationship. An additional 15 percent of married couples have a low-sex relationship. One in three nonmarried couples who have been together more than 2 years have a no-sex relationship.

The longer the couple avoids sexual contact, the harder it is to break the cycle. Avoidance becomes a self-fulfilling trap. The longer the partners are in a low-sex or no-sex marriage, the more they blame each other. The more shameful they feel, the harder it is to break the cycle. The couple that has not resumed sexual contact 6 months after the baby was born faces one set of problems, but the couple that has not been sexual for 6 years faces a more daunting task. Yet the strategy for change is the same—renew intimacy, engage in nondemand pleasuring, and add erotic scenarios and techniques. The more chronic the problem, the more difficult is the change process. Maintaining motivation is a major challenge. Confronting avoidance and inhibitions is more difficult for the couple that has stopped being affectionate. The good news is that motivated couples are able to reestablish touching, desire, arousal, and intercourse.

the nonconsummated marriage

The number of couples that do not consummate their marriages is difficult to estimate because it is a shameful secret. One in four couples has an unsuccessful or painful first intercourse. As many as 1.5 percent of marriages are not consummated the first year, and about half of those remain unconsummated. Most of these couples were sexually active premaritally, but ceased intercourse before marriage and were unsuccessful at resuming. Another pattern is that a specific dysfunction, such as vaginismus or ejaculatory inhibition, makes intercourse very difficult or impossible. Some couples maintain desire and enjoy nonintercourse sex. Most people in nonconsummated marriages avoid any sensual or sexual activity.

Embarrassment over a nonconsummated marriage dominates their lives. The woman avoids gynecological examinations because she does not want to answer questions about sexual activity. If she has never had intercourse or suffers from vaginismus (spasming of the vaginal opening so that insertion is very painful or impossible), she avoids a vaginal exam or having a pap smear. The stigma for the male is just as severe. He views the nonconsummated marriage as an attack on his masculinity. The couple treats this as a "shameful secret," not talking to friends, doctors, or a minister, which furthers alienation and stigma. The partners do not even talk to each other. It is important to realize that non-consummated marriages, no-sex marriages, low-sex marriages, and marriages controlled by inhibited desire are more common than thought. Sexual problems can be addressed and resolved. You can revitalize your sexual bond and rebuild desire and functioning. It requires motivation, focus, and working as an intimate team.

what is normal sexuality?

Before 1970, we lacked scientific information about sexual function and dysfunction, had only poor quality educational materials, and suffered from inhibition, guilt, and limited communication. Sexual myths and misinformation were rampant. An astounding increase in knowledge has occurred during the past 30 years. Unfortunately, this has not resulted in improved sexual functioning. There are as many sexual problems in the 21st century as in the 1950s, although the types of problems have changed.

We have better scientific information about sexual function and dysfunction than at any time in human history. There is a plethora of educational materials and self-help books. Sexuality is discussed in arenas ranging from pulpits to talk shows. Sexual themes dominate our culture, especially TV, movies, and music. There is an enormous amount of sexual discussion, although the quality is low, with a confusing medley of fact and fiction. Naive, repressive myths have been replaced by unrealistic, performance-oriented myths. Guilt has been replaced by performance anxiety. There has been no net gain for sexual pleasure. Sexual anxieties, inhibitions, and problems are still the norm.

Sexuality is a complex, crucial aspect of life and marriage. We are respectful of individual, couple, and cultural differences in the functions and meanings of sexuality. There is not "one right way" to be sexual.

Concepts that promote healthy sexuality are

1. Sex is more than genitals, intercourse, and orgasm. Sexuality involves attitudes, feelings, perceptions, and values. Sexuality is a natural, healthy element in life. It need not be a source of guilt or negative feelings.

2. Sexuality is an integral aspect of your personality. You deserve to feel good about your body and yourself as a sexual person.
3. The essence of sexuality is giving and receiving pleasure-oriented touching.
4. Express sexuality so that it enhances your life and your intimate relationship.

The four components of sexual functioning are:

1. Desire—Positive anticipation and feeling that you deserve sexual pleasure.
2. Arousal—Being receptive and responsive to touching and genital stimulation.
3. Orgasm—Letting go and allowing arousal to naturally culminate in orgasm.
4. Satisfaction—Feeling emotionally and physically bonded after a sexual experience.

Healthy sexual functioning allows both people to enjoy pleasure. A key element is having realistic expectations, accepting the inherent variability and flexibility of sexual experiences. Novels and movies emphasize free-flowing, nonverbal, powerful sexuality where desire is intense. Arousal is quick, orgasm always occurs for both (simultaneously), and it is marvelous. This sells movies and novels, but makes real people feel inadequate and deficient. If partners experience powerful desire, arousal, orgasm, and satisfaction twice a month, they can count themselves lucky and should celebrate those special times. Less than half the sexual experiences of well-functioning couples involve equal desire, arousal, and orgasm. Typically, one partner is more into sex, although the other enjoys the experience or at least appreciates going along for the ride. Five to 15 percent of sexual experiences are mediocre, unsatisfying, or failures. This, too, is normal. You are not a perfectly functioning sexual machine. You are two individuals sharing sexuality. There is built-in variability and, occasionally, dissatisfaction or dysfunction.

Fifty percent of married couples (and over 60 percent of unmarried couples) experience sexual dysfunction or dissatisfaction. Inhibited sexual desire and discrepancies in desire are the most common complaints, so you have plenty of company. One spouse (usually the male) initiates and encourages sexual contact, so even if dysfunctional or unsatisfying, marital sex continues. Some people with desire problems do not have difficulty with arousal and orgasm once they begin. As a client said, "Once stimulation starts, I get turned on and come; it's the wanting to be sexual that stymies me." Pundits call it "lack of wanta."

Occasional lack of desire is normal. At times, it is healthy. You wonder about people who have high sexual desire in times of couple conflict, dealing with an ill child, after a funeral, facing a financial crunch, or during a work crisis. It is unhealthy to use sex as a way of denying or avoiding reality.

It is normal to occasionally have differences in desire. Sometimes one partner wants a hug, the other wants an orgasm. What is not normal is chronic inhibited desire, a no-sex or low-sex marriage, or constant conflict over sex.

romantic love and sexual chemistry

We have been socialized by movies, songs, and novels to believe that romantic love and sexual chemistry are the powerful, driving forces that carry couples to the heights of ecstacy. Sex is smooth, passionate, spontaneous, and uninhibited. Movie sex is spectacular sex; the fact that it has nothing to do with real couples' sex lives is beside the point of the magical media hype.

Romantic love, with its idealization of the partner and the relationship, plays a powerful role in initial attraction. Romantic love is inherently unstable, usually ending before marriage or seldom lasting past the first year. Sexual chemistry is very explosive and equally short-lived. Couples report "hot" sex at the beginning when they see each other on weekends, but experience sexual disappointment when living together or married. "Where did the passion go?" Hot sex based on romantic love and passion disappears, as it should. These cannot maintain desire. Sexual desire is based on emotional and sexual intimacy, not on romantic love or passionate sex. Comfort, attraction, and trust nurture desire after the heat of sexual chemistry is long gone. The prescription for maintaining sexual desire is integrating intimacy, nondemand pleasuring, and erotic scenarios and techniques.

Couples who believe that the way to rebuild desire is to rekindle romantic love and reignite sexual passion are heading into a dead end.

The keys to revitalizing marital sexuality are building bridges to desire, increasing intimacy, enjoying nondemand pleasuring, and creating erotic scenarios. Broad-based, flexible sexuality provides a solid foundation for marriage. Sexual desire is essentially interpersonal, not individual. The partners learn to think, talk, act, and feel like an intimate team. Each spouse facilitates and reinforces the other's sexual feelings and desires, rather than colluding in sexual avoidance.

Maintaining comfort, attraction, and trust is an active process. Each person takes the initiative and designs a pleasurable or erotic scenario. The spouse is open and receptive. Inhibitions and avoidance are confronted. This requires commitment and working together. Change is usually gradual, rather than dramatic. There will be difficulties, setbacks, disappointments, and lapses, but if the partners stay with the process, they will succeed. Once sexuality is reestablished, they need to generalize and maintain gains. Benign neglect subverts sexual desire. Relapse prevention is an active process. Good intentions and loving feelings are necessary, but not sufficient, to maintain a vital sexual bond.

who we are and the plan of the book

We have been married 36 years and see sexuality as a vital, integral part of our marital bond. Since 1980 we have been a writing team; this is our seventh coauthored book. We have complementary skills—Barry is a Ph.D. clinical psychologist, and certified sex and marital therapist; Emily has a degree in speech communication. Our previous sexuality books include a conceptual book, *Couple Sexual Awareness* (1998); a book using sexual exercises to increase comfort and skill, *Sexual Awareness* (2002); as well as *Male Sexual Awareness* (1998) and *Female Sexual Awareness* (1989).

A significant part of Barry's clinical practice is with couples suffering from inhibited desire or stuck in no-sex or low-sex marriages. He has treated over 2,500 couples who have sexual problems and dysfunction. Typically, the problems have gone on for years, and the partners feel ashamed and embarrassed. They mistakenly believe that they are the only couple with this problem and approach therapy with a great deal of hesitancy. Layers of frustration, resentment, and blaming have built and are a greater threat to the marriage than is the sexual problem itself.

Our motivation for writing this book is to provide knowledge, support, and hope for couples facing inhibited desire and a no-sex or low-sex marriage. Sexual problems need not control a marriage or dominate the couple's feelings. Women are unfairly blamed for sexual difficulties; guilt and shame further inhibit desire. We believe in working as an intimate team and using a range of affectionate, sensual, playful, and erotic bridges to rekindle desire.

This is not meant to be read like a textbook. We encourage you to identify issues that are personally relevant and to focus on those. Each chapter is self-contained. The material can be read for information and ideas, but it is best used as an interactive learning medium. We encourage you to read together as a couple and discuss what is personally significant. One technique is to take turns reading aloud, stopping at important points to discuss. Another method is for both of you to underline or star the points you feel are relevant. Then read these, underlining or marking what is important to you. Discuss issues. Try suggested strategies, involve yourselves in relevant exercises, and develop communication and sexual skills.

This is a book of ideas, guidelines, and exercises, not a "do-it-yourself therapy." The more information and understanding the partners have, the better decisions they will make. Knowledge is power. We draw on case studies of clients Barry has treated (names and details are altered to protect confidentiality). Most chapters contain an exercise to make the assessment and change process personal and concrete. We encourage you to engage in exercises that are helpful and feel free to skip those that are not. Exercises are not rigid or set in concrete; feel free to modify them so that you get the most you can from these experiences.

self-help and therapy

This is a self-help book, not a substitute for individual, marital, or sex therapy. The most efficacious use is as an adjunctive resource while in therapy. We offer information, guidelines, case examples, exercises, and personal observations, and we suggest change strategies and techniques. Increasing awareness and reducing myths and stigma are crucial. Information, understanding, and attitude change will challenge inhibited desire, but this is not enough.

Sexuality has a major cognitive component—the most important element for desire is positive anticipation. Attitudes about deserving sexual pleasure and your rights as a sexual person promote healthy sexuality. Yet sexuality is not a cognitive activity. Sexuality involves emotions and interaction—sharing intimacy, pleasure, and erotic feelings. The more severe and chronic the inhibited desire, the harder it is to develop the courage to take risks and reinstitute touching and sexual expression.

Sex therapy has a number of advantages over a self-help book. Therapy promotes hope and maintains motivation in the face of frustration or disappointment. The change process is never as easy or straightforward as is portrayed in books. The typical process is "two steps forward, one step back." The therapist helps the couple to stay focused and reinforces motivation for change. Having a regular therapy appointment and feeling accountable are valuable in breaking the impasse of a no-sex or low-sex marriage. The therapist's empathy and insights are vital. The therapist's respecting and caring about each person promote self-respect and mutual caring. The therapist can guide the couple toward other valuable helping resources. Guidelines for choosing a marital or sexual therapist are presented in appendix 1.

can all marriages be saved?

The traditional view was that all marriages could and should be saved. Divorce was viewed as a failure. This is untrue and self-defeating. Marriages that are fatally flawed, abusive, or destructive or those that subvert well-being are not worth preserving. We are definitely pro-marriage, but divorce is the healthy alternative when the marriage is fatally flawed or destructive.

A marriage that meets needs for intimacy and security is of great value. The marital bond of respect and trust motivates the couple to revitalize sexual intimacy. When respect and trust are lacking, trying to restore intimacy is a useless struggle.

A no-sex or low-sex marriage robs the couple of intimate feelings, especially when affection and sensuality are absent. Unless this changes or there are other sources of satisfaction, the marriage probably will not survive. The marriage might have genuine strengths, but inability to resolve sexual problems overwhelms the relationship. We hope this book can revitalize your marriage or at least revive hopefulness and motivate you to seek marital or sex therapy.

secrets and hidden agendas

Inhibited sexual desire and no-sex or low-sex marriages have a multitude of causes, especially sexual secrets and hidden agendas. Most of these can be dealt with; others symbolize a fatally flawed marriage. Examples of secrets that can be dealt with are shame over childhood sexual abuse, guilt over an idiosyncratic masturbation pattern, and sexual avoidance due to fear of failure. Examples of secrets that reflect a fatally flawed marriage are a homosexual orientation and hidden sexual life, marrying for convenience or security but no genuine feeling for the spouse, and a continuing comparison affair that subverts the marital bond because emotional and sexual needs are being met through the affair.

Ideally, the trust bond is enhanced by openness. Disclosing secrets facilitates trust. Sharing secrets (such as embarrassing or traumatic childhood incidents) helps the individual. Other secrets (such as telling the spouse that one of his or her children was born through an affair) can destroy the marital bond. Secrets inhibit sexual desire and should be shared with someone—if not the spouse, then with a therapist, minister, sibling, or best friend.

Hidden agendas are even more sensitive and explosive. Some can be dealt with, whereas others indicate a fatally flawed marriage. Couples can deal with fear of pregnancy, fear of being abandoned, shame about a fetish arousal pattern, lack of desire caused by a side effect of medication, being afraid to raise sexual issues because the spouse would leave, or pretending you lack desire in order to protect a spouse who is obsessed with sexual performance. Hidden agendas destroy sexual anticipation—they need to be disclosed and dealt with. Hidden agendas that produce a fatally flawed marriage include the man who married because of a sexual attraction to the stepchildren and who has little or no attraction to his spouse, a woman who married her spouse for money or security and uses sex to placate him, a woman who has decided to leave the marriage after her child graduates high school and so avoids sexual contact, and a man who is homosexual and uses the marriage as a social cover for business or professional reasons. These marriages cannot and should not be saved. The healthy alternative is divorce—hidden agendas control the relationship, resulting in a sham marriage.

Dealing with secrets or hidden agendas by yourself is extremely difficult. Individual or couple therapy can help you understand the dilemma and reach a resolution. Hidden agendas are very hard to address without professional help. Even with an objective third party, there is unpredictability and potential explosiveness. Sometimes both spouses have a hidden agenda, but usually it is one spouse. People with hidden agendas fear (often rightly) that these will be used against them to blame them for all of the problems or be used by lawyers in a divorce proceeding. If the goal is to revitalize the sexual bond, the hidden agenda must be addressed and dealt with.

is the sexual problem a symptom or a cause?

The question of whether a marital problem causes a sexual problem or the sexual problem causes marital dissatisfaction is more than a chicken-and-egg argument. Human behavior is overdetermined, with many causes and many dimensions. Any simple answer is likely to be wrong or, at least, incomplete.

Sexuality is a positive, integral component of marital intimacy. Although no-sex or low-sex marriages can function satisfactorily, these are the minority. Some couples maintain a respectful, trusting bond and are good parents even though sexuality is dysfunctional or absent. Other couples have an angry, alienated, nonsupportive marriage, and the only thing that works is sex.

The most common pattern is a couple that has a good relationship, but struggles unsuccessfully with inhibited desire. Over time, the sexual problem becomes severe and chronic. Sexual problems undermine marriages by robbing them of intimate connection and energy. The sexual problem increasingly defines the marriage; blaming and resentment build. In well-functioning marriages, sexuality plays a 15 to 20 percent role in terms of vitality and satisfaction. With a chronic inhibited desire problem, sexuality plays an inordinately powerful role, draining positive feelings and tearing at the marital fabric.

Another pattern is that relationship conflicts, especially those involving anger, are played out through sexual conflict. Anger is the main cause of secondary inhibited sexual desire. Withholding or avoiding sex makes a statement, a way to fight back. Although this is usually a female reaction, males shut down sexually as a way to express anger. Sometimes this is a conscious choice; more often it is not. Anger can involve a sexual issue (demand for oral sex, a discovered extramarital affair, conflict over birth control), but more often anger involves a relationship problem. Common causes of anger may be concern about drinking and driving, not feeling supported in a family conflict, out-of-control arguments that include slapping and pushing, conflicts over spending, and feeling that your spouse is taking advantage of you. As alienation increases, "hot" angry thoughts build on themselves. Attempts to bridge the emotional gap with affectionate touching or sexual activity are met with angry rebuffs, increasing frustration and isolation. Emotional and sexual distance feeds the angry cycle. The partners find themselves trapped in an alienated low-sex or no-sex marriage.

No-sex or low-sex marriages happen; it is not the spouse's intention. The exception is when that is the hidden agenda. Examples of hidden agendas include when one spouse is gay and has married for a convenient cover or the spouse has a paraphiliac arousal pattern (exhibitionism, fetishism, pedophilia, obscene phone calls), with little desire for intimate sex. Seeking out Internet pornography and chatrooms can become a compulsive pattern, subverting desire for couple sex. These are male patterns. Female hidden agendas are fear of pregnancy or pain during intercourse, resulting in sexual avoidance. There are nonsexual hidden agendas, which include marrying for security, money, social approval, or religious pressure but with lack of caring and attraction. There is little hope for these marriages unless the core issues that block a genuine marital bond are addressed. Unless both individuals are willing to confront the hidden agenda and build a solid marital bond, divorce is the healthy alternative.

Fertility problems are a common cause of inhibited sexual desire. Sex with the intention of becoming pregnant is an aphrodisiac. For 85 percent of couples under 30 and 70 percent of couples over 30, becoming pregnant is usually easy (often, too easy). Couples in the unlucky minority find that as time goes on, frustration builds. The process of undergoing a fertility assessment, with increasingly intrusive, painful, and expensive tests and interventions, weakens the desire of the most ardent couple. Fertility problems are no fun. Self-blame and blaming the spouse are easy traps. Fertility problems can bring out the worst in people. Infertility dominates self-esteem, the marriage, and sexuality. They stop being sexual except during the high probability week. Sex becomes a pressured performance to achieve pregnancy, with little pleasure, warmth, or feeling of connection. Couples dealing with a fertility issue need a great deal of support, which includes using touching, sensuality, and eroticism to energize themselves during the non–high probability periods of the month.

Another problematic pattern is conflict about intercourse frequency. Instead of broad-based pleasuring and a variety of bridges to desire, it is a "yes–no" question—are we going to have intercourse? If not, there is no touching. If every touch is a demand for intercourse, the pressure is up and the pleasure is down. Emotional intimacy and non-demand pleasuring are sacrificed to intercourse pressure. The result is inhibited desire. Intimacy, comfort, and pleasure lead to sexual anticipation. Conflict and pressure lead to inhibited desire. Quality is more important than frequency. Sexuality is more than genitals, intercourse, and orgasm. Guidelines that promote desire include the beliefs that touching is valued for itself, touching occurs both inside and outside the bedroom, and not all touching must result in intercourse.

Another pattern is that if sexual dysfunction increasingly dominates the relationship, one or both partners would rather avoid than try to be sexual. The dysfunction, whether erectile problems, premature ejaculation, nonorgasmic response, vaginismus, or ejaculatory inhibition, controls the relationship. The dysfunctional spouse feels embarrassed or humiliated. To avoid bad feelings, she avoids sex. This is an especially destructive trap for males with erectile dysfunction. If he cannot be guaranteed an erection sufficient for intercourse, he does not want to try. Premature ejaculation or ejaculatory inhibition is frustrating, but does not cause the couple to stop being sexual. Female dysfunction subverts desire, but the couple is unlikely to stop sexual activity, especially when the male continues to initiate. With vaginismus (which blocks intercourse), couples can enjoy nonintercourse erotic scenarios and techniques.

If sexual dysfunction does not reverse within 6 months, it is unlikely to spontaneously clear up. The typical outcome is that the problem becomes severe and chronic, negating anticipation and desire. Functional sex alone does not build anticipation, but dysfunctional sex drains desire.

A myriad of factors inhibit desire and lead to a no-sex or low-sex marriage. Understanding the pattern is a helpful, and usually necessary, step in resolving the problem. Most important is the commitment to restore intimacy and sexuality. No matter what originally started the sexual slide, once the pattern is established, chronicity, blaming, and avoidance solidify the problem.

The individual cannot resolve sexual problems alone or by sheer willpower. The partners have to work together. Being an "intimate team" is the cornerstone of this approach. The way to rebuild desire is a one-two combination of taking personal responsibility for sexuality and being an intimate team. Trust that the spouse will make a good faith effort to deal with inhibitions, anxieties, and traps. Be open to renewed ways to connect physically and emotionally and build bridges to sexual desire.

maintaining a vital marital and sexual bond

The change process is complex and difficult, but doable. Couples begin to experience desire, break the sexual hiatus, enjoy pleasuring, and resume intercourse. Once the cycle of the low-sex or no-sex marriage is broken, you cannot rest on your laurels. To maintain a vital sexual bond, you have to commit time and energy. The most important components in maintaining desire are to be an intimate team; anticipate sexual encounters; realize that sex is more than intercourse and orgasm; nurture bridges for desire; be open to flexible, variable sexual scenarios; and maintain a regular rhythm of affectionate and sexual contact.

It is normal for 5 to 15 percent of sexual experiences to be mediocre, unsatisfying, or failures. Do not overreact to a negative experience; especially do not avoid touching. Keeping intimate contact is the best way to ensure that a sexual lapse does not turn into a marital relapse.

Value emotional and sexual intimacy. Both people can enjoy affection, sensuality, playfulness, eroticism, and intercourse. Not all touching can or should lead to intercourse. Both planned intimacy dates and spontaneous sexual encounters promote a vital sexuality. The greater the number of bridges for desire and openness to variable, flexible sexual scenarios, the more likely you will maintain your gains. Sexuality nurtures and energizes your marital bond.

using this book to revitalize marital sexuality

This book can help you understand and resolve the complex, draining problem of inhibited sexual desire and the low-sex or no-sex marriage. We encourage you to seek marital or sex therapy, rather than trying to do it on your own. Overcoming desire problems requires awareness, understanding, working as an intimate team, active confrontation of avoidance and inhibitions, maintaining motivation, not overreacting to difficulties and failures, and using all of your resources and supports. Increased awareness and knowledge are helpful, but not sufficient, to break the cycle of the low-sex or no-sex marriage. Increasing understanding is the first step in the 10–step change process.

Use this book as an interactive learning medium; do not just passively read. Read it aloud or highlight what is personally relevant. Discuss issues. Try exercises that are relevant; feel free to redo or individualize these to promote awareness and comfort. Discuss guidelines and case studies, and implement what is meaningful and helpful. Use suggested strategies and techniques to empower change. Confront guilt and shame; do not beat up on yourself or feel stigmatized because of sexual problems. You deserve to feel good about yourself as a sexual person and to allow sexuality to nurture and energize your marital bond. This book is a resource in the healing journey to renewed sexual vitality and satisfaction.

CHAPTER 2

Whose Problem Is It—
His, Hers, or Ours?

INHIBITED SEXUAL DESIRE and no-sex or low-sex marriages are not caused by one factor or one spouse. Sexuality is complex, with many causes and dimensions. In addition, there are individual, couple, and cultural differences in sexual attitudes, experiences, feelings, and values.

Sexual desire and desire problems are best understood as a couple issue. This facilitates a comfortable, productive way to think about, discuss, address, and enhance sexual desire. The couple approach is especially valuable when considering what maintains, as opposed to what caused, inhibited sexual desire. Regardless of what originally caused the problem, you become stuck in a self-defeating cycle. It is considerably easier to break this cycle if you approach and talk about sexual desire as a couple issue. The traps of guilt and blame help maintain this as a chronic sexual problem that is a drain on your marital bond. Viewing inhibited sexual desire as a couple problem reduces guilt, defensiveness, and blaming.

Sexuality as a couple issue is one of the most helpful, yet hardest to accept, guidelines. When initially presented, the couple approach is received enthusiastically as a way to break the deadlock and promote change. The concept of being an intimate team is particularly inviting. However, when you encounter inevitable setbacks, frustrations, and disappointments, it is easy to revert to blaming. It is easier to blame your spouse than to be responsible for and change your own attitudes and behavior.

A core concept in couple therapy is to take responsibility for yourself. You are not responsible for your spouse. Focus on making personal changes in attitudes, behaviors, and feelings—this takes thought, work, and discipline. It is neither your responsibility nor your role to change your spouse. Communicate with your spouse, share feelings, and make requests for change. You can influence your spouse, but cannot make that individual change. Especially, you cannot coerce your spouse to change.

Ideally, marriage operates through a positive influence process—each spouse is responsible for self, and you are respectful and trusting toward each other. You discuss feelings, make requests, commit to a change process, and support and reinforce individual and couple changes. In a low-sex or no-sex marriage, the positive influence process has broken down (at least, in regard to intimacy and sexuality).

You are caught in a vicious cycle. The more sex is avoided, the lower is sexual desire. You become trapped in a pattern of blame-guilt-alienation. The self-defeating cycle is anticipatory anxiety, tension-filled sex, and sexual avoidance. You are not an intimate team working together to understand and resolve the sexual problem. Instead, the sexual problem dominates and drains your relationship. You alternate between self-blame and blaming the spouse. You are stuck in a "Who is the bad guy?" struggle. When intimacy breaks down into "good guy–bad guy" roles, the possibility of resolution is nonexistent.

when one spouse always pushes sex

Many couples stay stuck in the struggle where one spouse reports high desire, always pushes sex, and bitterly complains of being rejected. The other spouse feels pressured and besieged; it is upsetting to be forced to say no. Consciously or unconsciously, that person avoids intimacy. This pursuer–avoider pattern is the opposite of the positive influence, intimate team approach.

The partner pushing sex rejects approaching it as a couple problem, preferring to blame the spouse. The partners clings to the belief that inhibited sexual desire is totally the spouse's fault. Typically, it is the husband who pushes sex, but it can be the wife. Whether it is the traditional pattern or a role reversal, the couple dynamic is amazingly similar. The higher-desire spouse blames the lower-desire spouse and claims there is no reason for him to change. The lower-desire spouse is mired in guilt and self-blame, which alternates with blaming the partner for being insensitive and coercive. It is hard for either person to stay with the concept of sexual desire as a couple issue. Even when the therapist presents it as a couple problem and the partners initially agree, it is easy to slip back into old attitudes and habits at the first disappointment. The higher-desire spouse claims it does not help to stop pushing intercourse, and anyway, he does not have a sexual problem. Even if he does not overtly push, his sexual intensity, blaming, and pressure are still felt. Frustration and anger do not invite emotional sharing, touching, or sexual intimacy.

No matter how the inhibited sexual desire pattern started, the higher-desire spouse's attitudes, feelings, and behavior exacerbate or, at least, maintain the pattern. His blaming and guilt-inducing are alienating and reduce her sexual desire. Seeing the spouse as your hostile, worst critic does not facilitate trust or desire. Sex then involves conflict and coercion, not pleasure and mutuality. This is not to blame the higher-desire spouse or make him the "bad guy," but to highlight his role in maintaining the problem. Inhibited sexual desire is best dealt with by thinking, talking, and acting as an intimate team. The higher-desire spouse does not make sex inviting. Sex is a pressured performance to placate him and avoid his anger.

The valid points the higher-desire spouse makes are that avoidance makes the problem worse, sex is a bonding experience, and rejection is emotionally alienating. The invalid points are that it is all the partner's fault and that increasing the frequency of sex is the key.

A prime guideline to successfully address inhibited sexual desire is that the quality of emotional and sexual intimacy is more important than intercourse frequency. To break the cycle of a no-sex or low-sex marriage, sexuality needs to be comfortable, inviting, and pleasurable for each spouse. Intimacy, affection, sensuality, playfulness, and eroticism, as well as intercourse, are valued by both spouses. The higher-desire spouse can change by adopting a nondemand approach to touching and by valuing broad-based sexuality. Not all touching can or should lead to intercourse. The single most important guideline for the higher-desire spouse is to respect and honor the partner's emotional and sexual feelings. Her feelings and needs are as important as his. Intimate coercion has no place in marriage. Coercion poisons sexual desire.

the spouse with lower sexual desire

In our sex-saturated society, it is hard not to feel deficient or guilty about lack of sexual desire. Yet it is a problem for one in three adult women and one in seven adult men (with the figures for males increasing with age). The more guilty, angry, depressed, and self-blaming the person is, the worse the problem becomes. You pile one negative emotion on top of another, which subverts self-esteem and sexual desire.

What can the lower-desire spouse do? First, increase awareness— do not avoid thinking and talking about intimacy and sexuality. Second, take a problem-solving approach; do not feel ashamed or self-punitive. Third, approach the spouse as your supportive, intimate friend, not as your worst critic. Fourth, carefully assess what you value about intimacy, affection, sensuality, playfulness, eroticism, and intercourse. Take responsibility for your sexuality. Identify aspects of intimacy and sexuality that you value for yourself and the marriage. Sex is not a way to placate the spouse.

You feel defensive, guilty, or angry and have lost track of the positive functions of touching, intimacy, and sexuality. Changing inhibited sexual desire is a one-two combination—first, increasing awareness and taking personal responsibility, and second, viewing desire as a couple issue and being an intimate team in revitalizing sexuality.

Are there special issues when it is the man with inhibited sexual desire? It is more acceptable for him to admit to erection or orgasm problems than admit to not being sexually interested. Traditionally, masculinity and sexuality are closely linked. Too much of the man's self-esteem is tied to his penis.

Male desire problems have a multitude of causes. Among these are pressure for perfect performance, fear of pregnancy, embarrassment due to sexual dysfunction, greater confidence with masturbation than with partner sex, alcohol or drug abuse, a way to maintain emotional distance or punish the spouse, a secret such as a fetish arousal pattern or sexual orientation issue, being distracted by work or money concerns, being involved with children or extended family to the detriment of couple time, not valuing marital sex, side effects of medication, few spontaneous erections so that he is hesitant to initiate sex, feeling intimidated by the wife's sexual desire, feeling that it is unmanly to ask for stimulation to facilitate arousal, low self-esteem, or depression. The man has to be aware of and take responsibility for his desire problem. He asks the spouse to be his intimate friend in rebuilding sexual desire and erotic functioning.

The spouse with inhibited desire wishes the partner would "back off" and "reduce the sexual pressure." This is necessary, but not sufficient. You have to build bridges to sexual desire. Enlist the spouse as a facilitator of desire and pleasure, rather than making him the one who pushes for sexual performance. Is it worthwhile for you to change your attitudes toward intimacy and sexuality? Do you trust the spouse to be your intimate friend?

desire discrepancy—an alternative way of thinking and communicating about sexual desire

When you chose to marry, you did not decide to enmesh your lives and become one person. A viable marriage involves a balance between individual autonomy and sharing your lives as an intimate couple. If you needed to feel equally desirous to engage in an activity, the marriage would be stagnant and blocked. One spouse likes dancing; the other is enthusiastic about board games. One spouse prefers the mountains to the ocean; the partner prefers bed-and-breakfast inns to resort hotels. One spouse enjoys creating elaborate salads; the other's favorite meal is meat loaf with macaroni and cheese. Yet even with those individual differences, couples are able to participate in and enjoy a range of activities. One enjoys certain experiences more, and that is okay. They reach a balance that recognizes individuality as well as coupleness. There is no need for a power struggle. Discrepancies in hobbies, vacations, and foods are accepted and even enjoyed.

Let us give a personal example. Emily is a quilter and an antiquer who loves craft shows, especially in small, historic towns. Barry appreciates and enjoys these activities, but not as much. Barry loves cities, ethnic foods, and plays, which Emily appreciates, but finds overwhelming as a steady diet. We accept these differences and work with them. Each spouse offers experiences that expand and enrich both partners' lives. Each person is able to say no to an activity that is aversive or excessive. For example, 2 hours is Barry's maximum at a quilt show— he does his thing (reading, biking, or writing) and we meet later for dinner. Emily finds more than 3 days in New York intolerable, so we do not plan more than a weekend trip. Desire discrepancies are successfully accommodated. We communicate feelings and requests and reach agreements, rather than settle for lukewarm compromises.

Can couples use this model in discussing and working with discrepancies in sexual desire? We believe not only that they can; this is the preferred approach. It ends the power struggle and breaks the blame/guilt cycle. Discrepancies in sexual desire are conceptualized as a couple issue. Each spouse states feelings, makes requests, and as a couple you develop agreements that nurture desire and sexuality. Accept the desire discrepancy; do not fall into the guilt/blame trap or be coercive. Commit to marital sexuality, enjoy touching, and adopt a broad perspective on intimacy and sexuality. This provides a solid foundation from which to revitalize sexual desire.

broad-based intimacy and sexuality

There is more to sexuality than intercourse and more to intimacy than sexuality. A key to change is awareness of the many dimensions of intimacy and sexuality. The prescription for satisfying marital sex is integrating an intimate relationship, nondemand pleasuring, and erotic scenarios and techniques. Even in the best marriages, a mutually satisfying sexual encounter does not occur all the time—in fact, the couple is lucky if it occurs most of the time. Contrary to movies, love songs, and magazines, not all sex is romantic, mutual, functional, or satisfying. There is normal variability in sexual expression.

Inhibited sexual desire often reflects an intimacy issue. How emotionally close does each spouse want to be? Is more intimacy better? Some couples prefer the best friend marital style, with a great deal of closeness; others prefer the complementary couple style of retaining autonomy with moderate closeness; others prefer the conflict-minimiz-ing style, where personal boundaries are strong; still others adopt the emotionally expressive style, where there are periods of great closeness mixed with periods of anger and distance. You need to develop a mutu-ally acceptable level of intimacy that fits your emotional needs and life situation. Sexuality is one way to express intimacy, but not the sole means or even the primary means. Sharing feelings, being affectionate, cuddling on the couch and in bed, disclosing hopes and fears, and shar-ing your lives as trusted, respectful friends are the core of intimacy.

Sensuality and nondemand pleasuring are the basis of broad-based sexuality. Sensuality involves pleasure-oriented touching—body mas-sage, taking showers or baths together, kissing, playful touching while clothed or semiclothed. Touching is valued for itself, occurring inside and outside the bedroom. Staying in touch is as likely to involve a hug as it is intercourse. A hug can evolve toward arousal and orgasm, but normally does not. Cuddling before going to sleep and on awakening provides a solid basis for loving feelings. Dancing in the living room to your favorite music, while engaging in playful touching and kissing, is inviting and at times serves as a bridge to sexual desire. Giving a neck or back massage while watching TV is a way to maintain connection. Showering together in the morning or before bed can be playful and pleasurable. Nondemand pleasuring is the bedrock of a healthy sexual relationship.

Eroticism includes a range of manual, oral, rubbing, and inter-course scenarios and techniques. Eroticism serves to turn you and the spouse on. Eroticism includes intercourse, but is not limited to inter-course. To increase eroticism, you can engage in multiple stimulation before and during intercourse. Multiple stimulation involves kissing, caressing, breast stimulation, testicle stimulation, anal stimulation, and the use of fantasy.

The broader the intimate, sensual, and erotic repertoire, the easier it is to maintain sexual desire. Both partners are open to a variety of ways to express intimacy, affection, sensuality, playfulness, and eroti-cism. Sometimes touching is for emotional intimacy, sometimes for affection; sometimes it is playful, sometimes sensual, sometimes erotic, and sometimes lustful. Communicating feelings and sharing touch help maintain sexual desire.

JILL AND STEFAN

When they finally arrived in the therapist's office, Jill and Stefan were a demoralized couple trapped in the power struggle of whose fault it was that they had a low-sex marriage. They had been married 6 years and had a 3-year-old daughter. Jill very much wanted a second child. Stefan was angry at the lack of sex and feared that Jill only wanted him for "stud" services; he would be trapped in a child-centered marriage. Jill felt that Stefan was being irrational and withholding; before marriage they had agreed on two children. Stefan counterattacked, saying that Jill had tricked him into believing that she valued sex. Both agreed that their best sex had been premaritally. When dating, they had sex each night they were together. When they began living together, sex was three to five times a week. This decreased to once or twice a week 4 months before marriage. During that time, Jill began experiencing inhibited sexual desire.

The 2-week honeymoon to Hawaii was the beginning of the intense struggle over sexual initiation and frequency. Stefan had the expectation of daily sex, while Jill's expectation was for a fun, scenic, romantic time. Jill felt coerced by Stefan's sexual pressure. Stefan felt betrayed and played with by Jill's sexual avoidance. Jill was not orgasmic during either of the two times they had sex. When the newlyweds returned from Hawaii, friends joked what a wonderful, sexy honeymoon it must have been, which increased the upset because the couple resented having to lie and pretend.

When you begin fighting about sexual initiation and frequency, it is easy to fall into the cycle of anticipatory anxiety, negative or mediocre experiences, and sexual avoidance. Guilt and blame become the dominant emotions. This pattern was broken when they had sex with the intention of conceiving their daughter, but they quickly regressed after Jill became pregnant. Since the birth, intercourse was once or twice a month. Stefan stopped initiating because of his anger at being rejected. Jill felt that Stefan rejected her affectionate overtures, and she felt emotionally abandoned. Even though there was severe alienation, Jill very much wanted a second child.

The therapist found it hard being in the same room with Jill and Stefan. The tension was palpable. It was easier for them to socialize with other couples and do things as a family than to be a couple.

Fortunately, neither was threatening divorce. Divorce threats add a destructive dynamic. Jill and Stefan shared life goals and religious values, parented well, and felt supported by family and friends, all of which reinforced marital stability. They thought of themselves as a viable couple, committed to their marriage. However, the sexual problem was tearing at and weakening their marital bond. Jill questioned her love for Stefan; she saw him as irrational and mean in regard to sex. Stefan confided to the therapist that he was thinking of beginning an affair. The therapist told Stefan that affairs usually become more emotional and complicated than planned. As well, affairs are much easier to get into than out of. Stefan committed to not have an affair while they were in couple therapy.

The first therapeutic task was to break the cycle of guilt and blame. Stefan and Jill began thinking of themselves as an intimate team, striving to revitalize marital sexuality. The therapist's optimism helped them craft an expectation that this was a changeable problem. Inhibited sexual desire was the mutual enemy. Their marital commitment was the best prognostic sign for revitalizing sexuality.

Marital sex had never gotten on track, and inhibited desire was a growing threat to their marital bond. Building marital sexuality would take a great deal of communication and effort on both people's part. Good intentions were necessary, but not enough. It is crucial to approach the problem as a couple, break the cycle of blame/guilt, and cease the attack/counterattack pattern that demoralized and drained them. Playing "Who's the bad guy?" was getting them nowhere. Stefan agreed to stop name-calling and blaming. Jill lowered her wall of alienation and emotionally reinvested in the marriage. Reluctantly, she agreed to postpone pregnancy until sexuality was reestablished. She would use a diaphragm until a joint decision was made to become pregnant. Stefan was hesitant to agree to a temporary prohibition on intercourse, but this acknowledged the reality of the situation. With the performance pressure of intercourse removed, they had the freedom to explore touching as a means to feel connected and share pleasure. This was very inviting for Jill, who missed affectionate touch and sharing intimate feelings.

Rebuilding intimacy and sexuality was a complex, difficult couple task. Without the support and suggestions of the therapist, they would have given up in frustration and reverted to the guilt/blame pattern.

One of the major functions of therapy is to keep motivation high enough so that couples persevere through frustrations and setbacks to achieve the satisfaction of a pleasure oriented couple sexual style. A breakthrough for Stefan occurred when he realized that Jill was not punishing him by withholding sex. Her anxieties and inhibitions were real, not manipulative. Most important, Stefan realized that his being an intimate spouse, rather than a coercive, angry person, helped reduce Jill's inhibitions. When Jill realized that she could veto a sexual activity and Stefan would honor her veto, her anxiety was reduced and she felt less need to veto.

Jill found that sensual experiences led to erotic feelings. Jill was receptive and responsive to manual and oral stimulation—she preferred the term *outercourse*. Stefan's rigid view that "only intercourse was sex" melted under these new experiences. It was Stefan who began insisting that not all touching had to lead to intercourse, an insight Jill greatly appreciated.

Intercourse was reintroduced as a "special pleasuring experience." Intercourse was part of the pleasuring process, not the pass–fail test of their relationship. A side effect of the pleasuring exercises was that Stefan became a slower, more sensitive lover. This made intercourse more appealing. Jill's sexual response was similar to that of the majority of women; orgasm with manual or oral stimulation is easier than during intercourse. With self-acceptance and partner acceptance, Jill and Stefan developed a comfortable, functional couple sexual style. Not all touching culminated in intercourse, which helped Jill build sexual anticipation and excitement.

Becoming pregnant with a planned, wanted child is a major impetus for sexual desire. This was true not only for Jill, but for Stefan as well. Intercourse with the hope of a second child was a strong sexual motivator. In addition, they continued broad-based affectionate, sensual, and erotic experiences. This provided the bedrock for sexual desire.

Jill and Stefan were motivated to maintain and generalize sexual gains. A relapse-prevention plan is integral to sex therapy. Sexual desire cannot rest on its laurels or be taken for granted. Jill and Stefan set aside couple time, when their daughter was being watched by another parent or was asleep. Jill's initiating sex was important, to reassure

Stefan that he did not have to stay in the rigid role of always being the initiator. Equally important, Stefan learned to accept a "no" without withdrawing or punishing Jill. Stefan did not regress to coercing Jill or calling her names. Jill did not regress to hiding behind a wall of alienation.

For Jill, the keys to generalizing sexual gains were to reinforce intimacy, be open to sensual touching, and enjoy outercourse scenarios. These continued to be her bridges for sexual desire. For Stefan, the keys were feeling that they were an intimate team, enjoying both outercourse and intercourse, and accepting sexual disappointments as normal, rather than as a source of defensiveness and blaming. Stefan and Jill agreed to implement the therapist's suggestion that once a month they have a sensual date where orgasm and intercourse were prohibited. This allowed them freedom to play and enjoy touching.

functions of sexuality

At its essence, sexuality is a couple, not an individual, experience. That is another reason that inhibited sexual desire is best understood as a couple issue. Sexuality is best when both spouses feel free to initiate affectionate, sensual, playful, erotic, and intercourse experiences. Equally important, both feel free to say no or suggest an alternative way to stay connected. It is optimal that both spouses value sexuality as a shared pleasure. Couples who are comfortable with touching inside and outside of the bedroom, who are aware of the value and dimensions of touching, and who realize that not all touching leads to intercourse have a solid base for sexual desire. Each component of the sexual prescription—an intimate relationship, nondemand pleasuring, and erotic scenarios and techniques—require couple involvement. Each person is responsible for her or his sexuality. For desire to remain vital, the couple continues to share as an intimate team.

EXERCISE—SEXUAL DESIRE
AS A COUPLE ISSUE

This exercise involves two steps—the first is that each spouse writes self-blaming or blaming-the-partner statements. Next to each statement, they each write a healthy counter-statement that challenges irrational, self-defeating blaming. The second step is to discuss new, healthy understandings about sexual desire as a couple issue. They should write down and save these new understandings so that they can use these as a resource in the coming weeks, months, and years.

Examples of self-blaming and partner-blaming statements (with counters) include

"It's all my fault."—Sexual desire is complex; there is not an angel and a devil.

"My spouse doesn't love me."—Love and sexual desire are not the same.

"It's guilt from my Catholic background."—Guilt inhibits sexual desire. However, Catholic couples report high desire and satisfaction. The new Catholic teaching (almost all religions agree on this) is pro-sex in marriage.

"If only my spouse would change, my desire would be fine."—You can only change yourself. You cannot change the spouse, although you can encourage and support your spouse in making changes.

"If only I hadn't gotten pregnant."—"If only" thinking is self-defeating. Deal with the present; you cannot change the past.

"I can't enjoy sex until I lose 20 pounds."—A positive body image is important, but sexuality should not be held hostage to weight or a perfect body image. Sexual desire is based in the relationship and on giving and receiving pleasure-oriented touching.

"Romantic love is gone; there's nothing I can do."—Romantic love is very fragile; it seldom lasts more than 2 years and typically dissipates after 6 months. Sexual desire is based on mature intimacy, not romantic love.

"The best sex is premarital or extramarital."—Marital sex is special and can be high quality and satisfying.

"We've been trapped in a no-sex marriage for so long, it will never change."—Chronic problems are difficult, but motivated couples do revitalize marital sexuality.

"We have the only nonconsummated marriage in the city."—Because of stigma and embarrassment, people do not discuss this problem. Nonconsummated marriages exist and the problem is resolvable.

"Since my spouse had an affair, I will never trust her or desire to be sexual with her."—Couples can and do survive affairs. Intimacy and sexuality facilitate the healing process and are an integral component in rebuilding the trust bond.

There are many more self-defeating cognitions, but happily, there are even more rational, problem-solving counters.

The second step is to discuss sexual desire as a couple issue. Write down understandings as a way to acknowledge and reinforce crucial insights. New understandings facilitate self-acceptance, spouse-acceptance, and being an intimate team.

Do this exercise together. Write two to five statements about inhibited sexual desire and the no-sex or low-sex marriage as a couple issue. Be sure these are clear and genuine. Examples are

"There is no good guy-bad guy; inhibited sexual desire is the enemy. We will fight it together and revitalize marital sexuality."

"Our love for each other and commitment to the marriage will help us overcome this sexual problem."

"We are good people and a good couple that deserves to enjoy sexuality."

"The sexual problem has been a drain and we have been terrible to each other, but now we are committed to being an intimate team and to developing a vital, satisfying sexual relationship."

"We want to have sex and a baby. We are going to support each other in doing this."

Develop your list of statements, which will allow you to maintain an intimate team approach even when you encounter the inevitable frustrations, disappointments, and setbacks.

confronting desire problems as an intimate couple

When Barry treats demoralized couples who have chronic desire problems and marriages where there has been no sex for years, the concept of being an "intimate team" is what keeps them motivated. A crucial aspect of the team concept is not to turn on or attack your spouse. You win or lose as a team. You acknowledge sexual successes and share intimate feelings. When you fail, support and encourage each other; do not engage in blaming. Learn from the problem and plan for the next encounter. Trust that the spouse has your best interest in mind and wants you to succeed. The most powerful aphrodisiac is two involved partners where each person's arousal plays off the other's to create an erotic flow. This is a natural extension of the "give to get" pleasuring guideline.

Sex works best when each spouse is open and receptive. This is the opposite of the self-defeating pattern in which one spouse demands and the other feels coerced and avoids. Each spouse's sexual desire and bridges to desire are acknowledged and accepted. Both the higher- and the lower-desire spouse think and talk about sexuality as a couple issue, with the shared goal of establishing a sexual relationship that nurtures the marriage. It is not "his way" or "her way"; it is finding "our way." Quality of intimacy and sexuality is more important than quantity of intercourse. A comfortable couple sexual style is more important than sexual prowess. The focus is on sharing pleasure, not on intercourse performance. Confronting and changing the no-sex or low-sex marriage are challenges you meet as an intimate team. When your sexual relationship is disappointing or gets off track, you view this as a lapse. Remaining on the same team ensures that it does not turn into a marital relapse.

Establish positive, realistic expectations for marital sexuality. Sex is not the most important factor in marriage. Sex is not even the most important aspect of intimacy. Emotional closeness and giving and receiving nondemand touching are the core components of the intimate bond. Eroticism, intercourse and orgasm are special, energizing experiences. When sex works well, it plays a 15 to 20 percent role toward adding to marital vitality and satisfaction. Unfortunately, inhibited sexual desire is more powerful as a marital stress than good sex is as a marital enhancer.

Intimacy includes emotional closeness, trust, affection, sensuality, arousal, intercourse, and bonding. The most satisfying marital sexuality integrates intimacy and eroticism.

Does this mean that the individual loses his or her sexual autonomy? Not at all. Each spouse remains responsible for her or his desire, arousal, orgasm, and satisfaction. Being an intimate team does not mean giving up autonomy or blurring personal boundaries. Healthy sexuality involves developing and maintaining a comfortable, desirous, and satisfying couple sexual style.

Should every sexual experience be functional and satisfying? This is an unrealistic expectation that will result in relapse. A positive, realistic expectation is that 40 to 50 percent of sexual encounters will be mutually satisfying, 20 to 25 percent will be good for one spouse and okay for the other, 20 to 25 percent will be good for one spouse with the other going along for the ride, and 5 to 15 percent of encounters will be mediocre, unsatisfying, or failures. This is a very different image than is portrayed in movies, on talk shows, and in novels. The reality that 5 to 15 percent of sexual experiences are mediocre, unsatisfying, or dysfunctional is particularly important. This is the kind of sex where one spouse looks at the other and says, "I hope you are enjoying this; it's for you" and the other says, "I thought this was for you." The partners who can laugh or shrug off these experiences and get together at a later time when they are awake, aware, desirous, involved, and responsive have the right attitude. The couple that is frustrated, angry, panicky, or blaming is likely to relapse. Occasional mediocre or poor sexual experiences are normal.

closing thoughts

Conceptualizing inhibited sexual desire as a couple problem has great advantages—specifically, breaking the guilt/blame cycle. The one-two combination of personal responsibility and being an intimate team is key. Developing a broad-based couple sexual style sets the framework for satisfying marital sex. Being an intimate couple allows you to confront the no-sex or low-sex marriage and to revitalize marital sexuality.

CHAPTER 3

Turnoffs:
Poisons for Sexual Desire

SEXUAL DESIRE IS easy to kill. The potential for desire and pleasure is natural for both women and men, but can be vulnerable. A myriad of emotional and sexual factors can poison desire. Chief among these are anger and other negative emotions, including depression, guilt, anxiety, inhibitions, obsessions, compulsions, and shame. The technical term is *inhibited sexual desire*. This reflects the core issue—identifying and assessing factors that block (inhibit) sexual desire. The terms we use are *turnoffs* or *poisons*. To understand what inhibits desire, you need to identify individual and couple poisons.

Of the four phases of sexual response—desire, arousal, orgasm, and satisfaction—desire is the easiest to disrupt. Positive anticipation is the key to desire. If that key is turned off, it affects the entire sexual process. Sexuality is natural, but it has to be nurtured and reinforced. Women and men deserve sexual satisfaction. However, when conflicts, inhibitions, and avoidance dominate, sexual desire is undermined. This is especially true when anger overrides desire.

how premarital sexual experiences and expectations poison marital sex

A depressing reality is that "hot" premarital couples are vulnerable to desire problems once married. Why? The factors that drive premarital sex—newness, illicitness, risk-taking, winning the partner over, romantic love, and exploring sexual boundaries—are unstable. By its very nature, romantic love/passionate sex disappears with time. Ideally, romantic love would be replaced by mature intimacy. Ideally, hot sex would be replaced by the combination of intimacy, nondemand pleasuring, and erotic scenarios and techniques. Yet too often, sex becomes routine, low quality, and infrequent. Many times, this occurs even before marriage. The joke is that marriage kills sex, but nonmarried couples who have been together more than 2 years have higher rates of no-sex and low-sex relationships than do married couples.

New romantic love couples meet for weekends and special occasions. They have time, energy, and enthusiasm for each other. They ignore the real world of jobs, laundry, and schedules. The person and the relationship are idealized. Once married, they spend seven nights together and have to deal with the nitty gritty tasks of sharing their lives. Within this context, sex is no longer idealized and supercharged. Ideally, couples would have both planned and spontaneous sexual experiences. Unfortunately, the reality is that sex becomes the last thing they do at night after watching the news or comedy program.

Premarital sex is a self-defeating and unrealistic standard of comparison. Barry tires of couples complaining that sex was best premaritally. The decrease in sexual frequency and romance frustrates, embarrasses, and angers the couple. Do not make premarital sexual comparisons—this poisons marital sexuality. Marital sexual desire is based on a radically different way of thinking, feeling, and being a couple. Marital sexuality involves dealing with the whole person and sharing the complexities of your lives, including emotional and sexual intimacy. Premarital and marital sexuality comparisons are "apples and oranges." They offer no help in resolving sexual issues, only causing blame and frustration. Disappointment, resentment, and feeling tricked or manipulated poison marital sexuality. The premarital comparison interferes with developing a marital style that nurtures intimacy, desire, pleasure, and eroticism.

anger

Anger has an extremely corrosive effect on marital sexuality. Couples can and do use sex to make up after an argument. This works as long as it is not associated with emotional abuse or physical coercion. Chronic anger poisons both the marital and the sexual relationship. Key elements in marital sexuality are feeling emotionally connected and trusting. Chronic conflict and anger break this emotional bond. The spouse is no longer your trusted, intimate friend, but an untrustworthy stranger who could hurt or even destroy you.

Feeling attacked or put down is the main precursor for anger. This is especially impactful if the attack involves your body or sexuality. For example, a woman intent on hurting the husband complains that his penis is smaller than an ex-boyfriend's. Later, she apologizes and says she did not mean it, but he continues to ruminate and feel put-down. Anger and alienation build. The therapist explains that penis size does not reflect sexual prowess nor does it affect female satisfaction. The clinician utilizes diagrams and suggests readings. Although this reduces myths, it does not reduce anger. Anger destroys intimacy and fuels sexual avoidance.

Women feel anger, usually unexpressed, at "intimate coercion." Intimate coercion is a major cause of female inhibited sexual desire. The man who pushes sex, despite the woman's reluctance and verbal protestations, is an example of winning a sex battle, but losing a satisfying intimate relationship. Intimate coercion is very different from marital rape. Marital rape is a repetitive pattern that destroys trust in voluntary, pleasure-oriented sexuality. Intimate coercion is an intermittent pattern which does not involve force, but is destructive to intimate sexuality. The essence of coercion is that it is a demand for sex at this time and in this way, and if not met, there will be negative consequences for the partner, such as harassment, put-downs, or not providing money or help around the house.

The husband and wife perceive intimate coercion dramatically differently. He denies that it occurs or says it is not his fault, and is shocked and baffled by her anger. His perception is that he is seducing or coaxing her, similar to premarital scenarios. She feels pressured and violated. Her preferences and desires do not matter; he puts his sexual needs over her emotional needs. Involved, mutual, pleasure-oriented sex decreases. Frequency of intercourse is more important than her psychological and sexual feelings. She feels taken advantage of and abused. Intimate coercion must be confronted, and this marital poison eliminated.

Another source of anger involves the aftereffects of an extramarital affair. Men react more angrily than women. The wife's affair is a reversal of the double standard. The most common female affair is a "comparison affair." This affair met her emotional and sexual needs instead of these being satisfied in the marriage. She compared the lover to the spouse. Even though the affair is over, the husband feels judged and insecure, which is expressed as anger. Angry thoughts feed the cycle, especially when he is alone and ruminates. Some men react by shutting down sexually. Others forcefully initiate sex as if to avenge the affair. Angry sex kills loving feelings, alienating the woman and poisoning her desire. The wife's response to the discovery of the husband's affair is angry withdrawal. This anger builds a wall of resentment that brooks no touching, affection, or caring. Anger and alienation build on themselves and poison desire.

Sexual issues are not the only, or even the chief, reason for marital anger. Major causes are hurt and disappointment in the spouse, marriage, or both. Hurt is caused by one spouse saying derogatory things about the other, discussing the other's weaknesses with a relative or friend, putting the partner down in front of others, revealing a secret one had promised to honor, telling a joke at the other's expense, using a slap or the threat of force during an argument, or reneging on a financial agreement. Disappointment is caused by finding that the spouse is less successful than claimed, that the spouse's family is fraught with conflicts and not the loving family the spouse depicted, that the move to a safer neighborhood is not financially possible, that caring and attentiveness have been replaced by compulsive TV watching, and that promises of intimacy have been substituted by a marginal relationship. Anger is a secondary emotion; hurt and disappointment are the primary emotions. Anger, whether caused by sexual or emotional factors, is a sexual turnoff. This is true for both men and women. In pornography videos, anger is portrayed as a sexual stimulus, but that is not how anger works for the great majority of couples.

Anger is best dealt with outside of the bedroom. Talk out issues over the kitchen table, on walks, or in a therapist's office. The bedroom is the worst place for anger. Being nude and prone increases personal vulnerability. It is too easy for arguments to degenerate into hurtful attacks on the person, marriage, or sexuality. Deal with conflicts clothed and sitting up. Argue your points, but do not put the spouse down or fall into the "attack–counterattack" mode.

guilt

Guilt is the most self-defeating of emotions. When you feel guilty, you lower your self-esteem and are likely to repeat the same destructive behavior. For example, the man sneaks off to a nude dancing bar and spends the $50 he planned to use for a couple night out. He keeps this secret and avoids his wife. He is afraid that if she knew, she would think he was a "scum." As his self-esteem decreases, he feels guilty and lonely and returns to the nude club, which reinforces the self-defeating cycle.

For women, a major source of guilt is fantasizing about or having an affair. Sometimes the affair does not involve intercourse, but does include flirting, kissing, hugging, late-night calls, fondling, caressing, or stimulation to orgasm. Feelings of adventure, illicitness, and attraction are powerful. Ambivalent feelings, fear of discovery, shame, or disruption of a work situation or a friendship burden the affair, whether consummated or not. When the relationship ends, especially if it ends badly (as it usually does), feelings of guilt poison sexual desire. The bad feelings generalize to marital sexuality. The husband's reaction of blaming or anger feeds the guilt and is a further turnoff.

Guilt causes the person to put herself down and to isolate from the spouse. Guilt disrupts the process of sharing intimacy and pleasure. To confront guilt, you need to take responsibility for the negative behavior, apologize, make amends, and, most important, use all your resources to stop that behavior.

anxiety

Sex and pleasure belong together. Sex and performance are a poisonous combination. Anxiety is the emotion associated with performance. The type of anxiety that most interferes is anticipatory anxiety. Desire is facilitated by positive anticipation, but subverted by anticipatory anxiety. Approaching sex with a fear of failure, a wish to procrastinate or avoid, fear of embarrassment, or wanting to get it over with is a turnoff. It is like going swimming, burdened by a 100-pound weight before you dive in.

A second form of anxiety is performance anxiety, which has a negative affect on arousal and erection. The man views erection and intercourse as a pass–fail test. Sex is not sharing pleasure, but a performance where fear of failure predominates. Performance anxiety also affects women, interfering with subjective arousal and vaginal lubrication. When arousal and orgasm are taken out of the context of sharing pleasure and made into a performance goal, anxiety increases and desire decreases.

inhibitions

Sex is fun. Allow yourself to experience pleasure-oriented sexuality. What types of inhibitions (roadblocks) interfere with the natural progression of desire, arousal, orgasm, and satisfaction?

Inhibitions include psychological, relational, or sexual factors that block pleasure. Typical inhibitions are poor body image, reluctance to initiate, unwillingness to let go in front of the spouse, embarrassment at being nude, self-consciousness about making sexual requests, reluctance to try an erotic scenario, and fear of embarrassment or rejection. Inhibitions take the fun out of sexuality. Inhibitions result in rigid sex roles and stereotyped sexual expression. Sex becomes mechanical and stale, draining desire. For example, the couple has sex only late at night, with no lights, after the male's nonverbal initiation, with limited foreplay, use of the missionary position, and perfunctory afterplay. Even if functional for both partners (it is less likely to be functional for the woman), how much fun is it? Few people look forward to that predictable, stereotyped scenario.

Inhibitions are a psychological form of withholding. You are not free with yourself or with the spouse. Psychologically and sexually, you are hiding behind a wall; you are guarded and inhibited. Allow sexuality to be open, flowing, and free.

obsessions and compulsions

Obsessions and compulsions are sexual turnoffs. Sometimes they are a symptom of obsessive-compulsive disorder, but usually the problem is linked to sexual expression. Obsessive thoughts interfere with spontaneity and communication. For example, the husband who is obsessed by a fetish is shut off from the spouse. A woman who obsesses that a wife and mother should not enjoy oral sex blocks pleasure. Compulsive behavior is off-putting. Washing genitals can increase sexual comfort, but compulsive, ritualistic washing is a turnoff. Compulsive behavior such as counting intercourse strokes, using three different forms of birth control, and immediately jumping up to wash off semen, are turnoffs.

Obsessive-compulsive sexual behavior is based on the irrational fear of dirtiness and contamination. In fact, genital secretions are healthy. There are more germs in your mouth than on your genitals. An advantage of a monogamous relationship is that you can enjoy sex without fear of STDs or HIV/AIDS. Sexual obsessions and compulsions rob the couple of healthy, vital marital sexuality.

shame

Shame refers to negative thoughts and feelings based on past experiences. The sad reality is over 90 percent of women and men were subject to negative sexual experiences in their past. This refers not only to the major traumas of child sexual abuse, incest, and rape, but to being sexually humiliated, guilt over masturbation or fantasies, being sexually rejected or ridiculed, having a sexual dysfunction, having an unwanted pregnancy or sexually transmitted disease, being exposed to or being peeped on, receiving obscene phone calls, or being sexually harassed. Unfortunately, it is common to have confusing, negative, traumatic, or guilt-inducing incidents in childhood, adolescence, adulthood, or during all of these life stages. This is not the way it should be, but is the reality. These experiences are better confronted and dealt with, then accepted, not kept secret. The worst thing about a traumatic incident is that it becomes a shameful secret that controls sexual self-esteem.

Like guilt, shame has no positive function. Shame is more irrational because people blame themselves for something they did not cause. Why "blame the victim"? They dealt with the situation as well as they could, given their awareness and resources at the time. The "victim" should feel pride in having survived. Guilt lies with the perpetrator; there is no reason for the survivor to feel shame or guilt. The adage "Living well is the best revenge" is an optimal way to think about negative sexual experiences. Do not blame yourself; take pride in being a survivor. Express sexuality in a manner that reinforces self-esteem and your intimate relationship. Be a proud survivor, not a victim controlled by shame.

confronting and changing sexual poisons

Realizing that you feel controlled by a sexual poison need not cause embarrassment or depression. Knowledge is power. Becoming aware of the poison and its self-defeating effects is a first step. Accept, rather than deny or minimize. With increased awareness, you reduce the poison's control. It is a "trap"; replace it with sexually healthy ways of thinking, acting, and feeling. For example, the poison is guilty withdrawal after an incident of masturbating to a "900" phone fantasy. Share that information with the spouse within 24 hours so that it does not become a shameful secret. You agree to a negative contingency (such as cleaning the bathrooms for a month or sending a $25 check to a cause you vehemently oppose) each time you use the "900" line. Rather than "hiding out" after an incident, the couple is urged to engage in an intimate date. The poison is challenged. It no longer controls couple sexuality. The one-two combination is to confront the poison so that it is eliminated and to reassert a healthy role for marital sexuality.

RICH AND ROBIN

Rich and Robin began dating as high school seniors. The "two "Rs" were envied by friends as a happy, stable couple. They dated through college with only two minor breakups and married exactly a year after graduation. When they entered therapy, they had been married 4 years and had an 18-month-old daughter. Rich was successful in computer marketing and actively involved in the care of their daughter. This enabled Robin to pursue her academic career as a Ph.D. student in literature. They were viewed by family and friends as a model couple, moving ahead with individual, couple, and family lives. Rich and Robin were affectionate in public, and because they had a baby, people naively assumed that they were a sexually active couple. People do not realize the difficulties and pain that occur behind a bedroom door.

Rich and Robin were controlled by turnoffs and poisons, including several remnants from their premarital relationship. Robin felt very guilty about contracting a sexually transmitted disease during that time when she had broken up with Rich. She transmitted chlamydia to Rich, who had been furious and blaming. Rich was viewed by friends as easy-going, but Robin knew how angry he could be. He never hit her, but had thrown things and put his fist through a wall. Robin was intimidated by his anger.

Early in the relationship, they used sex to calm the anger. Robin came to resent this, especially Rich's demands for oral sex. Robin viewed fellatio as Rich's pacifier and found this a turnoff. Even before marriage, sexual frequency and quality (especially the latter) dramatically decreased.

The honeymoon had been a disaster. Rich demanded and forced fellatio after heavy drinking at the wedding reception. This was their only sexual experience during the 2-week honeymoon. Awkwardness and resentment built, especially Rich's hostile satire of the couple as the only husband and wife in America who had not consummated their marriage (in fact, 1.5 percent of marriages are not consummated during the first year).

Robin wanted to get pregnant, and they developed a pattern of having sex in the middle of the night. Their daughter was conceived through a 2 A.M. intercourse. Although they seldom discussed the no-sex state of the marriage, each was privately ashamed and embarrassed. Robin blamed Rich's angry, demanding approach and unwillingness to share feelings. Rich blamed the problem totally on Robin, seeing her as cold and inhibited. Rich felt that Robin had lied during the premarital years, when they felt romantic love and had enthusiastic sex.

What brought the chronic problem to a crisis was that Robin discovered Rich was purchasing oral sex at a massage parlor on a weekly basis. Although he paid in cash, Robin became suspicious because debt was mounting. When confronted, Rich tried to finesse and minimize the problem. He finally admitted the paid sex incidents, but blamed

them on Robin for withholding sex. He assured her that he used condoms, but she insisted they both be tested for STDs and HIV. The
results were negative. The physician suggested consulting a marriage
therapist with a subspecialty in sex therapy.

Robin and Rich were extremely uncomfortable during the first
therapy session. They believed the cultural myth that couples in their
20s do not have sexual problems. In reality, sexual problems are the
main cause of divorce during the first 3 years of marriage. When they
realized they were not alone, feelings of stigma were reduced. The
therapist put the problem in perspective—like many married couples,
Robin and Rich had not developed a comfortable, functional couple
sexual style. Sex cannot be treated with benign neglect; this results in a
no-sex or low-sex marriage.

After the initial meeting, individual sexual histories were sched-
uled. Without the spouse present, each person had an opportunity to
review positive and negative elements of his or her sexual development
and to explore attitudes, behavior, and emotions. The therapist asked
each to focus on his or her role, rather than blame the spouse. Secrets,
turnoffs, and poisons were carefully assessed.

In the feedback session, the therapist observed that when Rich and
Robin began as a couple, they felt open and caring. Over the years, frustrations, secrets, resentment, bitterness, and poisons built and compounded. Respect, trust, and intimacy eroded. Living incongruent lives
increased emotional stress. It is draining to appear to be a happy couple while in reality feeling alienated and trapped in a no-sex marriage.
The goal of sex therapy is to confront personal, marital and sexual poisons and to revitalize the intimate bond. This entails dealing with
secrets and turnoffs and breaking down walls of alienation and avoidance. Rich and Robin needed to begin thinking, talking, acting, and
feeling like an intimate team.

The therapist pointed out "traps" each needed to monitor. Robin
had to stop seeing sex as Rich's domain, instead valuing sexuality for
herself and their marital bond. She needed to confront anger and
resentment, not use sex as a way of withholding or getting even. She
could use her veto power to stop a sexual activity that she experienced
as aversive. She reduced guilty feelings about the STD and did not
allow that to control her sexual self-esteem. Rich was understanding
and supportive of these changes, but reluctant to confront his traps. His

biggest issue was eliminating angry sexual demands and intimate coercion. The therapist advised instituting a 48-hour prohibition on sexual activity after an angry incident. Rich had to stop judging and blaming Robin.

Rebuilding the marital bond and revitalizing sexuality are not easy, but are doable. Rich and Robin were committed to their marriage and family, but the poisons were severe. They had to confront the poisons, with each spouse committed to eliminating (or at least significantly reducing) these. Each partner had to be responsible for his or her behavior. Gradually, they began feeling and acting like an intimate team. The marital bond of respect, trust, and intimacy was badly frayed, but was still intact and open to being revitalized.

The change process was uneven, two steps forward and one step back. It is easier to confront a poison before it takes hold, but for Rich and Robin their poisons were chronic. They liked the analogy of marriage as an emotional bank account. Premaritally, they had made big deposits and there were few withdrawals. Since marriage, there had been few deposits (their child was the main one) and many withdrawals, especially in the sexual area. They had to conscientiously make small, steady, intimacy deposits and guard against poisonous withdrawals.

The change process was arduous and required a great deal of psychological energy. Robin assertively vetoed what she found uncomfortable. Rich stopped intimate coercion. They did each trust that the other spouse was dedicated to revitalizing the sexual bond. If an incident got them off track, the partner who was resonsible assured that it was not intentional, and this took away the poison.

Rich was surprised at how much he enjoyed sensual, nondemand touching. Robin joked that they were better at pleasuring than at sex. The therapist reinforced the importance of emotional intimacy and nondemand pleasuring as a solid basis for couple sexuality. He encouraged them to confront poisonous attitudes and behavior. Sexuality could not bloom if poisonous feelings and turnoffs were present (like weeds overrunning a flower garden).

It was Robin who initiated the return to intercourse. She requested that they maintain the prohibition on quickie intercourses and fellatio to orgasm. Rich agreed to honor this. He was enthusiastic about interactive, giving, prolonged sexual experiences. Robin taking the role of requestor and guider was a significant breakthrough. Equally important was monitoring turnoffs. For example, if Rich became frustrated and angry, rather than acting out, he called a time-out. They left the bedroom, brewed herbal tea, and talked for half an hour over the kitchen table. Robin listened empathically and validated his feelings, even if she did not agree with his proposed course of action. They went to sleep as intimate friends, with the agreement that they would discuss the problem during therapy if they could not resolve it by themselves.

At therapy termination they planned follow-up meetings and relapse-prevention strategies. Poisons are never totally gone. You have to monitor poisons and be committed to not fall into old traps. Individually and as a couple, you must value and nurture emotional and sexual intimacy.

confronting and reducing sexual turnoffs

Changing behavior is seldom easy, nor is it total. Even people who have successfully stopped smoking and have not had a cigarette in years still experience urges to smoke. It is easier to totally cease a behavior than to moderate it; for example, it is easier to stop smoking than to moderate eating. Intimacy and sexuality are areas where balance and moderation should be the norm, which makes the change process challenging.

Couples with a no-sex or low-sex marriage must struggle to revitalize intimacy and desire. Some poisons are totally eliminated, but others need to be monitored. For example, a couple with a history of physical and verbal abuse is committed to abstain from abusive behavior. If conflict and anger intensify, there is fear of regression. It is hoped that they will learn to utilize emotional-regulation skills and the time-out technique. Fears and resentments never disappear, but they will no longer control the couple.

Individually and as a couple, you can confront marital and sexual turnoffs. They do not deserve power over your life or sexuality. Do not allow them to control your present or future. The person with obsessive thoughts about a sexually transmitted disease or an affair accepts the reality of the past, but does not let this control the present. You cannot change the past (although you can learn from it). Take responsibility for yourself in the present. Do not remain stuck in the victim role. You are a survivor who is aware of poisons and is committed to not repeat self-defeating behavior. You are empowered to view sexuality as positive, accept sexuality as an integral part of your personality, and express sexuality so that it enhances your life and marriage.

EXERCISE—IDENTIFYING AND CHANGING SEXUAL POISONS AND TURNOFFS

This exercise involves a concrete, personal assessment of sexual poisons and turnoffs. Develop a realistic plan to eliminate or drastically reduce them. Do the assessment phase separately, then work together on the change phase.

Each of you must list your poisons and turnoffs. Then list couple poisons and turnoffs. Focus on your turnoffs; do not second-guess your spouse's. Examples of individual poisons include dwelling on angry thoughts, resentment over a sexual incident, inhibition about making sexual requests, avoidance of sexual topics, a secret arousal pattern, obsessive-compulsive reaction to vaginal secretions, irrational fear of pregnancy, making yourself unattractive, feeling controlled by childhood sexual trauma, overscheduling so there is no time for intimacy, making sexual demands or threats, being afraid to try new erotic scenarios and techniques, and feeling that you do not deserve sexual pleasure. Make two columns. In the first column, list the advantages of maintaining this poison. Be honest. You maintain the poison because it protects you from anxiety or fear of failure, it is a way to control or punish the spouse, it gives you a sense of power, or it serves to maintain the status quo. Are these in your best interest? In the second column, write how your life and marriage would be better without the poisons. What would you be free to try? Would this facilitate sexual anticipation and desire? You owe it to yourself and to the marriage to challenge and reduce poisons and turnoffs.

What is your role (not your spouse's) in maintaining couple poisons? Examples include your role in the pursuer–distancer dance, the intimate coercion process, avoiding couple time, angry arguments, attack–counterattack cycle, using alcohol as a way to avoid intimacy, not making sexual requests yet resenting your spouse's insensitivity, maintaining an extramarital affair, comparing your spouse with a person you fantasize about, or blaming problems on family of origin. Next to each couple poison, draw two columns. In the first column, list the advantages of maintaining this poison. For example, you maintain the status quo; it is easier to blame your spouse than to take personal responsibility; it is a reason to avoid initiating; you desire to maintain emotional and sexual distance; you fear that if the issue is addressed, it will destroy the marriage; you need to maintain secrecy; or you get sympathy from friends and family. Is that what you want? Is that healthy for your marriage? In the second column, list the advantages for you and for the marriage of resolving the sexual problem. What will it take to confront couple poisons? How much time and energy? What attitudes and behaviors need to change? Do you value the benefits of a secure, satisfying marital bond? Be specific and concrete.

Exchange lists as you enter the change phase. It is easy to become defensive and counterattack when reading the spouse's material; that is counterproductive. The key to change is approaching sexuality as an intimate team. You trust that the spouse is on your side and will help you confront poisons. Sexuality is a team sport; do not turn against your intimate partner. Stay away from the "guilt-blame game." Your spouse is being vulnerable in disclosing turnoffs. Honor that vulnerability; do not turn it against that person. Listen to your spouse's requests of how you can support the change process. Overcoming turnoffs and poisons is a one-two combination: (1) each spouse takes responsibility for changing his or her attitudes and behavior, and (2) the partners work together to eliminate the poisons and revitalize marital sexuality.

Develop a specific, clear plan to confront and reduce individual and couple poisons. Your spouse states how he or she will be supportive. What specifically will you do to promote change? What is your spouse committed to stopping so that the process is not subverted? No change plan is perfect, but it will be successful if it is clear, positive, gradual, and you are willing to problem-solve when you encounter difficulties.

Change is a couple task. Sexuality is a shared, intimate process. You cannot force or coerce your spouse. This exercise and the follow-up experiences give you practice at being an intimate team. Instead of denying poisons and turnoffs, focus on changing so that these no longer control your marriage and sexuality.

closing thoughts

There are a myriad of personal and couple turnoffs that can poison the sexual relationship. When poisons are identified and confronted, they lose power. When people assume responsibility for their own turnoffs, recognize that each person has a right to express feelings, share problems with the spouse's, realize the spouse's intentions are not to poison the relationship, and work as an intimate team to confront and eliminate these problems, change is well on the way. Successfully confronting turnoffs is a source of pride.

Removing poisons is necessary, but not sufficient, for revitalizing marital sexuality. Intimacy, nondemand pleasuring, and erotic scenarios and techniques are integral to healthy sexuality. Affirming sex as a shared pleasure, a way to reinforce intimacy, and a tension-reducer allows sexuality to play a positive role in your marriage.

Personal and couple turnotts need to be monitored so that they do not regain power. You have devoted time and energy to identifying and eliminating poisons, but you cannot stop there. Be aware and vigilant so that negative attitudes and habits do not return. It is normal to have "lapses"; do not allow them to become relapses. An adage is "marriage cannot rest on its laurels." Be willing to address personal, relational, and sexual issues so that these remain free of poisons.

CHAPTER 4

The New Man: Overcoming Sexual Dysfunction

Do DESIRE PROBLEMS cause sexual dysfunction, or does sexual dysfunction cause desire problems? For the great majority of males, the causation is clear—sexual dysfunction results in desire problems. The main male sexual dysfunctions are premature ejaculation, erectile dysfunction, and ejaculatory inhibition. For males, sexual desire problems are almost always secondary. In other words, he once had desire, but it is now inhibited, low, or nonexistent. The destructive cycle is anticipatory anxiety, performance anxiety resulting in dysfunctional sex, and sexual avoidance due to embarrassment and failure.

There is a second pattern—variant sexual arousal. This can involve compulsive masturbation (often accompanied by use of "900" numbers, online sex, or pornography), a paraphiliac arousal pattern, or an issue of sexual orientation. These subvert desire for marital sex.

Males learn that desire, arousal, and orgasm are easy and automatic. Most males masturbate by age 16, usually beginning between ages 10 and 14. The combination of masturbation and the fact that masculinity and sexuality are so closely tied reinforces sexual desire for the adolescent and young adult. These experiences are valuable, but pose vulnerabilities with dysfunction and aging. Ease and quantity of sex are not solid foundations for sexual desire. For example, an 18-year-old ejaculates, has a short latency period before he is receptive to sexual stimulation, and then can have another orgasm. Is this the best measure of sexual satisfaction? The easy, automatic, autonomous quantity approach to sex sets the stage for sexual dysfunction as he ages.

By their mid-30s or early 40s most men find that arousal is no longer autonomous; they need partner involvement and stimulation. About one in three men finds this transition difficult and develops arousal (erection) problems. Valuing quantity, rather than sexual quality, is self-defeating. The focus on performance, rather than on pleasure, makes him vulnerable to dysfunction. The worst sexual learning is that autonomy is better than intimacy. Over time, especially in marriage, intimacy is a key bridge to maintaining sexual desire. The prescription for sexual desire is integrating intimacy, nondemand pleasuring, and erotic scenarios and techniques. Male sexual socialization emphasizes only the erotic component.

A common male fear (which becomes a self-fulfilling prophecy) is that if he reduces self-confidence and goal-orientation, he will begin a "slippery slope" of becoming sexually self-conscious and lose erectile confidence. In other words, the cycle of positive anticipation, enjoying intercourse, and frequent sex will disappear, replaced by anticipatory anxiety, anxious and failed intercourse, and sexual avoidance. What accounts for this self-defeating cycle? Self-consciousness and performance anxiety. Sex is an active, involved, participatory activity—not a spectator sport. The couple enjoys the erotic flow, in which each spouse's desire, receptivity, and responsivity enhances the other's. This is the basis of the "give to get" pleasuring guideline. At its core, sexuality involves giving and receiving pleasure-oriented touching. The spouse being "turned on" is a turn on for him. Sexual desire is integrated into the relationship, not something "on the side." Each person's arousal plays off and enhances the other's arousal. Distraction and self-consciousness break the erotic flow. When sex becomes a pass–fail performance, this creates conditions for sexual inhibition and failure.

The answer to the anticipatory and performance anxiety cycle is not a return to the youthful pattern of easy, autonomous erections. Once sensitized to sexual difficulty, a man cannot pretend it did not happen and resume automatic functioning. By the time he seeks help, the anxiety/failure pattern has become well-established, resulting in secondary inhibited sexual desire. Sex is now a source of anxiety, frustration, and angst, rather than of pleasure and satisfaction.

Sexual anxiety and avoidance are stigmatizing because sexuality is viewed as a measure of masculinity. The performance myth is that "A real man can have sex with any woman, any time, any place." You and your penis are human, not a perfect performance machine. How can you challenge this trap? Key strategies are establishing positive, realistic sexual expectations; viewing your spouse as your intimate friend; enjoying nondemand pleasuring; allowing pleasuring to flow into erotic scenarios and techniques; enjoying your own and your spouse's arousal; viewing intercourse as a special erotic experience, not a performance test; letting arousal naturally flow to orgasm; and enjoying afterplay. At its essence sexuality is about intimacy and pleasure, not pressure and performance. Desire and satisfaction are more important than arousal and orgasm. Sex is more than the penis, intercourse, and ejaculation. You can learn to value intimacy and partner involvement, rather than automatic, autonomous functioning. Sexuality is about sharing pleasure and eroticism. Males have been socialized to function in a sexually autonomous manner and only turn to the spouse when there is a problem. This is the model of pornography. The man becomes turned on by external stimuli, not by intimate, interactive sexuality. Being open to her stimulation and arousal is key to regaining erectile comfort and confidence.

These concepts are particularly valuable for desire, arousal, and ejaculatory inhibition, less so for the most common male problem, premature ejaculation. Even with that problem, it is crucial to view the woman as your intimate friend who helps you learn ejaculatory control.

premature ejaculation

Most males begin their sexual lives as premature ejaculators. As they gain comfort and experience, most men develop ejaculatory control. However, 3 in 10 adult males experience early ejaculation. The average time for intercourse from intromission to ejaculation is 2 to 7 minutes. Contrary to male braggadocio, most males ejaculate in less than ten minutes.

Some define premature ejaculation in terms of time (a minute after intromission), some in terms of activity (fewer than 20 strokes), and some in terms of whether the woman is orgasmic during intercourse (an extremely poor criterion because a significant number of women are orgasmic with nonintercourse sex, but not during intercourse). A reasonable approach is that if the couple is making good use of nongenital and genital pleasuring and the man's ejaculation is earlier than both partners wish and interferes with pleasure, then they can benefit by improving ejaculatory control. Learning ejaculatory control will enhance sexual pleasure for the man, as well as for the couple. Enhanced pleasure facilitates sexual desire.

Premature ejaculation is usually a primary dysfunction, although some men (especially when sex is infrequent or tension-filled) develop secondary premature ejaculation. The two most common male strategies make the problem worse. The first is using "do it yourself" techniques to reduce arousal. These include the man biting his lip, wearing two condoms, or thinking of the money he owes. The outcome of distraction techniques is reduced sexual arousal, not greater ejaculatory control. He risks creating an erectile dysfunction. The second strategy is to replace quantity for quality. This means having a second intercourse as quickly as possible. Second orgasms are usually less satisfying for the man, and the woman is more likely to feel like a sex object than a loved spouse. This negatively impacts the sexual relationship—desire decreases because of low satisfaction.

Learning ejaculatory control is a three-phase process. First, identify the point of ejaculatory inevitability, after which ejaculation is no longer voluntary. Second, use the stop-start technique as you approach the point of ejaculatory inevitability. The man signals his partner to stop stimulation as he approaches the point of inevitability. Stimulation stops for 30 to 60 seconds until he no longer feels the urge to ejaculate. The couple then resumes stimulation. This enhances awareness while maintaining arousal. Both phases are practiced with manual stimulation and involve communicating to the spouse when to stop stimulation. The third phase involves ejaculatory control with intercourse. The couple practices intercourse in the female-on-top position, using slow, long stroking (controlled by the woman). She stops stroking as he approaches the point of ejaculatory inevitability. As control increases, slow down stroking, rather than stopping. The couple experiments with intercourse positions, types of stroking, and rhythm of stroking. The hardest situation for ejaculatory control is with the man on top, with short, rapid thrusting.

Some men prefer to utilize medication to improve ejaculatory control. Anti-depressant medications can help to delay ejaculation. Some men prefer to take daily small doses; others take a moderate dose 4 hours before intercourse. The problem is that when the medication is stopped, premature ejaculation returns (a rebound effect)—sometimes more severely. For most men, the recommended technique is to practice the ejaculatory control exercises while taking medication and then gradually phase out the medication.

Learning ejaculatory control is a couple task, requiring time, practice, and feedback. Ejaculatory control is not about the man performing to a standard or proving that he can "give" her an orgasm during intercourse. The focus is on mutually satisfying, pleasure-oriented intercourse.

A common mistake is for sex to end at the man's ejaculation. Many women enjoy manual or rubbing stimulation after intercourse—either for orgasm or to share closeness. Afterplay is the most neglected phase of sexuality. Yet it very much affects the couple's (especially the woman's) sense of satisfaction.

Learning ejaculatory control is like learning any skill. It is a gradual process, requiring practice, feedback, and working as an intimate team.

erectile dysfunction

Far too much of a man's self-esteem and sense of masculinity are tied to his penis. Erectile dysfunction (commonly called "impotence" or "not getting it up") is a major male fear. A well-hidden fact is that by age 40, about 90 percent of men have experienced (at least once) a problem with obtaining or maintaining an erection adequate for intercourse. By age 50, over half of males report mild to moderate erectile difficulty. So a man's major fear is, in fact, an almost universal experience. Men are notorious liars and braggarts about sexual prowess. They deny sexual doubts, questions, or difficulties. The myth-based performance criterion of "A real man is able and willing to have sex with any woman, at any time, in any situation" puts tremendous pressure on the man, especially on his penis.

For men under 40 most erectile problems are caused by psychological or relationship problems, rather than by physical or medical factors. Physical vulnerabilities do increase with age. Common physical causes include alcohol abuse, smoking, drug abuse, side effects of medications (especially hypertension and psychiatric medications), spinal conditions, prostate surgery, chronic illness, poorly controlled diabetes, and vascular insufficiency. Common psychological and relational causes are antic-ipatory anxiety, performance anxiety, distraction, self-consciousness, viewing intercourse as a pass–fail test, a reluctance to request partner stimulation, and anger at the spouse. If an erection problem does not remit within 6 months, the man (and couple) becomes trapped in the cycle of anticipatory anxiety, performance failure, and avoidance. No matter what started the problem (alcohol, side effect of medication, fatigue, alienation, depression, anger, or trying to force sex), this self-perpetuating anxiety cycle maintains erectile dysfunction.

The hormonal, vascular, and neurological systems must be func-tional for adequate erectile response. With aging, beginning in the mid-30s, there is a gradual decline in the efficacy of these systems. That is why there are few professional athletes at age 40; the body is a less effi-cient performance machine. Testosterone affects sexual desire, which indirectly affects erectile functioning. An erection involves increased blood flow to the penis (vasocongestion), which fills the tissues and increases the size of the penis. As arousal builds, rigidity (hardness) increases—a neurological response. These systems remain functional, but are no longer at optimal efficiency. Psychological, relational, and erotic factors become crucial for erectile response.

Erection is vulnerable to distraction and anxiety. Intimacy, nonde-mand pleasuring, and erotic stimulation matter more. A 50-year-old man is not the easy, automatic, autonomous, sexual machine he was at 20. Sexual response is less predictable. Both spouses can accept sexual variability and flexibility, while maintaining positive sexual feelings and expectations.

If you have questions about physical or medical aspects of your sex-ual functioning, the doctor to consult is either a urologist or a sexual medicine specialist. Although not considered a male sex doctor, the urologist functions much the way a gynecologist does for women. Be sure the urologist is interested in doing a comprehensive assessment, not simply in promoting Viagra, penile injections, external pumps, or surgery.

The most important assessment question is whether the man is able to get erections during self-stimulation, with partner manual or oral stimulation, during sleep, or on awakening. If so, it is likely that the physical factors are functional, although operating less efficiently, espe-cially after age 50. Anxiety, distraction, fatigue, and negative emotions are major factors interfering with sexual functioning. Psychological factors of comfort, involvement, intimacy, and openness are necessary to regain erectile confidence. These include communication with and trust of the spouse, being turned on by her arousal, being open to her stimulation, and making sexual requests. Erotic factors, especially penile stimulation, her guiding intromission, awareness of personal and couple turn-ons, and enjoying orgasm with nonintercourse sex are crucial. If the couple chooses to use medical interventions such as Viagra, injections, or external pumps, the partners have to communicate about how to integrate these into their lovemaking style.

Guidelines for treatment of erectile dysfunction emphasize intimacy, nondemand pleasuring, erotic scenarios and techniques, and positive, realistic expectations. As with other sexual problems, seeking the counsel of a sex therapist is superior to working on your own.

The foundation for regaining erectile comfort and confidence is non-genital and genital pleasuring. A crucial technique is that the man (and woman) become comfortable with the waxing and waning of erections. Men are used to going to intercourse and orgasm on a first erection, so when an erection fades, they panic. The man is afraid that the sexual opportunity is lost. In fact, continued involvement and erotic stimulation ensures that the erection will wax again. The process of waxing and waning of an erection can occur two to five times in a 45-minute pleasuring session. The next step is to be orgasmic at least twice while erect during nonintercourse sex (manual, oral, or rubbing stimulation). This increases awareness and comfort with the interplay between subjective and objective arousal. During the free flow of penile stimulation (without switching to intercourse), the man can reach orgasm. Subjective arousal (feeling turned on) usually precedes objective arousal (becoming erect). Without the worry of intercourse failure, arousal and orgasm flow. The next step is to play with the penis around the vagina to desensitize performance anxiety and give the woman practice at stimulating and guiding the penis. She decides when to transition to intercourse, what position to use, and guides intromission. During intercourse, the couple is encouraged to use multiple stimulation (he touching her breasts, she stroking his testicles, kissing, fantasizing), which builds eroticism and heightens arousal.

Since 1998, an increasing number of men are using Viagra to improve erectile functioning. Viagra is the first user-friendly medical intervention; men take a pill approximately an hour before initiating sex. Viagra has two advantages: First, it is a vasodilator that enhances blood flow to the penis and allows the erection to maintain. Second, it serves as a positive psychological stimulus to reduce performance anxiety. The partners need to be comfortable and open in integrating Viagra into their intimacy, pleasuring, eroticism style.

Men who overcome erectile dysfunction do not go back to easy, automatic erections. They are aware, better lovers who have comfort and confidence with erections and appreciate variable, flexible sexual experiences. Approximately 85 percent of their sexual experiences flow into intercourse, another 5 to 10 percent involve nonintercourse sex to orgasm, and 5 to 10 percent are sensual experiences. Mediocre or disappointing sexual experiences (5–15 percent) are accepted. Neither the man nor the spouse overreacts. If sex gets off track, it is seen as a lapse, not a relapse. Men (and couples) who can shrug off or laugh about disappointing or unsuccessful sexual experiences are in a solid position to maintain erectile comfort and confidence.

ejaculatory inhibition

This is the least known male sexual dysfunction. The old terms *retarded ejaculation* or *ejaculatory incompetence* had a negative, put-down connotation. Ejaculatory inhibition or male orgasmic disorder refers to the man wanting to reach orgasm, but his sexual response is blocked (inhibited). The most severe form, primary ejaculatory inhibition (inability to ejaculate by any means), is very rare. Among young men, the most common manifestation is the inability to ejaculate during intercourse, although they do during masturbation (and usually with manual or oral stimulation). This can continue for years, not being addressed until the couple wants to become pregnant.

Ejaculatory inhibition is most common in the intermittent form, affecting as many as 15 percent of men, especially after age 50. Difficulty in ejaculating stems from a range of inhibitions—the inability to let go, beginning intercourse at low levels of arousal, not being comfortable requesting additional erotic stimulation, fear or ambivalence about pregnancy, or feeling sexually guilty or fearful.

Some males reach orgasm with a very narrow type of stimulation—rubbing against bedsheets, a fetish arousal pattern, or self-stimulation with partner present. They feel inhibited during intimate, interactive sex. Sex is a cooperative, sharing experience between two people who are actively involved in giving and receiving pleasure. With ejaculatory inhibition, this process is blocked. Rather than orgasm being the natural culmination of arousal, it becomes an anxiety-provoking goal the man fails to achieve.

As with other sexual dysfunctions, ejaculatory inhibition is best viewed as a couple issue. The couple—not just the man—has to increase involvement and erotic stimulation, which allows arousal to naturally flow to orgasm. You cannot will or force an orgasm—the key is to increase arousal, especially subjective feelings of being involved and turned on. Erections (objective arousal) can occur at low levels of subjective arousal, so the woman mistakenly believes that the man is highly aroused. A common inhibition is feeling shy about requesting additional erotic stimulation. Males with ejaculatory inhibition can have intercourse for half an hour, an hour, or longer. Those suffering from early ejaculation or couples worrying about erectile performance envy these men. What nonsense! This type of intercourse is mechanical (and sometimes aversive), not pleasure-oriented. Involvement and arousal do not increase. Intercourse is more to service the partner than to give and receive pleasure.

Two techniques facilitate orgasm—multiple stimulation and using orgasm triggers. A guideline is not to initiate intercourse until the man's subjective arousal is at least a "6," and preferably a "8." Another is to request erotic stimulation to increase arousal—this can involve fellatio while he moves rhythmically, and she strokes his buttocks or testicles, or combining kissing and manual stimulation. Requesting erotic stimulation during intercourse enhances involvement and arousal. Why should multiple stimulation cease when intercourse begins? Erotic stimulation involves giving, as well as receiving, stimulation. You can switch intercourse positions. She does testicle or buttock stimulation, while he gives breast or clitoral stimulation. He verbalizes sexy feelings, fantasizes, or tells erotic stories.

Orgasm triggers are idiosyncratic. One of the best ways to identify orgasm triggers is to tune into the touches, thoughts, fantasies, and movements you utilize during masturbation right before the point of ejaculatory inevitability. You can transfer these to partner sex. Orgasm triggers include verbalizing or making sounds, moving your body, focusing on a fantasy, giving stimulation, watching the partner, and doing rhythmic thrusting. Use orgasm triggers to move from high arousal to letting go and coming.

sexual dysfunction and inhibited sexual desire

Sexual dysfunction often results in secondary inhibited sexual desire. Sex is no longer an anticipated pleasure. It becomes a source of disappointment and frustration. Sex is something to be feared and avoided. This is exacerbated when the man employs "do it yourself" techniques, such as using two condoms or a desensitizing cream for ejaculatory control; using a "cock ring" or doing an injection for erection problems without telling the spouse; or buying a herb or potion that is supposed to force ejaculation. These either do nothing or cause more severe sexual or relationship problems. Sex is a "team sport." You need to communicate and work as an intimate team to resolve the problem. Focus on rebuilding a comfortable, functional couple sexual style. It is a gradual process, not a miracle cure. Engaging in couple sex therapy is more successful than trying it alone. There is a positive reciprocal relationship between sexual pleasure and sexual desire. Inhibited desire and performance anxiety subvert pleasure for both spouses.

variant sexual arousal

Approximately 2 to 5 percent of males have a variant arousal pattern. The most common types are fetish arousal, cross-dressing, using "900" numbers with a speciality in "kinky" fantasies, cybersex, and sado-masochistic behavior. A second type is a "noxious paraphilia," involving a sexual arousal pattern that is abusive and illegal. This includes exhibitionism, voyeurism, frotteurism, obscene phone calls, and pedophilia.

The variant arousal is very narrow, but very powerful. It combines high eroticism with high shame, a poisonous combination. It is quite difficult, and usually impossible, to transfer variant arousal to couple sex. Premaritally and early in the marriage the man might be functional, but over time he develops inhibited sexual desire. There is low desire for intimate, interactive sex. Sexual desire is trapped in the narrow dead end of variant arousal.

This problem absolutely requires clinical intervention. Typically, the man is in denial or minimizes the impact of the variant arousal. He is intent on keeping this secret from his spouse, especially a noxious paraphilia. The secret is exposed when he is arrested or loses his job— a major crisis for the man and the marriage. Preventative intervention is preferable to crisis management. This problem will not be resolved unless addressed therapeutically.

Let us consider the more serious problem first, the noxious paraphilia. This is both illegal and harmful to others. The pattern develops in childhood or early adolescence and is reinforced by thousands of experiences of masturbating to images of deviant arousal. It is best thought of as a compulsive, addictive behavior that serves as the man's "secret sexual world." He distorts reality by thinking it is okay and does not harm others. Couple sex cannot compete with this distorted fantasy and secret world.

Fetishism, cross-dressing, masturbating to pornography, going to massage parlors or prostitutes, and telephone or online sex do not involve illegal activity (in most American cities) or harm to others. However, they are very impactful on the marriage, subverting couple intimacy. The woman feels relieved when the problem is revealed because she has blamed herself or felt "crazy." Rather than feeling involved and turned on during partner sex, the man tries to shut her off and to focus on the variant fantasies. Most men, and many women, use fantasies as a bridge to desire and arousal, a healthy form of erotic stimulation. However, variant fantasies serve as a wall to block out the partner. Intimacy is a victim of variant sexual arousal.

The therapeutic strategy is a one-two combination of the male confronting and stopping the variant arousal pattern and the couple developing an intimate, interactive sexual style. The woman is not responsible for changing the man's variant arousal; he is. It is a joint responsibility to develop a comfortable, functional couple sexual style.

sexual orientation issues

Sexual orientation issues are extremely disruptive to the man and a major threat to the marriage. This type of issue is a powerful secret he tries to hide from his wife. Emotionally and sexually, he is leading a double life.

Sometime in their lives (most often in adolescence or early adulthood), approximately one of four men has a sexual experience with another man. Sexual fantasies or experiences with men do not mean the person is homosexual. Sexual orientation means an emotional and sexual commitment to a woman (heterosexual) or a man (homosexual). In clinical practice, Barry has seen a range of situations, from someone who is clearly gay and uses the marriage as a convenient cover; to a man who is aroused by being fellated in an anonymous encounter, but is not emotionally or sexually attracted to men; to men who are passive in anal intercourse (the most dangerous behavior for HIV/AIDS); to men who obsess about and are afraid of being homosexual, yet are clearly heterosexual; to men who use sex with males as a way to get back at the spouse. In cases where the husband's orientation is homosexual, trying to convert him to heterosexuality for the sake of the marriage or children is self-defeating. Most of these marriages will end in divorce, and that is for the best. Trying to pretend about a desire that is nonexistent is in no one's interest. Because of emotional closeness, concern for children, convenience, or any combination of these, some couples choose to stay in a no-sex marriage (often with one or both people having affairs). These decisions are best made in the context of couple or individual therapy.

Where the male is ambivalent about sexual orientation, the treatment of choice is individual therapy, with couple therapy occurring concurrently or sequentially. Sexual orientation is a major life commitment. Although it is possible to be sexual with both men and women, this does not mean the person's orientation is bisexual. If bisexuality is defined as equal emotional and sexual commitment to both sexes, the number of true bisexuals is small. To rebuild desire, the man's sexual commitment must be heterosexual. He cannot pretend or try to convert to save the marriage.

EXERCISE—CONFRONTING MALE SEXUAL PROBLEMS

This exercise has two components. The man honestly and objectively examines past and present sexual functioning in regard to premature ejaculation, erectile problems, and ejaculatory inhibition. Is sex functional or dysfunctional? How does this affect sexual desire? The man should not blame the spouse, but take responsibility for his sexual attitudes, behavior, and feelings.

The second component is sharing understandings with the spouse. The man proposes a strategy to address the sexual problems, whether through individual therapy, marital therapy, sex therapy, or a self-help approach. He should be clear about how he plans to change and what he needs from his spouse.

If there is a problem with a variant arousal pattern or sexual orientation, this exercise might cause it to surface for the first time. It has been the man's shameful secret. He needs to confront this, rather than to deny or minimize. Is he open to change? Is he willing to seek therapy? Does this problem mean the marriage is not viable? Is he motivated to maintain the marriage and resolve the problem? What is a healthy role for the wife?

In sharing information about sexual dysfunction or other sexual problems, the wife has an opportunity to present her perceptions and feelings and to add a helpful perspective. She can suggest alternative ways to approach the problem or support his proposed strategy. She clarifies what she is willing to do, as well as her limits. How can she be an active, intimate team member in confronting the sexual problem and revitalizing marital sexuality?

DOUG AND ALICIA

Doug and Alicia fell into the traditional trap, where he wanted to ignore or minimize the sexual problem and she wanted to cure it for him. When this did not happen, Alicia became angry and Doug's worst critic. Doug married Alicia at 27, making jokes that he finally got caught. In reality, he was glad to be married and looked forward to a secure marriage.

Although Doug had engaged in sex with over 20 women, he never discussed the problem of premature ejaculation. He focused on sexual quantity rather than quality, lasting longer the second time. Alicia had not raised the issue of early ejaculation, either. Alicia had had fewer premarital partners, but the relationships lasted longer. In her experience, ejaculatory control usually improved after some months. She naively hoped this would happen with Doug.

The "magic of romantic love/passionate sex" lasted 8 months, ending 4 months before marriage. Doug and Alicia admitted that the quality of their premarital sex was not high, but fondly remembered it as a very special time.

Romantic love fades even among the most loving, sexually functional couples. Unless romantic love is replaced by mature intimacy, the sexual relationship is vulnerable. Three months before marriage, Doug threatened to call it off because Alicia was saying no to sex with increasing frequency. Rather than deal with the issues of sexual desire and premature ejaculation, Alicia tried to placate Doug. This proved disastrous for both. Alicia felt sexually anxious and pressured. Increasingly, she resented Doug, feeling more alienated and less aroused. Alicia's desire and orgasms decreased. Doug felt it was on his shoulders to keep sex alive, and his focus was frequency.

A year and a half into the marriage, the problem of premature ejaculation was raised, this time with more vehemence and less empathy. After a frustrating experience, Alicia accused Doug of being uncaring and sexually selfish. He was shocked and offended and counterattacked by calling her a "frigid bitch." Alicia saw him as mean and she withdrew. Impulsive sexual fights in bed are volatile and counterproductive.

Doug decided that he would show her by achieving ejaculatory control on his own. He used as his resource an advertisement in a men's magazine, offering a desensitizing cream with a money-back guarantee. All it did was irritate his penis. Doug then consulted a male sex clinic that prescribed a low dose of antidepressant medication (Prozac, the miracle drug). He did not tell Alicia about this, but was pleased that his ejaculatory control improved. When Alicia found the medication, she was very concerned about Doug's depression. This made him so self-conscious, he threw out the pills. Premature ejaculation returned with a vengeance. Medication can help with ejaculatory control, but is not a miracle cure. If incorporated into a couple's ejaculatory control program, medication can be a valuable resource. However, if done alone, especially if kept secret from the spouse, it is likely to backfire and cause sexual alienation and inhibited desire.

Doug's strategy had been to do it himself, reduce excitement, and prove something to Alicia. Unfortunately, he wound up with a worse problem—erectile anxiety. He inserted as soon as he became hard, ejaculated at or right after intromission, and blamed it on Alicia's sexual disinterest. This is an example of the iatrogenic effect of focusing on sexual performance; it creates a more severe sexual problem. It was not long before Doug and Alicia were avoiding not only intercourse but affectionate touch. They were stuck in the cycle of emotional alienation, inhibited desire, avoidance, and a low-sex marriage.

It was Alicia who challenged the cycle by suggesting couple sex therapy. Alicia had been in individual therapy as a college student and benefited from 2 years of group therapy as an adult. Doug was distrustful of general psychotherapy, but open to the idea of sex therapy.

Regaining comfort and confidence with arousal and erection was the initial therapeutic focus. Doug began to treat Alicia as an intimate friend and to share sexual concerns and anxieties, as well as sexual requests. Alicia was a willing and supportive sexual friend. Pleasuring exercises made Alicia feel very good, and her sexual enthusiasm transferred to Doug. This is the usual pattern—women find sex therapy concepts and techniques easier to accept than men. Intimacy and nondemand pleasuring greatly enhanced Alicia's sexual anticipation and desire. Her openness and desire increased Doug's involvement and arousal. With manual and oral stimulation, Doug was surprised at how quickly his confidence with erections returned. Sex was no longer a race toward erection, intercourse, and ejaculation. Slowing down the process, while increasing erotic stimulation, improved ejaculatory control.

A breakthrough occurred when they began the stop-start technique. Alicia used manual stimulation, and when Doug approached the point of ejaculatory inevitability, he signaled her to stop. They did this for 10 to 12 minutes. They openly communicated and enjoyed erotic feelings. Although Alicia found it less fun after the first week, they knew they could master ejaculatory control if they worked together. Being intimate friends, where each spouse's arousal enhances the other's, was particularly valuable. Doug was not performing for Alicia; they were sharing pleasure and eroticism.

For the transition to intercourse, Alicia guided intromission. She began with slow, long thrusting. They used the stop-start technique before and during intercourse. What worked even better was changing the type and rhythm of coital thrusting. Alicia could be orgasmic with both intercourse and nonintercourse stimulation. Doug particularly enjoyed Alicia being orgasmic during intercourse. Doug was learning ejaculatory control not for Alicia to have orgasms during intercourse, but to make the sexual experience comfortable, pleasurable, erotic, and satisfying for both.

male functioning and sexual desire

The male (and the couple) can enjoy the process of desire, arousal, orgasm, and satisfaction. A sign of healthy male sexuality is replacing unrealistic demands to be a perfectly performing sexual machine with a mutual pleasure orientation. Adolescent and young adult sexual experiences take place in a double standard context, which ultimately undermines male sexuality, especially after age 40 and in marriage. Easy, automatic, autonomous sexual functioning can transition into valuing intimate, interactive, variable, and flexible sexuality. Arousal or orgasmic dysfunction is a sign that this transition has been unsuccessful. The stage is set for a collapse into inhibited sexual desire and avoidance. Male inhibited desire is more likely than are female desire problems to lead to a no-sex marriage. Male sexual problems are harder to treat, interfere more with intercourse, and are more disruptive to the marriage.

Male sexual dysfunction is best conceptualized and treated as a couple problem—the wife's role as the intimate sexual friend is crucial. It is a one-two combination. He takes responsibility for changing his sexual attitudes, behavior, and feelings. They work together to develop a comfortable, functional, and flexible couple sexual style. This will inoculate the man and the couple against a no-sex or low-sex marriage with his aging and the aging of the marriage.

closing thoughts

Male sexual dysfunction usually precedes inhibited sexual desire. The man feels embarrassed and humiliated because he cannot meet the rigid performance demands he grew up with. He retreats into blaming of self, blaming of spouse, and sexual avoidance. The key to change is to adopt a broad, flexible, pleasure-oriented approach to sexuality. The couple is an intimate team that develops a comfortable, satisfying sexual style. The man's trying on his own is likely to be iatrogenic and to cause more serious marital and sexual problems. Couple sex therapy facilitates the change process. When the problem is a secret—involving sexual variations or orientation—therapy is vital.

CHAPTER 5

Finding Her Voice: Overcoming Female Dysfunction

Woman have the same right to desire, arousal, orgasm, and satisfaction as men. The biggest mistake people make is to define female sexuality narrowly and mechanically. Sex does not equal intercourse. Sexual satisfaction does not equal orgasm. The myth is that if a woman has an orgasm, she will not have inhibited sexual desire. We are strong advocates for female orgasm, but this is not the cure for desire problems.

Sexual function includes desire (anticipating being sexual and feeling that you deserve sexual pleasure), arousal (receptivity and responsivity to genital stimulation, resulting in feeling turned on and in vaginal lubrication), orgasm (letting go and allowing arousal to naturally culminate in orgasm), and satisfaction (feeling good about yourself, the spouse, and your intimate bond). The most common female sexual dysfunctions (in order of frequency) are

1. Secondary inhibited sexual desire
2. Primary inhibited sexual desire
3. Secondary nonorgasmic response during partner sex
4. Painful intercourse
5. Arousal dysfunction
6. Primary nonorgasmic response during partner sex

7. Primary nonorgasmic response
8. Vaginismus

A primary sexual dysfunction means that there has always been a problem (i.e., primary inhibited sexual desire means she has never felt deserving of sexual satisfaction). Secondary dysfunction means that she was sexually functional, but has become dysfunctional (i.e., secondary inhibited sexual desire means she once anticipated and enjoyed sex, but now has little or no desire). Some women experience arousal and orgasm, but have inhibited desire. More typically, arousal and orgasm problems result in secondary inhibited desire.

It is crucial to resolve the dysfunction when that is the main factor inhibiting desire. For example, if the woman had a history of sexual desire, but develops pain during intercourse and secondary nonorgasmic response, these are the focus of treatment. Pain-free and orgasmic sex will result in increased desire. On the other hand, when the desire problem is primary and chronic (whether or not she experiences orgasm), desire is the focus of treatment. For most women, both desire and dysfunction issues need to be addressed.

As with desire problems, arousal and orgasm dysfunction are best considered a couple issue. The traditional trap was to label the woman *frigid*. Happily, that term has fallen into disrepute. The "politically correct" explanation is to blame the partner—"Males are selfish, lousy lovers." The old trap was to blame the woman; the new trap is to blame the man. It is a cop-out to label the woman frigid or the man a lousy lover. Blaming makes the problem worse.

The therapeutic strategy is the one-two combination of the woman increasing awareness and taking responsibility for her sexuality and the couple working as an intimate team. She increases feelings of comfort, deserving, and anticipation. She takes an active role in the pleasuring process. Keys to arousal are receptivity and responsivity to genital and erotic stimulation. She communicates and guides the spouse (either by putting her hand over his or making verbal requests), showing him what turns her on. They learn to talk, feel, problem solve, and share as an intimate team. He is open to her requests and guidance, instead of playing the "macho" role of the sex expert. They are trusting, equitable partners.

In the traditional scenario the woman remains passive, while the man "services" her during foreplay to get her ready for the main event of intercourse. Although some women prefer this scenario, most prefer "pleasuring." Pleasuring refers to giving and receiving sensual and erotic touching, especially the "give to get" pleasuring guideline. They enjoy each other's pleasure. One's arousal plays off and builds on the other's. The husband is an involved, caring partner. Pleasure and arousal are good in and of themselves; they do not have to be goal-oriented (i.e., intercourse). Unfortunately, our culture labels erection as the measure of male sexuality and orgasm as the measure of female sexuality. These rigid performance criteria inhibit sexual desire and satisfaction.

Major misunderstandings are rampant concerning female arousal and orgasm. Old myths involved female passivity and less sexual capacity. Women felt pressure to be like men—have one orgasm during intercourse. Old repressive myths have given way to new performance myths. These include the belief that the woman must have an orgasm each time, that orgasm is the only measure of satisfaction, that nothing equals a "G" spot orgasm, and that being multiorgasmic is superior to having a single orgasm.

The scientifically valid concept is that female sexual response is more variable, flexible, and complex than is male sexual response. Male response is more predictable and stereotyped (i.e., he has one orgasm during intercourse). The woman can be nonorgasmic, singly orgasmic, or multiorgasmic, which can occur in the pleasuring/foreplay period, through intercourse, or during afterplay. More variable and flexible does not mean better or worse.

There is not "one right way" to experience orgasm. Only one in four women follows the male model of a single orgasm during intercourse. The most common pattern for "Jane and Joe Average" is for Jane to be orgasmic with manual or oral stimulation, or both, during pleasuring and for Joe to be orgasmic during intercourse. Most women can be orgasmic during intercourse, but many find it easier and more satisfying to be orgasmic with nonintercourse sex or with multiple stimulation during intercourse. Most women do not have an orgasm at each sexual opportunity. Approximately 20 percent of women have a multiorgasmic response pattern. If she has six orgasms, does that mean she is six times more satisfied? There is no evidence that women who are multiorgasmic feel more satisfied than do women who are singly orgasmic. The healthy concept is to develop an arousal and orgasm pattern that allows the woman to enjoy sexual experiences and be orgasmic most of the time. The woman, as well as the couple, can enjoy the variability and flexibility of female sexual response.

What does this mean for desire, arousal, orgasm, and satisfaction? The key is accepting and enjoying variability and flexibility. Competing with a male performance standard subverts female desire. Each woman and each couple develop their sexual response pattern—differences and preferences are respected and accepted. The woman—not the man or an arbitrary performance criterion—is the expert on her sexuality.

orgasm during intercourse

Freud made the distinction between "vaginal orgasm," which he labeled as mature, normal, and occurring during intercourse, and "clitoral orgasm," which occurred during self-stimulation or partner manual, oral, or rubbing stimulation. Freud labeled clitoral orgasms as immature, less than normal. Scientific research by Masters and Johnson and clinical work by sex therapists found this to be inaccurate. A rigid performance criterion is scientifically incorrect and psychologically self-defeating.

Physiologically, an orgasm is an orgasm—whether resulting from masturbation, partner manual stimulation, intercourse, cunnilingus, vibrator stimulation, or rubbing stimulation. There are differences in women's preferences and satisfaction. The woman develops an arousal and orgasm pattern that she feels comfortable and satisfied with. This may or may not include being orgasmic during intercourse.

Nonorgasmic response during intercourse is *not* a sexual dysfunction—it is a normal variation of female sexuality. If she is aroused and orgasmic during partner sex and enjoys intercourse, this is optimal for her. One in three women never experiences orgasm during intercourse. There is nothing "better" or "more mature" about orgasm during intercourse. Many women who are orgasmic during intercourse utilize multiple stimulation—their own or their partners' manual clitoral stimulation, vibrator stimulation, or indirect clitoral stimulation provided by certain intercourse positions and movements. This is neither superior nor inferior to women who are orgasmic with manual, oral, vibrator, or rubbing stimulation. It is neither superior or inferior to women who are orgasmic with only intercourse stimulation. Orgasm is not a competitive performance. Orgasm is a natural result of involvement, pleasure, arousal, erotic flow, and letting go emotionally and sexually.

Let us review the most common arousal and orgasm dysfunctions.

secondary nonorgasmic response during partner sex

Secondary nonorgasmic response during partner sex has increased in the last decade and is a major cause of inhibited sexual desire. The woman had been orgasmic, but no longer is or rarely is (less than 20 percent). Part of the problem is performance anxiety and unrealistic expectations caused by the media's emphasis on the "big O." Orgasm has received inordinate focus, more than any other area of female sexuality. It is as if female sexuality = orgasm. It has become a measure of the man to ensure she has an orgasm. This performance focus is self-defeating, resulting in secondary dysfunction.

Orgasm is integral to the desire-comfort-pleasure-arousal cycle, not something separate from it. Orgasm is the natural culmination of involved erotic stimulation. Women have fallen into the male trap of pressuring themselves to be orgasmic each time, and, if not, they feel sex was a failure.

You do not need the "right" orgasm to prove something to yourself or the spouse. Orgasm is an erotic, flowing process. It begins with feeling comfortable and responsible for your sexuality, being receptive and responsive to stimulation, and letting go and allowing arousal to flow to orgasm. Personal responsibility includes making sexual requests and guiding the partner. The spouse cannot make you have an orgasm, nor is he responsible for your orgasm. He can be caring, cooperative, and sharing—your intimate friend.

Common causes of secondary nonorgasmic response are performance anxiety, anger, and emotional alienation. As is usually the case, sexual causes are easier to deal with than are emotional inhibitions or conflicts. The approach is to increase sexual comfort, pleasure, and arousal, while decreasing performance pressure. This begins with nondemand pleasuring and a temporary prohibition on intercourse. Put intimacy, pleasuring, playfulness, and eroticism back into sexuality. Nondemand pleasuring is the underpinning of sensuality and sexual response.

Allow sensual and sexual touching to move at the woman's pace, rather than at the man's. She makes requests and he is open to her guidance. For example, some women prefer beginning genital touching with breast stimulation, others with vulva stimulation. This is not a matter of right or wrong—identify your receptivity-responsivity pattern(s) and share it with your spouse. Most women prefer indirect, rather than direct, clitoral stimulation. A common female complaint is that the male tires of rhythmic stimulation and switches to stimulation that meets his needs. This breaks her arousal rhythm. The strategy for dealing with this is communicating your feelings and utilizing multiple stimulation. Arousal involves maintaining rhythmic clitoral stimulation while adding erotic stimulation, including manual or oral breast stimulation, stimulation of the mons or anal area, kissing and caressing, intravaginal finger stimulation, vibrator stimulation, or rubbing the penis against her breasts or vulva. Some women enjoy passively accepting stimulation; most prefer actively giving and receiving. Examples of being active include touching and stimulating him, focusing on a sexual fantasy, moving her body rhythmically to increase sensations, giving and receiving oral stimulation simultaneously, being in a standing or kneeling position that allows erotic touch and movement, and multiple stimulation during intercourse. Increasing involvement and eroticism are key.

Letting go and allowing arousal to flow into orgasm involves psychological, sexual, and relational factors. The more the problem is caused by emotional and relationship inhibitions, the more the couple has to become an intimate team. The change process is complex, and is undermined by miscommunication, misunderstanding, and frustration. When psychological and relational factors are the predominant cause, you are strongly encouraged to seek sex therapy, rather than to attempt change by yourself.

Anger, more than anxiety, interferes with sexual expression. The woman who has turned off sexually because of anger or alienation finds it difficult to think of herself as being part of an intimate team. Anger is a powerful inhibitor of sexual desire. Negative emotions, such as depression, boredom, sadness, frustration, and feeling put-off, block sexual response. Relational factors, such as lack of couple time, conflict over money, irritation concerning personal habits, disappointment in the spouse or marriage, repeating negative patterns from the family of origin, and conflict over intimacy, inhibit sexual desire. Situational factors, such as lack of privacy, the phone ringing, the kids coming in, no lock on the bedroom door, an uncomfortable bed, no time to be sexual, work stress, drug or alcohol abuse, and side effects of antidepressants or other medications, interfere with sexual response. Making the psychological, relational, and situational changes that are necessary to enjoy pleasure, arousal, and orgasm is doable, but not simple.

Sometimes the couple loses motivation and focus. The longer the dysfunction exists, the more likely it will result in inhibited sexual desire.

arousal dysfunction

For many women the problem is lack of arousal. Her subjective and objective arousal is low or nonexistent. Subjective arousal refers to feeling involved and turned on. Objective arousal includes vaginal lubrication, increased muscle tension, blood flow to the vulva, the nipples become hard, and she is physically receptive to intercourse. Some women are orgasmic at low levels of arousal, but typically, arousal flows to high levels, culminating in orgasm. Arousal dysfunction can be primary, but usually is secondary. A common theme is higher arousal from erotic stimulation than during intercourse. Another theme is that premarital sex was more arousing than marital sex is. Some women feel more aroused with their clothes on. Others say sex was more fun in the back seat of the car. The overfocus on goal-oriented intercourse robs sexuality of playfulness, seductiveness, and eroticism.

A key to understanding arousal problems is recognizing the different sexual socialization of women and men. Males typically learn arousal and orgasm through masturbation. Men learn that arousal is easy, predictable, and automatic. The man gets spontaneous erections, arousal is autonomous—he needs nothing from the woman. Female arousal is variable, slower, and can be lost because of distracting stimuli. Some women learn to masturbate to orgasm in childhood or during adolescence. However, for many women, masturbation begins later or does not occur. Interestingly, rates of female masturbation increase after marriage. A significant number of women are unsure of their arousal pattern. It is hard to share if you are not aware of your body's sexual receptivity/responsivity pattern.

Experiences with manual, oral, and rubbing stimulation are unsatisfactory. She reacts to the man's sexual style and needs, rather than establishing her own. The rhythm of touching is his, not hers. Very few women experience autonomous sexual arousal. Arousal is an intimate, interactive experience involving receptivity and responsivity to partner stimulation.

The most common sexual block is poor stimulation technique. Rather than blaming the spouse or labeling men as uncaring or insensitive lovers, she must take responsibility for her arousal. This includes awareness of her conditions for good sex—psychologically, relationally, and situationally. One woman's arousal dramatically increased after asking the husband to put a lock on their bedroom door, brush his teeth before kissing, and being sexual between 7 and 7:30 in the morning. For some women, a prime condition for good sex is feeling emotionally close before beginning erotic touching. For others, kissing and touching promote intimacy. For some, talking builds intimacy and arousal—for others, talking distracts from arousal. Be aware of your conditions for arousing sex and communicate these.

Her sexual feelings and needs are as important as his. When there is an arousal dysfunction, the couple is better to follow her rhythm of touching and stimulation. The main mistake men make as arousal builds is to increase the speed and hardness of stimulation. He does this not to subvert her arousal, but because that is his arousal pattern. She needs to establish and communicate her rhythm of arousal, focusing on steady, slow, gradually building erotic stimulation. Some women prefer one focused stimulation at a time. Most prefer multiple stimulation. Some prefer receiving; others find give-and-take stimulation most arousing. Many women find stimulating the spouse arousing. Be aware of your psychological, relational, erotic, and situational conditions for good sex. Make clear, specific requests; you are an active member of the intimate team.

medical interventions to enhance female arousal

The physicians women turn to for sexual concerns are gynecologists or endocrinologists. The most common concern is lack of vaginal lubrication, especially among perimenopausal and menopausal women. Yet there are women in their 20s who feel subjectively aroused, but are poor lubricators. Gynecologists assess for underlying pathology, such as low estrogen, vaginal infections, or side effects of medication. The physician can prescribe estrogen-based creams or hormone replacement therapy for some women. The most common intervention is an over-the-counter water-based lubricant.

There are two new trends in the medical treatment of female sexual dysfunction. The first is to use supplemental testosterone therapy. This is especially true for those menopausal women who report a total lack of sexual thoughts, fantasies, and sexual urges. The second is Viagra (an oral medication developed to treat erectile dysfunction). Although in early phases of development and testing, oral medications or creams to facilitate arousal show promise. As with any medical intervention, it is important to view this as an additional resource to promote desire and arousal, not a magic cure. Lubricants or medications need to be integrated into the couple's lovemaking style of intimacy, pleasuring, and eroticism.

painful intercourse

Painful intercourse (the technical term is dyspareunia) occurs on occasion to the great majority of women. This is a chronic problem for 10 to 15 percent. It is crucial to consult a gynecologist for a comprehensive assessment of hormonal, vascular, neurological, and structural factors. If a specific physical cause is not found, the woman concludes that it is all in her head and feels put-down. Pain is real; it is in your vulva, not in your head. Pain is a complex psychophysiological process. Often, the best way to deal with painful intercourse is through psychological and behavioral changes, rather than with medication or surgery. Medication is most effective when there is an acute infection.

Two techniques are especially valuable for pain occurring during intromission. The first is for the woman to initiate and guide intromission. This makes sense because she is the expert on her vagina. Her guiding intromission will sometimes reduce or eliminate discomfort. The second technique is to use a lubricant to facilitate intromission and coital thrusting. Many women use K-Y Jelly because it is a sterile substance they are familiar with from gynecological exams. Other women prefer lubricants that feel or smell sensuous—be sure they are hypoallergenic and water-based to prevent infection. Favorites are Astroglide, abalone lotion, aloe vera lotion, or flavored lotions. This is especially helpful for women who feel subjectively aroused, but experience limited lubrication. There are a number of causes of decreased lubrication, including aging. Forty-year-old women lubricate less do 20-year-old women, and 60-year-old women lubricate less than do 40-year-old women.

A common cause of painful intercourse is discomfort resulting from prolonged coital thrusting. The average time spent in intercourse is 2 to 7 minutes (the average time for the entire lovemaking experience is 15 to 45 minutes). Less than 10 percent of intercourse experiences extend longer than 10 minutes. Women who are orgasmic during nonintercourse sex do enjoy intercourse. Involvement and arousal decrease after 10 minutes of thrusting, and vaginal irritation increases. Especially if he engages in hard, prolonged thrusting, she is in danger of irritation, which can be painful, as well as can heighten the risk of tearing the vaginal walls, developing an infection, or both. It is important to communicate when discomfort begins, so that you avoid pain.

One way to increase involvement and arousal is multiple stimulation during intercourse. Why should kissing, caressing, playful touching, and erotic stimulation stop when the penis enters the vagina? Touching during intercourse can include breast stimulation, buttock stimulation, clitoral stimulation, and testicle stimulation. Switch intercourse positions or types of stroking if there is discomfort. Many women find circular thrusting particularly pleasurable, or they enjoy longer, slower thrusting. Men prolong intercourse with the hope that the woman will reach orgasm, not realizing she is becoming less turned on. Communicating and working as an intimate team are crucial.

There are a number of gynecological interventions for difficult, complex, or chronic cases. The most intrusive is surgery. Alternatives include exercises to strengthen vaginal muscles, hormone replacement therapy, suppositories, and medication. Be sure you have a good rapport with the gynecologist, and she takes the pain problem seriously. Referral to a subspecialist in gynecological pain might be advisable. Ask the spouse to accompany you to appointments. Be clear about how he can be helpful, practically and emotionally, in reducing painful intercourse.

primary nonorgasmic response

Primary nonorgasmic dysfunction (also called pre-orgasmic) means the woman has never experienced orgasm by any means (5 to 10 percent of adult women). The more common problem is primary nonorgasmic dysfunction during partner sex (10 to 15 percent of women complain of this). In this case, she has been orgasmic with self or vibrator stimulation, but not during partner sex. Approximately half of young women learn to be orgasmic during masturbation, the other half with partner manual, oral, or rubbing stimulation. Less than 10 percent of women have their first orgasm during intercourse.

The treatment of choice for pre-orgasmic women involves increased sexual awareness, body exploration, and masturbation. This can be done individually, augmented by self-help materials and exercises, or through a 10-session women's sexuality group. The group reduces stigma and provides practical and emotional support and motivation for change as women see others progressing. Masturbation as a treatment technique was revolutionary a generation ago. Self-exploration and masturbation are now recognized as the most natural, easiest way of learning to be orgasmic. Men have few problems reaching orgasm, in part because of masturbation experiences. The woman who is aware of her arousal and orgasm pattern can transfer this knowledge to partner sex. Masturbation promotes a healthy, self-affirming attitude toward your body and personal responsibility for sexuality. Use of vibrator stimulation as an adjunct to masturbation has become popular in the past 25 years. The speed and intensity of vibrator stimulation break down inhibitions and self-consciousness and serve as an orgasm trigger. Although women fear becoming "hooked" on the vibrator, most find the transition to hand or partner stimulation relatively easy. Women use vibrator stimulation (either alone or during partner sex) as a special turn-on to facilitate orgasm.

Self-stimulation allows the woman to be aware of and use "orgasm triggers." This facilitates moving from high levels of arousal to orgasm. Orgasm triggers are variable and individualistic. They include tightening leg or thigh muscles, or both, to build tension until it bursts forth in orgasm; verbalizing you are "going to come"; doing breast and clitoral stimulation simultaneously as you move toward orgasm; and using vibrator or intravaginal finger stimulation to enhance orgasmic sensations. Erotic stimulation is focused and rhythmic. Reinforce orgasm triggers. Then transfer these learnings to partner sex.

Many women find it easier to learn to be orgasmic through masturbation than through partner sex. For some women, the transition to orgasm with a partner is easy; for others, difficult. If nonorgasmic response during partner sex involves a specific sexual inhibition, it is simpler to resolve than if there is an emotional inhibition. The most direct technique is stimulating yourself to orgasm with the spouse present. Sexually and emotionally, this is a major breakthrough. He can observe how you become aroused and reach orgasm (which is motivating and exciting). Then, he (with your guidance) stimulates you to orgasm. For women who feel self-conscious, asking him to be vulnerable and do it first can be freeing.

Key concepts are for the woman to take the sexual lead, develop her "sexual voice," make requests, and set an erotic rhythm. He is open and responsive to her requests. A key component in a healthy marriage is the husband's openness to the wife's influence. Discard the belief that it is his responsibility to "make her come." This pressure wilts her sexual desire and arousal. The pressure on him results in frustration and anger, which negates his role as the intimate spouse. Neither he nor she can force an orgasm. Orgasm is a natural result of erotic stimulation and letting go. Orgasm cannot be willed, forced, or coerced. Focus on the scenarios, positions, feelings, and erotic techniques that heighten arousal. If you think of arousal being on a scale of 0 (neutral) to 5 (moderate) to 10 (orgasm), most women find that the problem is getting from 2 to 5. Neither cunnilingus nor intercourse is arousing unless feelings are at least 5 before beginning erotic activities. Otherwise, erotic stimulation can be counterproductive, resulting in self-consciousness.

Traditionally, couples transition to intercourse at the man's initiative when he feels she is ready. Let the woman initiate the transition to cunnilingus or intercourse. Many women find it easier to be orgasmic with oral stimulation. Being orgasmic is more than just prolonging stimulation. Moving from 5 to 8 on the arousal scale involves making verbal and nonverbal requests to enhance erotic feelings. These include multiple types of stimulation, such as combining manual clitoral stimulation, oral breast stimulation, and stroking the penis; involving yourself in an erotic fantasy as you enjoy cunnilingus; switching positions to kneeling or standing while moving your body in rhythm with his stimulation; and rubbing your clitoris against his penis or thigh while he is playing with your breasts or buttocks. Use of orgasm triggers allows arousal to flow from 8 to 10. Orgasm triggers in partner sex are similar to or the same as orgasm triggers with masturbation.

Some women either prefer or need intercourse for orgasm. Female sexuality is about individual differences. Starting intercourse at level 5, or preferably level 7, facilitates arousal during intercourse. Let her set the rhythm of thrusting—this is easier in the woman-on-top or side intercourse positions. Use of additional clitoral stimulation by her hand, his hand, or vibrator allows arousal to build toward orgasm. Asking him to make specific movements, putting your hands on his buttocks, or guiding his movements are valuable techniques. Communicate and experiment to develop an arousal pattern that allows you to enjoy orgasm during partner sex.

vaginismus

This is an infrequent sexual dysfunction, but one that disrupts the sexual relationship and can drain desire. Vaginismus refers to the tightening or spasming of the vaginal introitus, which makes intercourse impossible or very painful. A gynecological examination is necessary for appropriate diagnosis. Vaginismus requires sex therapy using *in vivo* desensitization (often using vaginal dilators). Active involvement and support of the spouse are crucial. The good news is that the likelihood of successful treatment is high; the bad news is that it is a gradual, sometimes frustrating, process. Maintaining motivation and working as an intimate team are critical, but can be emotionally taxing. Couples do best when they are open to nonintercourse sensual and erotic experiences. Physical and emotional connection makes it easier to rebuild desire. Couples who have stopped physical contact are faced with a double task of rebuilding connection and confronting vaginismus.

Often, what motivates the couple is a desire to become pregnant. The need for intravaginal ejaculation challenges the pattern of avoidance. Although gynecologists do insemination with the husband's sperm, most couples prefer trying to become pregnant naturally—that is, through intercourse. Desire for a child is a powerful impetus. The couple works as an intimate team, using the resources of a gynecologist, a sex therapist, and sometimes a physical therapist. The woman increases awareness and control of her vaginal muscles. She gradually guides intromission. Use woman-on-top intercourse with slow, comfortable thrusting. One benefit of treating vaginismus is that it increases the woman's awareness, responsivity, and valuing of sexuality, which inoculates her against desire problems in the future.

FAITH AND SAM

Faith and Sam had been married 4 ½ years. They were convinced that they were the only couple in American who had been married that long and not consummated their marriage. Faith's vaginismus had been diagnosed by the gynecologist before marriage, but he had not made a treatment recommendation. The minister who married them counseled love and patience, but said nothing specific about sex. Premaritally, Faith and Sam had been sexually active, utilizing oral and rubbing stimulation. This decreased over time.

Faith developed secondary arousal dysfunction, secondary orgasmic dysfunction, and secondary inhibited sexual desire. Sam remained sexually functional, but became hostile and emotionally distant. He had two one-night affairs and threatened an ongoing affair. Faith felt that would be devastating and would throw the marriage into crisis. She had manual sex with Sam one to two times a week, but it was one-way sex, in which she was uninvolved, just "servicing" him. These experiences further reduced Faith's sexual desire. Sam enjoyed orgasm, but felt emotionally isolated. It was a self-defeating cycle. This pattern protected them from addressing the desire and vaginismus problems.

The motivation that led to therapy was a shared desire to have a child. Sam viewed a baby as a bond that would hold the marriage together (a questionable rationale, but helpful for Sam and Faith). Children were an integral part of Faith's life plan and a strong motivation to resolve vaginismus. The gynecologist recommended bypassing the sexual issue by using artificial insemination. Neither partner was enthusiastic about that technological solution, so the gynecologist made a referral to a female sex therapist with expertise in treating vaginismus.

Sam and Faith were relieved to learn that other couples have nonconsummated marriages and that vaginismus is a treatable problem with a good prognosis. The fact that Faith's desire, arousal, and orgasm dysfunctions were secondary showed she had the ability to enjoy sex.

Inadvertently, Sam's sexual attitudes and behavior exacerbated Faith's sexual difficulties. Sam was surprised when the therapist asked if he wanted to be Faith's intimate friend or sexual critic (the role he now played). Desire had been subverted by frustration; they were working at cross-purposes. Each had to take responsibility for his or her behavior. Sam had to begin thinking, acting, and feeling like an intimate friend and spouse. Faith had to reinvolve herself in pleasuring and realize that she deserved arousal and orgasm. Faith set the pace for approaching vaginal intromission. Sam was her active supporter and "cheerleader."

With Faith taking initiative, Sam being the intimate friend who enjoyed giving, and performance pressure reduced, she enjoyed being sexual. The transition to outercourse for arousal and orgasm was relatively easy. Viewing erotic videos and Sam verbalizing sexual fantasies significantly enhanced Faith's arousal. At a different time, they did the slow, painstaking exercises to confront vaginismus. Faith learned general relaxation techniques, specific pelvic relaxation, pubococcygeal muscle control, use of dilators for vaginal insertion, movement with fingers and dilators, and playing with Sam's penis around her vagina. Faith felt in control of the process. Fear and discomfort gradually decreased, and Faith was open to intravaginal sensations. Once intromission occurred, they did not immediately go to thrusting, but became comfortable with intercourse sensations and minimal movement (the "quiet vagina" exercise). Faith had to experience intercourse as functional before she could perceive it as pleasurable. Luckily, they were a couple that easily became pregnant (at their 4th month trying). Faith did not begin to enjoy intercourse until 6 months after the baby was born. Sam and Faith were satisfied with their lovemaking style, which integrated manual, oral, and intercourse stimulation.

EXERCISE—IDENTIFYING SEXUAL PROBLEMS AND DECIDING HOW TO PROCEED

This exercise is for the woman to do alone and then share with the spouse. Do an honest, objective assessment of past and present sexual attitudes, behavior, and feelings. Write this down to make it concrete. Create four categories: desire, arousal, orgasm, and satisfaction. Consider self-stimulation experiences, as well as partner experiences.

When has sexual desire (anticipation and deserving) felt the highest? When has arousal (being receptive and responsive to stimulation) been the highest? When have you been orgasmic (by self, partner manual stimulation, cunnilingus, vibrator stimulation, rubbing stimulation, intercourse, afterplay)? When have you felt the most satisfied, emotionally and sexually? Do not be surprised if your answers are at different times and different circumstances for each component. Some women remember a time when desire was high, even though they were not orgasmic. Some find they were sexually responsive even though, in retrospect, it was an unhealthy relationship. Be especially aware when arousal was high and you were easily orgasmic. If this never occurred, then the dysfunction is primary. If it has occured before, the dysfunction is secondary. This is a good way to assess whether the arousal or orgasm dysfunction, or both, preceded or followed the desire problem. The woman who is regularly orgasmic, but experiences inhibited desire, is in a different position than the woman whose desire decreased after developing an arousal or orgasm dysfunction.

How do you assess desire, arousal, orgasm, and satisfaction at present? Do you view arousal and orgasm as your responsibility, the spouse's, or joint? Taking responsibility is very different than blaming yourself or blaming the spouse!

In conveying your insights to the spouse, be clear in differentiating the past and present. Share understandings about your sexual function and dysfunction; do not do an assessment of his sexuality. Rather than blaming and counterblaming, describe the present state of sexuality. This allows the spouse to be nondefensive and give feedback on how he perceives and feels about the sexual problem.

Most important, make a proposal of how to address the problem. Our usual recommendation is couple sex therapy. Consider other alternatives, including a self-help individual or couple program, individual therapy, a woman's sexuality group, consulting a gynecologist or endocrinologist, or talking to a minister or marriage therapist. Tell your husband the alternatives you have considered and why you chose the one you did. Some women discuss two or three alternatives. The spouse's perceptions and feedback are a vital part of the problem-solving process. A self-defeating reaction is to give up and decide to do nothing. Benign neglect makes sexual problems more chronic and severe.

Decide on a strategy to address the sexual problem and make a good faith effort for it to be successful. If this does not help after a reasonable time and effort, explore a different alternative. Couples often decide to address the problem themselves, and if it does not change in 3 to 6 months, then seek professional intervention. Remember, sexual problems are changeable. Enhanced sexual desire and functioning increase personal and marital well-being.

closing thoughts

A woman learns to value sexuality for herself and for the marriage. The bad news is that rates of sexual dysfunction are higher for women than for men. The good news is that successful resolution of sexual problems is easier for women. Women do better in, and feel they get more from, couple sex therapy. There is not a direct relationship between sexual function and sexual desire. Usually, both issues have to be addressed, as well as the broader issue of intimacy.

PART 2

Changing

CHAPTER 6

The Second Step:
Nurturing Anticipation—
Bridges to Sexual Desire

PEOPLE BELIEVE THAT sexual desire is something you are born with—and that it cannot be changed. You either have it or you do not. People believe that those with low desire are somehow deficient or abnormal, that inhibited sexual desire is a character flaw. Our culture teaches that men are supposed to be the sexual experts and initiators, thereby increasing the stigma of inhibited sexual desire for men. No wonder so many men and women suffer in silence.

In truth, sexual desire is complex, with many causes and many dimensions. Desire involves physical, psychological, relational, cultural, and situational factors. Sexual desire can and does vary among individuals and between couples. Desire can be facilitated and strengthened— or it can be damaged and destroyed.

Inhibited sexual desire is best thought of as a "couple problem." Building bridges to desire is likewise best thought of as a couple process. Bridges to desire means ways of thinking, anticipating, and experiencing a sexual encounter that make sex inviting. Ideally, each person develops individual bridges to desire, as well as couple bridges to desire. Each bridge need not be mutual. Some sexual initiations and scenarios work better for one spouse than for the other; this is normal and healthy. For example, many men enjoy visual stimuli such as erotic clothing or an X-rated video to ignite desire. Many women prefer a scenario of extended, involved pleasuring to build sexual anticipation.

Sexuality is a one-two combination. First, you are responsible for your sexuality, including desire. Second, is being part of an intimate team. Intimate sexuality is about sharing, facilitating, encouraging, and supporting. It is not only normal, but preferable, for each spouse to have his or her bridges to desire. When you have multiple ways to anticipate and initiate sexual encounters, once the cycle of sexual avoidance is broken, desire will remain vital. You have a variety of ways to emotionally and sexually connect. Choice, rather than obligation, enhances desire. When sex degenerates into "Are we going to have intercourse or not?" the relationship is in trouble. When one spouse demands intercourse and the other wants to avoid pressure, the result is a power struggle and a no-sex or low-sex marriage. It is important to identify personal and couple poisons that subvert desire, but even more important to develop healthy attitudes, initiation patterns, and feelings that promote sexual desire.

core strategies

Strategies to facilitate sexual desire include:

1. Nurturing anticipation;
2. Owning your sexuality;
3. Feeling that you deserve sexual pleasure;
4. Enjoying arousing, orgasmic sex; and
5. Valuing intimate sexuality.

Desire is the core of sexuality. The prescription for sexual desire is positive anticipation, an emotionally intimate relationship, nondemand pleasuring, erotic scenarios and techniques, sharing orgasm, feeling emotionally bonded and satisfied, and maintaining a regular rhythm of sexual activity. Sexuality is a core means of expressing intimacy. Feeling intimate and connected is not dependent on intercourse. Touching can occur both inside and outside the bedroom. Not all touching has to, nor should it lead to, intercourse.

nurture anticipation

Anticipation is the central ingredient in sexual desire. Anticipation cannot be willed, forced, or coerced, but can be facilitated and nurtured. You undermine anticipation by bowing to internal or external pressure, faking sexual desire when you do not feel it.

There are two ways you can build sexual anticipation. First, look forward to sexual encounters in the same way that you look forward to a sporting or musical event. Our culture idealizes romantic, spontaneous, swept away, nonverbal sex. This makes for sexy movies and love songs, but is not helpful to married couples (especially those with jobs and children). Romance and spontaneity are fine, but being dependent on these is too limiting. "Intentional, planned sexual dates" can generate anticipation and desire. Be open to both planned and spontaneous sexual encounters. Set aside time and anticipate a sexual experience. Afterward, acknowledge and savor the experience. This establishes a positive feedback cycle—anticipation, satisfying sex, and enjoying a regular rhythm of sexual experiences. Unless you set aside couple time, sex becomes relegated to late at night in bed (which can be functional and fine, but is unlikely to be intimate or special). Being awake and aware facilitates anticipation.

The second way to build anticipation is being free to make requests, especially for special turn-ons. Requests improve sexual quality, increasing involvement and arousal. Ten minutes of foreplay, 5 minutes of intercourse, and 30 seconds of afterplay do not promote anticipation. Sex that has settled into a mechanical routine is not inviting. Erotic scenarios and turn-ons add a special dimension. When you feel comfortable talking about sexuality, can make requests, and are free to play out erotic scenarios, your desire will be robust.

Anticipation is inhibited by routine or mediocre sex, lack of intimate communication, taking for granted that all touching leads to intercourse, and sex in bed late at night with the lights out. You can enhance anticipation by setting aside couple time, planning intentional sexual dates, making requests, allowing sexuality to be fun and pleasure-oriented, and feeling free to play out erotic scenarios and turn-ons.

own your sexuality

You are responsible for yourself as a sexual person. It is not the spouse's job to make you desirous or turn you on. This is more easily accepted by males because men and women experience such different sexual socialization. The media emphasize how different sex is for women than for men. In truth, there are many more sexual similarities than differences between women and men. Psychological and relational factors are more important than physiological or hormonal factors in sexual desire.

One gender difference involves experience with masturbation. Over 90 percent of males have masturbated to orgasm by age 16. Female rates are less than half that, and a significant number of women do not masturbate until after marriage. Masturbation had been a source of guilt or embarrassment, but that view is based on ignorance. In truth, masturbation is normal, natural, and healthy. Masturbation helps men and women own their sexuality, learn about arousal and orgasm, and be in a better position to make requests and guide the partner.

You deserve sexual self-esteem. Sexuality enhances your life and marriage when it is comfortable, pleasure-oriented, and mutual. Owning your sexuality and feeling personal responsibility enhance desire. You feel free to assert your sexual rights (including freedom from unwanted pregnancy, STDS, HIV/AIDS, and sexual coercion). You are free to discuss sexual desires and wants, make requests, share vulnerabilities, disclose personal turn-ons, and feel accepted (not criticized or judged).

It is crucial to accept your sexual past, including negative or traumatic experiences. These include child sexual abuse, incest, and rape, as well as being exhibited to, being peeped on, receiving obscene phone calls, dealing with an STD, having an unwanted pregnancy, being sexually humiliated or rejected, having a sexual dysfunction, being sexually harassed, being caught masturbating, or feeling guilt over sexual fantasies. Negative sexual experiences are an almost universal phenomena for both females and males. It is normal to have negative sexual experiences, whether as a child, adolescent, young adult, or adult. You can accept these experiences and integrate them into your sexual self-esteem. You are a survivor, not a victim. Feeling controlled by guilt about past trauma cheats you from sexual self-acceptance and enjoyment of marital sexuality.

you deserve sexual pleasure

The essence of sexuality is giving and receiving pleasure-oriented touching. A focus on pleasure, rather than on performance, facilitates desire. Sexual performance to prove something to yourself or to the spouse, or to meet the spouse's demands, subverts sexual desire. You deserve to feel good about marital sex. Your sexual feelings, preferences, and desires count.

Males are socialized to focus on performance, especially on being orgasm-oriented rather than pleasure-oriented. The most common cause of male inhibited sexual desire is a sexual dysfunction (premature ejaculation, erectile problems, ejaculatory inhibition). The male feels that if he does not function perfectly, he does not deserve sexual pleasure, so avoids sex. Another performance trap is to focus on his wife's sexual performance—believing that she needs to be orgasmic each time and he is responsible for her orgasm. Performance orientation (whether his or hers) turns sex into a pass–fail test. This sets the stage for failure, avoidance, and inhibited desire. It is healthier (for both the man and the marriage) to adopt a pleasure orientation.

Feeling deserving of pleasure is particularly important for women. Our culture has not supported female sexuality, especially women valuing eroticism. Traditionally, female sexuality is contingent on romanticism, love, and body image. It is easy for the woman to fall into the trap of feeling that she does not deserve sexual pleasure and of turning herself off. It is as if sex is a reward for being a perfect woman in a perfect relationship. Loss of sexual pleasure is a punishment for any deficiency. She deserves to feel good about her body, to enjoy sensual and sexual touch, to have sexual thoughts and fantasies, to be erotic, and to anticipate sexuality—because she is a woman, noncontingent on any other factor. Women who are overweight deserve to feel sexual, women with a history of sexual trauma deserve to feel sexual, nonorgasmic women deserve to feel sexual, and women in conflictual marriages deserve to feel sexual. Feelings of being undeserving subvert self-acceptance and exacerbate inhibited sexual desire. Sexual pleasure is an inherent right for women (as well as for men).

enjoy arousing, orgasmic sex

Sometimes desire problems exist by themselves; more often, a desire problem coexists with an arousal or orgasm dysfunction. This is especially true of males with erectile dysfunction. Sexual comfort and confidence are important for both men and women. Sexual confidence requires changing attitudes and emphasizing a broad-based, flexible approach to sexuality—sex is so much more than intercourse. If desire is contingent on each experience being an "A" performance, you are vulnerable to inhibited sexual desire. When sexuality is broad-based, with a variety of bridges and pleasure-oriented scenarios, desire will be robust.

We are proponents of arousal, orgasm, and intercourse, but there is more to sexuality than that. The seductive, but false, assumption is that if both people had guaranteed orgasms, there would not be a desire problem. Many people, once they become involved, reach orgasm; the problem is anticipating and initiating sex. They "want to want to have sex," but do not.

You can increase awareness of your emotional and practical conditions for good sex, enhance intimacy, build sexual comfort, and be responsive to your spouse's feelings and requests. This provides a solid basis for sexual expression, but is not enough. Eroticism is key—increase manual and oral stimulation, experiment with erotic scenarios and techniques, utilize multiple stimulation during intercourse, and vary intercourse positions. An involved, aroused partner is the main aphrodisiac.

Some people prefer taking turns, others mutual stimulation. Some find intercourse most arousing; others prefer manual or oral sex. Some find one type of focused stimulation most erotic; others enjoy multiple stimulation. Be aware of and communicate your preferred arousal pattern(s).

Orgasm involves letting go and allowing arousal to naturally flow to climax. Men find it easiest to be orgasmic during intercourse. Female orgasmic response is more variable and individualistic—some women find it easier to be orgasmic with manual stimulation, others with oral stimulation, some with rubbing stimulation, some with vibrator stimulation, and others with intercourse stimulation. You can develop a mutually satisfying arousal-orgasm couple style.

value intimate sexuality

Intimacy is a major bridge for sexual desire. Marital sex involves integrating intimacy and eroticism. Traditional socialization taught men to value sex and women to value intimacy. Sexual desire is robust when each spouse values both emotional and sexual intimacy. The famous Ann Landers adage that 90 percent of women prefer affection to intercourse did not promote sexual communication. Ideally, both men and women value emotional intimacy, affection, pleasuring, eroticism, and intercourse.

Not valuing intimacy is primarily a male trap. Males learn about sex as a short, intense, easy, and, unfortunately, autonomous function. Men under 30 need little from the woman in order to experience desire, arousal, and orgasm. This does not serve the man well after 30, especially in marriage. If sexual desire is to remain vital, the man needs to be open to and to value intimate, interactive sexuality. An involved, aroused partner is the main aphrodisiac for both men and women. Valuing emotional connection and sexual intimacy is easier for the woman—that is the mode in which she learned to be sexual. It is a more challenging transition for the man. According to male mythology, "A real man has sex with any woman, any time, any place." He has to confront this attitude and learn to value intimate, interactive marital sexuality. He is used to being the giving sexual partner, receptive to her stimulation only after he is aroused. He assumes an easy, automatic erection and worries that he is a "wimp" or "impotent" if he wants or needs her help in the arousal process. The "give to get" pleasuring guideline had been one-way rather than mutual.

He must become aware that she receives pleasure from stimulating and arousing him. He learns to value intimate sexuality, sees her receptivity and responsivity as a cue for his arousal, is open and responsive to her manual and oral stimulation, and sees her as his intimate sexual friend. Desire is inhibited by self-consciousness, competitiveness, and performance orientation. Desire is enhanced by intimacy, giving and receiving erotic stimulation, and having a pleasure orientation.

LYDIA AND VICTOR

Like many couples in a no-sex marriage, Lydia and Victor were trapped in the cycle of embarrassment, guilt, blame, and resentment. Lydia's simple explanation was that Victor's incessant sexual pressure turned off her desire. Victor's simple explanation was that Lydia had sexually rejected him, and it was all her fault. Attack–counterattack and blaming increased emotional alienation. Affectionate touch was abandoned. They traded divorce threats.

Lydia consulted their minister, who wisely noted that this was a serious problem that required referral to a specialist who could treat both relationship problems and sexual dysfunction. Victor reluctantly agreed. When they presented at the therapist's office, they were a demoralized couple who easily fell into traps of anger and blaming. The therapist helped them confront these traps. The clinician asked each to say what he or she was afraid of. Under the anger was a great deal of hurt. Anger and blaming protected them from experiencing feelings of sadness and loneliness.

In individual meetings to assess psychological and sexual history, the therapist encouraged a self-focus. Sexual initiation was difficult for each spouse, although for different reasons. Victor was shy and unassertive. His nonverbal initiations were late at night. Lydia desired romantic, seductive initiations, but wanted them to come from Victor. She was put off by his initiation style, but felt uncomfortable initiating. Unfortunately, the rigidity and passivity she had learned in premarital experiences plagued marital sex. Lydia felt trapped in a no-sex marriage, felt hopeless about breaking the pattern, and was the one likely to leave.

In the couple feedback session, the therapist empathized with their feelings and frustrations, but was confrontative about the need to end the blame/attack cycle. Lydia and Victor agreed to a 6-month good faith effort to revitalize marital sexuality and build bridges to sexual desire. They ceased threats of divorce and stopped refighting old battles. If they wanted to discuss past issues, they agreed to do so in the therapist's office. At home, Victor and Lydia focused on increasing emotional and sexual intimacy and engaging in exercises to rebuild sexual desire.

Lydia found the structure of the sexual exercises helpful; they promoted a comfortable way to initiate touching and break the avoidance cycle. Reintroducing nongenital touch and sensuality made a great difference. This became Lydia's favorite bridge for sexual desire. Nondemand touching tapped her need for closeness and intimacy. Victor enjoyed showering together and found touching in the shower erotic. This became his favorite bridge for sexual desire. Both realized how much they missed touching. Realizing that sex was not a "good guy–bad guy" conflict opened the door to renewed intimacy. Victor's verbalizing that he loved and valued her meant a great deal to Lydia. Her initiation of spontaneous affection in public helped them feel like a vital couple. Affectionate touch was an affirmation that theirs was a viable marriage and that sexuality could be revitalized.

The value of couple therapy, as opposed to trying to resolve problems on their own, is that when there are stresses and disappointments, the therapist helps to assess these in a rational, objective manner, rather than the partners falling into old traps. The therapist helped Victor and Lydia maintain motivation and not feel overwhelmed by difficulties and setbacks. In movies and sitcoms, change is intense and dramatic; love conquers all. Lydia and Victor found that reestablishing desire and sexuality was gradual and sometimes difficult. The therapist's support, insight, processing exercises, suggestions, and explorations of couple dynamics were vital in the change process.

Seeing desire as a couple issue and working as an intimate team were key for Lydia. She became comfortable with sexual initiation; touching was a bonding and energizing experience. It was through Victor's initiation of sex play in the shower that Lydia realized that her orgasm pattern was with manual and rubbing stimulation, not intercourse. Lydia's favorite term was "outercourse." Interestingly, Victor found it more arousing to give cunnilingus than Lydia found receiving oral sex. Lydia enjoyed cunnilingus and intercourse, but arousal was highest and orgasm most likely with Victor's manual stimulation around her clitoral shaft, using two-finger rhythmic stimulation or she rubbing her vulva against his thigh. Victor took great pleasure in Lydia's arousal. He accepted and enjoyed her style of orgasmic response. Lydia felt sexually validated by Victor, which increased her desire. Another bridge to desire for Lydia was dancing. She loved to dance and much preferred home to crowded, smoky bars. Combining dancing with seductive touching and undressing Victor was an inviting bridge.

Victor's initiation repertoire and bridges to desire expanded. He liked planned sexual scenarios, which Lydia accepted as long as he did not spell them out in detail (she found this too clinical). Lydia said, "Doing it is more fun than listening to you plan it." An inviting bridge for Victor was being sexual early in the morning after he showered. Another bridge was viewing an R-rated movie, touching during it, and being sexual afterward.

When they had reestablished a regular rhythm of affection and sexual expression, Lydia felt closer to Victor. When Victor felt good about their sexual relationship, it brought out the closeness and couple connection Lydia valued. These were very different feelings from the sexual pressure of the past. Victor was pleasantly surprised by the broad, varied sexual repertoire they developed and found Lydia's sexual responsiveness gratifying. This was not the "meat and potatoes" intercourse sex Victor was used to. Victor read that broad-based sexuality would inoculate him against sexual problems with aging. This was reassuring, but an added dividend, because he very much enjoyed the sexuality they were experiencing now.

A special scenario was that once a month Lydia and Victor set aside time for a sexual date, with an agreement that it not culminate in intercourse. Sometimes it was a sensual evening with dancing and playing. Most of time there were high levels of erotic stimulation, resulting in orgasm for both. Lydia found it especially satisfying to bring Victor to orgasm orally because he felt so uninhibited. Lydia enjoyed intercourse, but when it came to high intensity sex, nothing beat outercourse.

They realized that not each bridge to sexual desire would work every time. They felt secure enough to accept occasional mediocre sex or lack of desire by one or both. Lydia and Victor are aware that sexuality cannot rest on its laurels. Sexual desire must be nurtured and bridges to desire expanded and reinforced.

anticipation as the key to desire

For many couples, sex is tied to romantic love—the best sex is new and swept away. By its very nature, romantic love is a fragile, time-limited phenomenon that seldom survives more than 2 years. For romantic love couples, sex ends with time and marriage. What a self-defeating approach!

Sexual desire can and should remain a vital part of marriage. You can enhance desire by developing one or two favorite bridges; varying bridges, depending on your mood; creating special bridges for special occasions; and devising exotic bridges to experiment with. The function of developing bridges to desire is to build anticipation. Some bridges are planned, others spontaneous; some are mutual, others preferred by one partner; some are complex, others simple; some require accouterments, others just the two of you. What fits your couple style? Be sure the sexual bridge is comfortable and facilitates anticipation. Some couples enjoy a romantic country inn. Others prefer their own bed and lighting a fragrant candle as a cue. For some couples, a regular Friday night or Sunday morning sexual date facilitates anticipation. For others, having varied days and times enhances excitement. Some couples enjoy a rhythm of being sexual once or twice a week. Others find desire high one week (they will be sexual four times) and will not be sexual again for 10 days. What facilitates your anticipation and desire?

EXERCISE—BUILDING BRIDGES TO SEXUAL DESIRE

There are many sources of sexual desire, including (but not limited to) sharing pleasure, feeling "horny," reinforcing intimacy, using sex as a way to connect, being turned on by a fantasy or movie, using sex as a way to relax before sleep, taking advantage of time away from children, sharing loving feelings, making a special date for a birthday or anniversary, indulging in the novelty of staying at a hotel, making up after a disagreement, and feeling erotic after sensuous caressing. Be open to a variety of individual and couple bridges to sexual desire.

A persistent myth is that the spouse should be the source of all sexual desire. According to this myth, if you have fantasies of another person or a movie star, you are being disloyal. In truth, fantasies and other external stimuli (movies, TV, novels, people on the street, sexy pictures, erotic videos, songs) are a major source of sexual desire. Few people fantasize about intercourse in bed in the missionary position with the spouse. Much erotic imagery involves nonsocially desirable (unacceptable) acts, people, and situations. If individuals were prosecuted for their sexual thoughts and fantasies, almost everyone would be in jail. Sexual fantasies are a natural, healthy bridge to desire. Sexual fantasies spice up and enhance sexual desire, and increase response during partner sex.

For this exercise, each spouse lists at least 3 and up to 10 bridges for sexual desire. Share 2 or more with the spouse, but keep at least 1 to yourself. Sexual desire is subverted by sharing all and describing everything in detail. Share erotic turn-ons and scenarios, but remember to keep seductiveness, uncertainty, and playfulness alive in your relationship. Instead of "bread and butter" ways of having sex, think of erotic scenarios and techniques you would like to experiment with.

One of the most interesting things about being a sex therapist is discovering the range of experiences that individuals and couples find erotic. There are the traditional romantic scenarios of dressing up and having a gourmet dinner that includes wine and candles, with sex being tender, loving, and prolonged on silk sheets. There are the traditional erotic scenarios of going to a motel, watching X-rated videos, dressing in sexy lingerie, and having intercourse under a ceiling mirror. For some people, the key is location: being sexual in front of a blazing fire, in the shower, on an antique bed at an historic inn, or on a deserted beach. For others, the key is external stimuli: erotic dancing, sex videos, using lotion to cover each other's genitals, feeding the spouse gourmet snacks in bed, or reading erotic fantasies aloud. Some couples emphasize sexual techniques: simultaneous fellatio and cunnilingus (69), vibrator stimulation during intercourse, mutual manual stimulation while standing in front of a mirror, taking a 10-minute wine break and then returning to intercourse, engaging in one-way sex to arouse the partner to total abandon, use of multiple stimulation during intercourse, switching intercourse positions three times, or using light bondage as an erotic stimulus.

Anticipation of a sexual encounter is a powerful bridge to desire. Rather than waiting for desire to occur "naturally" or expecting all desire to come from the spouse, use fantasies or a planned erotic scenario to facilitate desire. For example, if you have a sexual daydream or see an attractive person in a store, allow that image to "simmer" through the day so that at night it serves as a bridge for sexual initiation. If a favorite erotic scenario is surprising your spouse, who had fallen asleep on the couch, by taking off your top and rubbing your breasts on his face, think of this as you put your children to sleep. Erotic cues and scenarios facilitate anticipation and desire.

maintaining sexual desire

Maintaining sexual desire is not the same as building sexual desire. You can reinforce anticipation by establishing a rhythm of pleasure-oriented sensual and erotic experiences. The excitement of developing new bridges is replaced by the challenge of maintaining vital marital sexuality. The difference is between starting a new business and maintaining an ongoing business—it requires different attitudes and skills.

Routine, mechanical sex subverts desire. You devoted the time and energy to explore and develop bridges; do not negate these gains by treating sex with benign neglect. Both the man and the woman affirm the value of intimate, interactive sexuality. The most powerful bridge is anticipating an experience where the spouse is involved, giving, and aroused. Couples who anticipate giving and receiving pleasurable and erotic touch will maintain a vital and satisfying sexual relationship.

The more varied the bridges, the easier it is to maintain desire. A variety of turn-ons, initiation patterns, times, and places facilitates robust sexual desire. The more each spouse feels that he or she deserves sexual pleasure and anticipates a satisfying experience, the stronger the desire. A key element in maintaining desire is a regular rhythm of sexual contact—whether twice a week or every 10 days. Sexuality is like anything else; if it is neglected or unused, you lose enthusiasm. When you resume sexual activity, you both feel awkward and self-conscious, which interferes with pleasure and erotic flow. A prime way to maintain desire is through touching. Touching occurs both inside and outside of the bedroom. Not all touching can or should lead to intercourse. Touching is a way to stay connected and serves as a bridge to desire, pleasure, and eroticism.

Desire and satisfaction are more important than arousal and orgasm. Quality of the sexual experience is more important than quantity. These two guidelines help to maintain a vital, satisfying sexual bond in marriage.

reinforcing old bridges, building new ones

Sexual desire needs continued nurturing; it cannot be taken for granted. Emily's father was a factory foreman who emphasized the importance of preventative maintenance and repairing equipment, rather than letting it rust or waiting until it broke. This is the strategy we advocate for marital sexuality.

Keep your desire bridges in good repair and spice them up so that they remain vital. What worked in previous months or years becomes less inviting if you do not at least spruce up sexual scenarios. For example, a couple found that being sexual before or after an afternoon nap on the weekend served as a bridge for desire. With time, this fell into a mechanical routine, rather than being an exciting cue. To revitalize this bridge, the man purchased a body lotion and awakened the woman with a sensual massage. Or, she awakened him by doing "fish kisses" on his stomach and inner thighs. They were creative, having wine and a munchie in bed as an appetizer, with sex as the main course. Putting new energy and playfulness into a tried-and-true bridge revitalizes excitement.

Building new bridges can be particularly important. A favorite analogy is between sex and ice cream. Some people prefer 2 or 3 favorites, sometimes will try another, and for special occasions will experiment with an exotic flavor. Other people want to try all 33 flavors, look forward to the flavor of the month, and invent their own flavors. For those with the latter preference, building new bridges and erotic scenarios is vital. The spouse accepts this, rather than being defensive or resistant. Be open and receptive to each other's sexual preferences.

You have a right to veto anything that is uncomfortable or opposed to your moral values. Intimate coercion has no place in marriage. Coercion does more than inhibit sexual desire; it kills it. Within this guideline, both people are free to play, experiment, and enjoy erotic scenarios and techniques. Some bridges are better for one spouse than for the other, which is fine. Sexual desire is about sharing and playing; sex is not a competition, nor is it a zero-sum game. Develop at least one new bridge that is inviting for both people.

closing thoughts

Building bridges to sexual desire is a powerful strategy to break the cycle of the low-sex or no-sex marriage. Sexual desire is not a biological given. It is influenced by psychological, relational, and situational factors that can be nurtured and enhanced. Developing both individual and couple bridges facilitates anticipation and enhances desire.

CHAPTER 7

The Third Step: Feeling Close—Enhancing Intimacy

Dᴇsɪʀᴇ ғᴏʀ ᴀɴ intimate, secure relationship is a major driving force in the decision to marry. An intimate marriage facilitates sexual desire. Intimacy is broad-based, not limited to sexual intercourse or even sexuality. Intimacy involves both emotional and sexual dimensions. A prime function of marital sexuality is to reinforce and deepen intimacy. Intimacy is higher during pleasuring and afterplay—less so during intercourse itself. Traditionally, intimacy has been strongly valued by women and undervalued by men. Intimacy is of as much value for men as for women. Most important is the role of intimacy in nurturing, energizing, and strengthening the marital bond.

The essence of intimacy is feeling emotionally close, connected, and valued. At its core, marriage is a respectful, trusting friendship. Intimacy provides energizing, special feelings. People have emotionally close relationships with friends, siblings, parents, and mentors. The integration of emotional and sexual intimacy makes marriage special.

No-sex and low-sex marriages have a major negative impact on intimacy. Unfortunately, sexual dysfunction and conflicts have stronger negative effects on the marital bond than do the positive effects of satisfying sexuality. Lack of intimacy drains loving feelings and threatens marital viability. Intimacy and sexuality play a significant, but not dominant, positive role in good marriages (contributing 15 to 20 percent to marital vitality and satisfaction). Inhibited sexual desire and other sexual problems play a major negative role. Sexual problems subvert the relationship, often resulting in separation and divorce, especially in the first 3 years of marriage.

The three most common sexual problems are sexual dysfunction, fertility problems, and an extramarital affair. Of these, affairs have the most impact on intimacy because they are a direct challenge to the trust bond. People do not choose to have a dysfunction or a fertility problem, whereas an affair is at least partly a choice behavior. Affairs are a violation of the trust bond, subverting emotional and sexual intimacy.

Which is more important—emotional or sexual intimacy? This makes a great talk show debate or argument at a bar, but is not psychologically helpful. Emotional intimacy and sexual intimacy are different, but complementary and well-integrated in a healthy marriage.

Traditionally, men and women learn very different lessons about intimacy. Women are socialized to value feelings, emotional connection, and an intimate relationship, but to devalue sexual expression and eroticism. Males are socialized to identify masculinity with sexuality and to emphasize sexual prowess. Men are not socialized to value emotional closeness, intimacy, or a committed relationship. It is no wonder that with such different socialization and peer influences, husbands and wives have a difficult time understanding and communicating the meaning of intimacy and sexuality.

There are more similarities than differences in intimacy needs between women and men, especially for married couples. The idea of an innate "war between the sexes" or that "men and women are from different planets" is nonsense. Both women and men are capable of desire, arousal, orgasm, and satisfaction. Both are capable of empathy, closeness, sadness, and anger. Gender struggles are not based on biological differences, nor are they predestined. Misunderstandings and conflicts are primarily a function of socialization and media hype, rather than of genetic or hormonal differences.

Our premise, which has strong empirical support, is that an intimate, satisfying marriage recognizes shared feelings, capabilities, and values of the woman and man. This promotes a respectful, trusting friendship, which is the foundation for a satisfying, stable marriage. Emotional and sexual intimacy generates special feelings and energizes the marital bond.

Healthy sexuality plays an integral role in marital satisfaction. The main functions of sexuality are as a shared pleasure, to deepen and reinforce intimacy, and as a tension reducer to alleviate the stresses inherent in life and marriage. Intimacy and sexuality energize and make special the marital bond. When sexuality is problematic or non-existent, it serves as a major drain, robbing the marriage of intimacy and good feelings.

emotional intimacy

Emotional intimacy has a more subtle role in marital satisfaction than sexual intimacy has, but is just as important. Mature intimacy is quite different from the romantic love that initially brought the couple together. Romantic love is an intense emotional experience; the partner and the relationship are idealized. You feel special because the partner has chosen you. Romantic love dissipates by the time of marriage or within the first year. When replaced by mature intimacy, the marriage has a solid foundation. Feeling cared for and caring for the spouse, sharing positive and negative feelings, experiencing empathic communication, feeling personally validated, enjoying a sense of "we-ness," and establishing closeness are integral to emotional intimacy. Being in an emotionally intimate relationship brings out the best in each person. Emotional intimacy blends autonomy and coupleness. Both emotional caring and a positive influence process are reinforced. There is a positive, reciprocal relationship between emotional intimacy and sexual satisfaction. Sexual problems subvert emotional intimacy. Decreased emotional intimacy makes sexual problems worse and sets the stage for a no-sex or low-sex marriage. Maintaining emotional intimacy is a positive prognostic sign for resolving sexual desire and dysfunction problems. Emotional intimacy has value in itself. It is a major factor in both psychological well-being and marital satisfaction.

Intimacy is an overused term, centered on "feeling good." Intimacy is more than positive feelings. Genuine intimacy includes the entire range of personal and couple feelings and experiences. Intimacy involves sharing weaknesses, vulnerabilities, fears, and negative experiences, as well as strengths, assets, competencies, and positive experiences. Intimate couples share a range of feelings—from anger to disappointment, boredom to numbness, joy to excitement, closeness to love. The core of marriage is respect and trust. Without this, intimacy is vulnerable and unstable.

We emphasize being an "intimate team." Intimacy does not mean giving up your personhood—you retain autonomy and individuality. The challenge is maintaining a healthy balance of individuality with coupleness. Either extreme can cause problems. People who are isolated or overly protective of personal boundaries are unable to feel close and share their lives. The other extreme is enmeshed or fused couples. These couples are so reactive, they cannot make requests, incorporate negative feedback, or express sexual needs. They think of themselves as extremely intimate, but clinicians view this as a self-defeating pseudo-intimacy. Healthy intimacy allows for both individuality and coupleness.

Emotional intimacy includes freedom to express feelings without needing the spouse's approval. It helps to have the spouse's emotional validation. This has to be genuine, not given in order to placate or accommodate. Healthy marriages accept differences in feelings, attitudes, and behavior without negating intimacy. Being an intimate couple does not mean being the same person. Feelings are listened to in a respectful, caring manner. Your spouse does not have to agree with you. Each person has a right to his or her feelings and thoughts. A strength of intimate relationships is that your spouse knows you psychologically and emotionally. You feel loved and accepted for who you are, strengths and weaknesses, competencies and idiosyncrasies.

sexual intimacy

Ideally, emotional and sexual intimacy are integrated. Some couples have difficulty with emotional intimacy, but do well sexually. More typically, couples enjoy emotional intimacy, but are troubled sexually. The most common pattern is that the couple has difficulty with both emotional and sexual intimacy. The traditional marriage therapy adage was that if the couple resolved emotional and relationship problems, sex would take care of itself. Although true for some couples and some sexual problems, it is not the norm. Sexual intimacy is a unique dimension that needs to be specifically addressed.

Sexuality is more than genitals, intercourse, and orgasm. Sexual intimacy is more than functional sex. The essence of sexual intimacy is openness and comfort, the ability to share your body, especially sensual and erotic feelings.

People can be sexually responsive and functional with no intimacy—consider the one night stand or angry sex. Sex is at its most human when the sexual relationship combines eroticism with emotional intimacy. Sharing yourself, your body, and your feelings is the essence of sexual intimacy. Partners share sexual thoughts and feelings, enjoy sensuality and nondemand pleasuring, give and receive erotic stimulation, come together during intercourse, allow arousal to flow to orgasm, and enjoy afterplay as a bonding experience.

The main functions of marital sexuality are a shared pleasure, a means to deepen and strengthen intimacy, and a tension-reducer to deal with the stresses of life and marriage. Marital sex can be a mix and match, depending on the couple's feelings, needs, situation, and time constraints. Sometimes it is very intimate—tender, warm, extended, and loving. Other times, sex is short, intense, and lustful. Intimate sex can be loving, erotic, or both. Intimate sexuality involves awareness of feelings and needs. Intimacy includes freedom to take sexual risks and communicate desires. The prescription for vital sexual desire and satisfying marital sexuality is integrating emotional intimacy, nondemand pleasuring, and erotic scenarios and techniques.

Nondemand pleasuring is a key. Affectionate (holding hands, kissing, hugging) and sensual (massages, bathing or showering together, cuddling on the couch semiclothed, snuggling at night or in the morning) experiences have value in themselves. Couples enjoy touching both inside and outside the bedroom. Not all touching can or should lead to intercourse. Touching can serve as a bridge to sexual desire. Other times, it is a way to stay connected. Sometimes you want an orgasm, sometimes you want a hug. Men have a hard time asking for a hug, so they initiate sex. Women have a hard time saying they feel lustful, so they initiate a hug. Optimally, the woman and man are comfortable initiating both nondemand pleasuring and intercourse.

Touching is a request, not a demand. Intimate coercion has no place in marriage. Coercion poisons sexual desire. Intimate coercion includes the implicit threat of an affair, withholding love or money, being angry or belittling, or using sex as a bribe. Genuine intimacy respects the autonomy and personal boundaries of each spouse. Requests do not carry the implicit threat of a negative consequence if there is not sex.

The spouse has the right to accept, say no, or offer an alternative. A demand says, "Do this my way, now, or there will be negative consequences." A request says, "this is how I feel and what I want, I am open to your feelings and needs, I want this encounter to be enjoyable for both of us." With demands, you win the sexual battle, but lose the intimacy bond. With requests, both individuals and marital intimacy win.

EXERCISE—EMOTIONAL INTIMACY

In discussions of intimacy, the traditional focus is on the spontaneous expression of feelings. We are in favor of spontaneity and naturalness, but it is naive and self-defeating to believe that this alone sustains a marriage, especially a marriage plagued by sexual problems. This exercise asks you to have a planned, intentional "intimacy date."

Traditionally, males have undervalued intimacy, so let the man be the initiator. Be sure you are both alert and awake, have time (at least half an hour—an hour is preferred), and will not be interrupted (the children are asleep or out of the house, the answering machine is on, you do not answer the door). The man can enhance the milieu by having a glass of wine or speciality coffee, playing music in the background, and sitting on the porch or in the family room. Initiation is personal and inviting, not "we have to do the exercise."

Discuss an experience where you felt especially emotionally intimate. Examples include walking on the beach and feeling close, disclosing hopes and dreams, remembering your most intimate lovemaking, showing the spouse the neighborhood you grew up in and discussing your childhood, deciding you want to start a family, going on a picnic or hike and talking about your lives, feeling romantic and loving after attending a friend's wedding, reacting to a loss and crying together, sharing excitement after a promotion, staying up all night to wallpaper your first apartment, walking in the rain, or after your first child was born realizing that you were a family and not just a couple. Focus on feelings, not on the event. How open were you? How close did you feel? How trusting were you?

What is the present state of emotional intimacy in the marriage? Be honest and specific. What do you say or do that facilitates intimacy? How frequently does it occur? How genuine are the feelings? How do you feel afterward?

The next topic is sensitive and difficult. What attitudes, behaviors, and feelings inhibit intimacy? Focus on your own feelings and behavior, not on what the spouse does or does not do. It is a cop-out to blame the spouse. Be responsible for your behavior. Specifically, what do you do or not do that blocks emotional intimacy? Is it intentional or unintentional? What are the advantages for you of maintaining barriers to intimacy? Are you willing to give up these barriers?

Make three specific requests that will enhance feelings of intimacy. Remember, these are requests, not demands. What do you want the spouse to say or do that would increase your feelings of intimacy? Examples include talking by phone during the day (at least every other day); nondemand touching before going to sleep or on wakening; taking a walk and talking about feelings at least once a week; disclosing a painful experience or feeling, with the spouse empathically listening; saying, "I love you" in a genuine manner; once a week going out for dinner or coffee and dessert and discussing hopes and plans; after the children are asleep, putting on music and dancing; making birthdays and your anniversary special; making a romantic gesture like bringing flowers or a personal gift; in the midst of a conflict, not calling names or engage in dirty fighting; and greeting each other with a hug. Each spouse makes three specific, personal requests.

Intimacy does not mean you get everything you ask for or want. The spouse is a separate person with separate feelings, perceptions, and needs. The spouse does not have to give you everything the way you want it. Losing personal autonomy or giving up a sense of self to please the spouse does not promote genuine intimacy. In fact, it subverts intimacy. The spouse does commit to listening in a respectful, caring manner. Both partners are committed to increasing intimacy, expressing feelings, and being a respectful, trusting couple.

the interplay between emotional and sexual intimacy

Emotional and sexual intimacy are different, but complementary. Emotional intimacy usually involves affectionate touch, sometimes sensual touch, but usually not erotic touch. Sexual intimacy focuses on erotic touch and usually, but not necessarily, includes intercourse. Wives often say they need to feel emotionally connected before having sex. Husbands often say that sex facilitates emotional connection. Ideally, the wife and husband value both emotional and sexual intimacy. These are not dichotomous dimensions, nor are they gender-specific. Emotional intimacy can be as valuable for the husband as for the wife. He has a right to emotional closeness, a hug, a supportive spouse. She has as much right to eroticism and orgasm as the husband does. Desire, arousal, and orgasm promote her well-being (as well as marital satisfaction).

Intimacy dates can be primarily talking, primarily touching, or a blend of talking and touching. Intimacy dates can evolve into intercourse, but that is not their purpose. The primary function of intimacy dates is to enhance feelings of closeness and validation. Touching, whether affectionate, sensual, playful, or erotic, facilitates intimacy. Think of the spouse as an intimate friend with whom you express a range of feelings, sharing good and bad times. Intimacy dates keep couples connected and set the stage for sexual desire.

EXERCISE—SEXUAL INTIMACY DATES

This exercise focuses on enhancing sexual communication and pleasure. Because, traditionally, it is the man who initiates sexual activity, let the woman take the lead. Ideally, both the husband and wife are comfortable initiating and both feel free to say no to a sexual request and suggest an alternative means to physically connect. To establish a comfortable milieu, begin by taking a shower or bath together. Cleanliness (especially washing genitals) facilitates sexuality. Showering or bathing can be a sensual experience. If showering, experiment with types of spray or temperature; if bathing, try a new bath oil or soap to increase awareness of sensual stimuli.

Start by soaping your spouse's back. Trace muscles and contours; rub and gently massage, ask him to face you. Soap his chest, stomach, genitals, hips, and legs. Let him soap and wash you. Many couples find sexual play in the shower particularly inviting and erotic. As you rinse off, play with his body, including his genitals.

Proceed to the bedroom, feeling natural being nude. Pleasuring and erotic stimulation are best done in the nude. Begin touching, using the giver-receiver format. Midway through, switch to mutual stimulation. Most couples prefer mutual stimulation; be aware of your feelings and preferences. Explore and see what feels good. What is the best way to transition from pleasuring to erotic stimulation?

Traditionally, the sexual script was to move from "foreplay" to intercourse, with the man directing foreplay to get the woman ready for intercourse. Be intimate partners; engage in nondemand pleasuring; evolve into erotic stimulation, which includes intercourse, but is not limited to intercourse.

In pleasuring, the giving partner enjoys touching for herself, without second-guessing him. The man is passive with his eyes closed, taking in pleasurable sensations. She mixes genital with nongenital pleasuring. Couples are used to short, intense male arousal—experiment with moderate and fluctuating levels of pleasure. Be aware that subjective arousal waxes and wanes, as does his erection. This is a new experience for couples who always go to intercourse on the first erection. Then switch roles. The man enjoys being the giver in a pleasure-oriented manner, rather than in goal-oriented foreplay. Enjoy exploratory touching rather than trying to "turn her on." Experiment with playful, teasing pleasure, mixing nongenital and genital touching. Let her decide when to transition to mutual give-and-take erotic stimulation.

Experiment with multiple stimulation in the context of nonintercourse sex. Later, utilize multiple stimulation during intercourse. Examples of multiple stimulation include: kneeling while facing the spouse, who is also kneeling—kissing, mutual manual stimulation, with the man doing oral breast stimulation; the woman standing, the man kneeling, utilizing manual vulva stimulation, combined with oral breast stimulation; engaging in mutual manual stimulation while she verbalizes a fantasy of him being her sexual slave; the woman lying on her side, the man kneeling, rubbing his penis against her breast as he manually stimulates her vulva; the woman lying on her back, the man between her legs, giving oral stimulation and simultaneously manual anal stimulation, while she caresses her breasts and verbalizes feelings of arousal. If she desires, continue erotic stimulation to orgasm.

Let the woman initiate the transition from pleasuring to intercourse. She initiates intercourse and guides intromission (i.e., guides his penis into her vagina). Integrate multiple stimulation during intercourse. Traditionally, men focused solely on thrusting. Most men (and women) find that multiple stimulation during intercourse increases involvement and arousal. Examples include from the man-on-top position, she caresses his testicles as he stretches and licks her breast; from the rear entry position, caressing her vulva as she verbalizes erotic feelings and he fantasizes; in the woman-on-top position, he watches her arousal as he plays with her breasts and she uses circular thrusting; from the side-by-side position, she strokes his chest as he rubs her buttocks and they kiss each other's bodies.

Afterplay is an integral part of sexuality. Many couples feel emotionally closer after sex than at any other time. Strengthening intimacy is a prime function of sexuality. You feel emotionally bonded after a sexual experience. Afterplay is the most ignored element in sex. Do you like to lie and hold each other, sleep in each other's arms, engage in playful tickling or a warm kiss, take a walk, read poetry, nap and start again, or talk and come down together? Find one or two afterplay scenarios that are comfortable and satisfying.

KATHARINE AND ERIC

When they first heard about the concept of an intimacy date, Katharine was thrilled, but Eric was put off. They had had intercourse only four times since their son was born 18 months earlier. Eric worried that intimacy dates would be another way to avoid sex. Tension over their no-sex marriage had steadily built and was interfering with all aspects of the relationship, including parenting. Sexual tension was expressed through irritability, especially Eric harping about Katherine's judgment and not trusting her. Although he considered separation, Eric was afraid Katharine would cut him off from their son as she had cut him off sexually. Katharine worried about Eric's anger and blaming, and feared that he would withdraw financial support if they separated. Trust and intimacy were at a low ebb.

Intimacy requires willingness to be open to and to trust the spouse. Their minister suggested therapy, but Katharine was not willing to engage in sex therapy. Eric was willing to see a therapist about the sex problem, but was not willing to enter marriage therapy. When Eric was 9, his parents began marriage therapy. After several therapies and therapists, they divorced when Eric was 13. This made him cynical about marriage therapy.

The church sponsored a weekend retreat for couples, which the minister encouraged Katherine and Eric to attend. There they were introduced to the concept of intimacy dates as a way to maintain emotional connection. Over the next 2 months Katharine and Eric stayed with the structure of weekly intimacy dates, usually initiated by Katharine. Katharine made it clear that she did not want intimacy dates to turn into sexual dates. After initial resistance, Eric accepted this and learned to value these experiences. He especially enjoyed dates where they went for a walk while a neighborhood friend watched their son. Katharine valued time with Eric when she could share feelings and discuss life issues. They had an understanding that they would not talk about sex, parenting, or money on intimacy dates. Katharine's attachment to and trust in Eric increased. Eric did not see intimacy dates as a substitute for a sexual relationship, but they increased his desire to revitalize the marriage. An unexpected side effect is that they became cooperative and supportive parents. Emotionally and parentally, they were a team.

Instead of being angry and blaming, Eric shared with Katharine his puzzlement that emotional intimacy did not transfer to sexuality. Instead of feeling hurt and counterattacking, Katharine admitted that she shared his puzzlement. They agreed to again seek the minister's counsel. The minister congratulated them on the positive changes and growth.

The traditional view is that if the couple dealt with conflicts and reestablished emotional intimacy, the sexual problem would naturally improve. Yet this is not true for the majority of couples (and was not true for Katharine and Eric). The minister strongly recommended that they consult a female sex therapist whose core training was in pastoral counseling. This was the impetus Katharine needed to begin couple sex therapy. Katherine's trust and intimacy with Eric were strong; she felt comfortable seeing a female therapist and reassured that the therapist utilized a spiritual-based approach.

The therapist was very supportive of intimacy dates and strongly encouraged continuing them. The clinician utilized feelings and insights from the intimacy dates to help assess what was inhibiting sexual desire. During intimacy dates, Katharine was her own person. Eric accepted her and enjoyed being with her. In the sexual relationship, Katharine was not her own person. In the past Katharine had been aroused and orgasmic, so Eric felt that there was no problem, except her withholding. Eric considered himself the sexually interested and sophisticated partner, seeing Katharine as less sexual.

A core element in revitalizing marital sex was that Katharine needed to be her own sexual person. She said, "I need to have my sexual voice." Eric had to accept that her sexual desires and preferences were different than his. This did not make them inferior or better, just different. Having learned to accept different preferences in intimacy dates made sexual differences easier for Eric to understand and accept.

In reviewing her sexual attitudes and experiences, Katharine realized that she had been primed to develop inhibited sexual desire. Katherine's dating and premarital experiences reinforced what she had learned from her mother and the church: Males were more sexually oriented than females. Katharine was surprised that arousal and orgasm were easy for her, but she felt that sex was driven by the man and he got more from it. When Eric and Katharine began as a couple, this pattern was reinforced. Katharine felt attracted to Eric and from the beginning enjoyed emotional and sexual intimacy. However, Eric did not attend to Katherine's need for a relationship that integrated eroticism and intimacy. After 2 months, they stopped discussing sexual feelings and requests.

Eric felt that sexual problems began after the birth of their son, but Katharine dated it to the pregnancy. For Katharine it was very special to have sex with the intention of trying to become pregnant. She was put off that Eric cared only about increased frequency.

A major disconnect occurred after she became pregnant. Katharine was aware of changes in her body—from nausea to breast tenderness, then excitement mixed with worry when the baby moved. Eric seemed oblivious. He wanted to continue intercourse for the whole 9 months. It was as if Katharine's body and feelings did not count. They went to prenatal classes together and experienced prepared childbirth. However, when it came to sexuality, Katharine did not see Eric as her intimate friend.

After their son was born, Katharine felt even more emotionally and sexually alienated. Mothering and breast feeding were a major transition, especially dealing with interrupted sleep and sleep deprivation. She saw Eric as uninvolved, and felt that he was as sexually demanding as the baby was physically demanding. One time Eric sucked on her breasts when she was full of milk—he thought it was funny, whereas Katharine felt it was gross. Eric knew that Katharine was upset, but had not known why.

Awareness of what causes inhibited sexual desire can be helpful, but only if awareness facilitates positive changes in the intimate and erotic relationship, especially building bridges to sexual desire. It is counterproductive when used as ammunition for blaming.

Eric affirmed that Katharine's emotional and sexual needs were as important as his. Eric no longer pushed sex at the expense of her feelings. Katharine began to think of Eric as her trusted, intimate friend. Eric was open to following her sexual lead. Katharine was open to using intimacy dates as a transition to sexual dates, but Eric needed to wait for her verbal invitation, not push. Eric preferred initiating sexual dates in a different manner, but accepted Katharine's preferences. If she did not say that she wanted to transition into intercourse, he enjoyed intimacy and affection for itself. Eric had a hard time understanding that Katharine put less importance on orgasm; for him, orgasm was central. They had one particularly intimate, close experience where he was orgasmic and Katharine was not. Katharine enjoyed and got more out of the experience than Eric did. This helped him understand the multidimensional aspects of her sexual feelings.

Sexuality was a more satisfying part of their marriage than ever before. Katharine felt pleased with the quality of the sexual relationship. Katharine and Eric were an intimate, equitable team. Katharine believed that the key to maintaining gains was weekly intimacy dates. Eric committed to initiating an intimacy date if they went more than 10 days without a sexual connection.

maintaining intimacy during hard times

A measure of marital viability is the ability to stay emotionally connected during times of stress or conflict. Intimacy is easy when things are going well. Intimacy energizes the marital bond. Yet intimacy is more than that. Maintaining a view of the spouse as your intimate friend even when there are disappointments or frustrations is a sign of a viable marriage. Conflict does not have to negate emotional intimacy. Anger need not be a reason to stop being sexual. Learn to deal with hurt, angry feelings, and resolve conflicts outside the bedroom. The sexually intimate couple is motivated to deal with conflicts and negative feelings. Couples who have confidence in their ability to deal with and resolve conflict have a crucial marital resource. Couples who do not sacrifice intimacy while dealing with conflict are especially healthy.

What happens when anger and conflict center around sexual issues, especially an extramarital affair or a sexual secret such as compulsive use of pornography? It is doubtful that what we say in this book will successfully address that problem. This type of issue requires professional therapy. Rather than letting the problem fester and destroy intimacy, it is a sign of good judgment to seek marital or sex therapy (Appendix 1 has suggestions and guidelines for choosing a therapist).

closing thoughts

Enhancing emotional and sexual intimacy is a powerful means to build sexual desire. Partners who reestablish intimacy are in a better position to challenge the no-sex or low-sex state of their marriage. Intimacy is a couple process; being an intimate couple makes it easier to deal with sexual problems. This does not take away personal responsibility, but does challenge the guilt-blame trap that paralyzes the couple.

Intimacy has the positive function of energizing the marital bond and building feelings of caring and closeness. Just as important, the couple is aware of how draining the sexual problem is and feels motivated to confront it. Both partners value an emotionally and sexually intimate marriage.

CHAPTER 8

The Fourth Step: Let's Play Feely-Touchy—Nondemand Pleasuring

THE ESSENSE OF sexuality is giving and receiving pleasure-oriented touching. Touching and sensuality is the core of sexual response. In many, if not most, marriages, when intercourse ceases, so does sensual touch and often affectionate touch. Revitalizing touch and sensuality is crucial in breaking the cycle of the no-sex or low-sex marriage.

Nondemand pleasuring is integral to sexual desire. The prescription for a vital marital sexuality is integrating intimacy, nondemand pleasuring, and erotic stimulation. A pleasure orientation contrasts with a performance orientation. "Foreplay" is used to get the woman (and, with aging, the man) ready for intercourse. "Pleasuring" includes affectionate touch, sensual touch, playful touch, and erotic touch. Pleasuring has value in itself, not just as foreplay. This includes touching both inside and outside of the bedroom. Not all touching is oriented toward intercourse. Pleasuring confronts the rigid dichotomy in the no-sex marriage—either no touching or foreplay to intercourse. Nondemand pleasuring is a healthy bridge to revitalize sexual desire.

Pleasuring is a couple concept. Affectionate (holding hands, kissing, hugging) and sensual touch (massage, bathing together, cuddling on the couch semiclothed, snuggling at night or in the morning) has great value. Couples are open to and can enjoy a range of sensual and playful touching experiences. Pleasuring can serve as a bridge to sexual desire and intercourse, but that is not its chief function. Touch is not a pressure or demand for sex. Nondemand pleasuring is just like it sounds—a way of maintaining physical contact, feeling connected, and sharing pleasure. Each spouse communicates his or her feelings and desires.

Nondemand pleasuring is in direct contrast to the game-playing and miscommunication that characterize dating couples. Pleasuring challenges the couple to communicate in a clear, comfortable, trusting manner. Touching is a source of closeness, warmth, and intimacy, not miscommunication, pressure, or conflict. Sometimes you want an orgasm, sometimes you want a hug. Men have a hard time asking for a hug, so they initiate sex. Women have a hard time saying they want sex, so they initiate a hug. Through the process of nondemand pleasuring, each spouse becomes comfortable with feelings and desires for affectionate, sensual, playful, and erotic contact. Optimally, both the husband and wife are open to initiating nondemand pleasuring. Pleasuring is valued as a means to reinforce marital intimacy and connection.

requests, not demands

Touching is a request, not a demand. Intimacy and touching involve trusting the spouse. Intimate coercion has no place in marriage. Marital rape is the extreme of coercion in that it involves physical force. Intimate coercion does not involve force, but rather demands and pressure. Coercion says, "I want sex my way, at this time, and if you do not go along, there will be negative consequences." This includes the implicit threat of an affair, withholding love or money if a specific sex act does not occur, being distant or angry if there is no sex, or using sex as a bribe. Coercion kills intimacy and desire.

Nondemand pleasuring involves requests and cooperation. You respect the spouse's individuality and autonomy. Each partner has a right to his or her feelings and to express desires and wants. The spouse has the freedom to enthusiastically accept, say no, or offer an alternative. A request says, "This is what I feel and want, I am open to your feelings and needs, you do not have to worry about negative consequences." Requests facilitate intimate communication. Demands set up an adversarial, performance situation. Demands let you win the sexual battle, but you lose the intimate bond. With requests, both individuals and the marriage win.

Nondemand pleasuring facilitates sexual desire. Pleasuring forms a bridge between affection and eroticism. It is the vital link between an emotionally intimate and a sexually satisfying relationship.

Replacing foreplay with pleasuring and goal-oriented performance with pleasure orientation facilitates marital intimacy. Pleasuring requires the partners to be aware of and communicate how they are feeling and what they want. This replaces the rigid male–female sex roles we learned as adolescents. You learn to engage as an equitable, intimate team. Pleasuring challenges the rigid view that sex equals intercourse. The couple adopts a flexible, interactive approach to touching, sensuality, and sexuality. Rigid thinking and a dichotomous view of sex keep couples stuck in the guilt/blame power struggle. Pleasuring facilitates physical and emotional connection.

Couples with chronic inhibited sexual desire are reluctant to experiment with nondemand pleasuring. Interfering factors include fears and inhibitions, but primarily, it is the reluctance to reengage in touching. It is easier to avoid than to try again. They fear falling into the yes–no struggle of intercourse. One way to introduce nondemand pleasuring is through semistructured exercises, with the clear understanding that there is a temporary prohibition on orgasm or intercourse. This provides a comfortable milieu to explore pleasuring.

EXERCISE—NONDEMAND PLEASURING

The focus of this exercise (preferably, a series of exercises) is to enhance communication and pleasure, while reducing performance orientation. There is a prohibition on orgasm and intercourse. This facilitates increased awareness and helps you focus on feelings, touch, sensations, and sensuality.

Traditionally, it has been the man's role to initiate, so let the woman take the initiative. Ideally, both the man and woman feel comfortable initiating and each feels free to say no and to suggest an alternative way to experience physical connection. Begin by taking a shower or bath together; this sets a comfortable milieu. Cleanliness (especially washing genitals) facilitates comfort and openness.

Showering or bathing is a sensuous activity. When showering, experiment with different types of spray or temperature. When bathing, try a new bath oil or bubble bath to increase awareness of sensual stimuli. Soap your spouse's back. Trace the contours and muscles; rub and gently massage. This is not a rigorous back-rub, but a sensual exploration. Ask your spouse to face you; look into his eyes. Eye contact facilitates closeness and trust. Soap his neck and chest. Move downward to the stomach—soap and touch in a gentle, exploratory manner. Wash his genitals as you would any body part. Genitals are an integral, natural part of your body. The focus is not stimulation and arousal, but exploration and pleasure. Touch and soap his hips and legs. Switch roles—be open to his touching and washing you. He treats your breasts and vulva like any other body part. Be aware of what feels particularly sensual.

Dry each other. Take your time, be tender, stand still, and take a good look at each other. Notice two or three physical attributes you find particularly attractive.

Proceed to the bedroom, feeling natural being nude. If you are not comfortable walking through the house nude, put on a robe or towel, but take it off when you reach the bedroom. Pleasuring is best done in the nude. In subsequent pleasuring experiences, experiment with sensual clothing or being semidressed. Keep the room at a comfortable temperature, with a moderate amount of light. If one spouse prefers to darken the room, that is fine, but be sure you can see the partner's body. To enhance the milieu, put on your favorite music, burn a candle with a pleasant fragrance, or both. Experiment with mood enhancers during subsequent experiences—for example, some couples find that classical music facilitates sensuality, others find that multicolored candles enhance the milieu, and others use a lamp with a blue or red light.

Start with the giver-receiver format, and let the woman take the first turn as pleasure giver. Be sure that each spouse has an opportunity to be giver and recipient. In subsequent experiences, experiment with mutual pleasuring. A sexually satisfying relationship involves both spouses being comfortable receiving and giving pleasure. Interestingly, men find it harder to receive than to give.

The recipient (in this instance, the man) has three tasks. The first is to be passive and receive pleasure. The second is to keep his eyes closed, focusing on feelings and sensations (this reduces the giver's self-consciousness). The third is to be aware of what parts of his body and what types of touch are sensual and pleasurable.

She looks at his body in an open, exploratory manner. She is free to play, giving a variety of touch and body stimulation. Rather than try to second-guess him, she touches for herself. She engages in stimulation that she enjoys giving. This is as an opportunity for her to enjoy touching, to not be distracted by past frustrations or disappointments. She savors the simple pleasures of giving and receiving touch and does not try to turn on her partner. The following are guidelines, not hard and fast rules. Both partners should feel free to be creative and innovative.

Have the man turn over on his back. He keeps his eyes closed, getting as comfortable as possible. The woman notices signs of relaxation and is aware of the difference between this and the tension she has observed during prior sexual experiences. She gently massages his forehead. She outlines favorite facial features with her fingertips. She tenderly kisses his closed eyes. She kisses his face, ears, and neck.

She massages his nipples. Does this touch feel sensual? Males inhibit their natural response because they think that men are not supposed to feel pleasure there. When exploring his chest, she uses smooth, tender strokes, covering the sides as well. She lightly strokes his body hair. She runs her hands sideways around his stomach. Do his stomach muscles react to her touch?

She looks at the front of his body. Does he have an erection? She accepts this as a natural response to pleasure. She is aware of touching the penis when it is flaccid, as opposed to when erect. Women view erection as a demand. Remember, there is a prohibition on orgasm. A common myth is that when the man has an erection, the woman must *do* something, have intercourse or at least bring him to orgasm. Interestingly, the man, too, believes that an erection *must* mean sexual arousal, and rushes to intercourse even when he does not feel like sex. Both partners can enjoy the erection as a natural response to touching and pleasure, without feeling any demand.

She explores the genitals as she would other parts of his body. She is aware of the penis—glans, shaft, frenulum. As she explores his testes, she notices which is larger and what the shapes remind her of. She notices how the testicles move inside the scrotum.

If her spouse is circumcised (most American men are), she traces the glans with her fingertips. If he is uncircumcised, she moves back the foreskin and gently explores the glans. She massages and caresses his inner thighs, perineum, and scrotum. She notices how the scrotum changes as he becomes aroused. When her touching stops, she notices that his erection subsides. Erections naturally wax and wane (as does vaginal lubrication). Men become anxious when the erection wanes because they are used to going to intercourse and orgasm on the first erection. Waxing and waning of erection is a natural, physiological response to prolonged pleasuring. During a 45-minute pleasuring session, the erection might wax and wane two to five times.

For both the man and woman, awareness that sexuality is more than genitals, intercourse, and orgasm is crucial. She can touch for herself—enjoy rubbing, caressing, and playing. If at any point she (or he) feels anxious or uncomfortable, she should not stop or avoid. Both partners can lie and hold each other until she feels secure and comfortable. Then she returns to nondemand pleasuring. The female giver proceeds at her own pace and comfort level.

She continues body exploration, enjoying slow, tender, rhythmic, flowing touch. She enjoys his whole body, including the penis as a natural part of him. When she feels comfortable with his body and sensual touch, they switch roles.

The woman lies on her stomach, allowing herself to be open and relaxed. The man finds a comfortable position for giving, whether sitting, kneeling, or lying. He does touching and pleasuring for himself, not trying to repeat her pattern, second-guess what she wants, or turn her on. Traditionally, men touch as foreplay to get women ready for intercourse. This exercise focuses on comfort, exploration, and sharing pleasure. The man touches and strokes the back of her body. Let stroking be slow, rhythmic, and tender. Do not rush the process. He explores from the top of her head to the soles of her feet, with a focus on pleasure and sensuality.

When it is time to turn over, he gently helps her move to her back. She keeps her eyes closed, focusing on feelings and sensations. He touches the front of her body, and does not zero in on the breasts or vulva. He integrates nongenital pleasuring with genital touch. He thinks of her breasts in a sensual manner. He explores a variety of touches, while she is aware of sensations and feelings. With the palm of the hand, he starts at her waist and moves to the neck with one long motion. He is careful not to press hard; breasts can be sensitive.

Sometimes the difference between pleasurable and irritating touch is less than an inch or a minor difference in pressure. He traces her nipple with his fingertips. Does it become erect?

He massages her torso, strokes her stomach. He tickles and plays with her belly button. He explores her genitals. He runs his fingers gently through her pubic hair and caresses the mons. He spreads the labia with his fingers. He becomes comfortable with the sight and feel of her genitals. He identifies the clitoris and clitoral shaft by gently pulling back the clitoral hood. He looks carefully at her labia, noticing how the labia surround the vaginal introitus (opening). As he explores her genitals, he touches and strokes her arm, kisses her face, or both. He spreads the vaginal opening with two fingers and notices the color and texture of the interior. He gently inserts one finger into the vagina and notices the sensations of containment. This is not a medical exam, but a comfortable, gentle exploration. If at any time there is pain or either person becomes uncomfortable, he stops touching, but keeps contact by holding. During intravaginal exploration, he feels the warmth and dampness. Is he comfortable with the feel and smell of vaginal lubrication? This is a natural process that waxes and wanes in the same manner as erections. He touches and explores the mons and perineum. He moves slowly and gently to ensure that touching and exploration are inviting.

He explores her legs, thighs, and feet in a sensuous, unhurried manner. He does a whole body massage, intermixing nongenital and genital touching. He is aware of favorite body parts and favorite touches. He focuses on openness and pleasure, not on arousal or orgasm.

End this exercise by holding each other, experiencing warmth and intimacy. Lie in bed and share feelings. What have you both learned of sensuality and pleasure? Is once enough or would you benefit from repeated experiences with nondemand pleasuring? What can you focus on in subsequent exercises? Verbally and nonverbally, guide your spouse in the type of touching that is most pleasurable. Do you enjoy multiple stimulation or is one touch at a time preferable? Does talking enhance intimacy, or does it distract from pleasure? Is mutual touching more pleasurable than the giver–recipient format? Do you want more or less kissing? Is playfulness more pleasurable than slow, deliberate touching? How can you generalize what you have learned from nondemand pleasuring to lovemaking and intercourse?

the value of nondemand pleasuring

We strongly believe in the value of nondemand pleasuring. We have considered writing an entire book on sensuality and nonintercourse eroticism. The sex therapy concept of reducing performance anxiety by placing a temporary prohibition on intercourse is understood, if not totally accepted. It is seen as temporary, a way to reintroduce intercourse. It is hard to get away from the cultural mandate that "real sex is intercourse." We are not opposed to intercourse; in fact, we are unequivocal supporters of intercourse. Nondemand pleasuring and intercourse are complementary, not in opposition or conflict.

If forced to say whether intercourse alone or nondemand pleasuring alone most contributes to marital intimacy, we would choose nondemand pleasuring! Why? The main functions of marital sexuality are that it is a shared pleasure, a means to deepen and reinforce intimacy, and a tension-reducer. Nondemand pleasuring serves these needs better than does intercourse. Intercourse is better for conception. You cannot get pregnant through pleasuring. What about orgasm? Intercourse is a better producer of orgasms for males than for females. Erotic stimulation is a natural transition from pleasuring. Most males are able to be orgasmic with manual, oral, or rubbing stimulation. Most women find it easier to be orgasmic with manual, oral, or rubbing stimulation than during intercourse, although many women value orgasm during intercourse.

Although an interesting conceptual point about pleasuring versus intercourse, it misses the main point. Nondemand pleasuring has value in itself—to promote emotional and physical connection, facilitate intimacy, emphasize the value of pleasure over performance, and, most important, promote a varied, flexible sexual repertoire that challenges the rigid roles that cause inhibited sexual desire. A vital function is as a bridge to sexual desire.

the value of nondemand pleasuring
in relation to intercourse

When sex becomes a pass–fail test of intercourse, your intimate relationship is vulnerable. This is true even if there is not a sexual dysfunction. We are sexual people, not perfectly functioning sexual machines.

If only perfect intercourse is acceptable, you are setting yourselves up for failure, if not this year, then 5 or 10 years hence. Orgasm and intercourse are a natural, integral part of sexuality. It is when intercourse and orgasm become a rigid performance mandate that problems occur.

Nondemand pleasuring puts intercourse in a healthy, integrated perspective. Not all touching is destined to end in intercourse. This frees both spouses to enjoy touching, including erotic touching. The analogy we employ is five touching gears, like a five-speed car transmission. Gear one is affectionate touching while clothed—hugging, kissing, holding hands; gear two is sensual, nongenital touching that can be nude or semiclothed; gear three is playful touching that combines nongenital and genital touch; gear four is erotic stimulation to orgasm (manual, oral, or rubbing); and gear five integrates pleasuring and eroticism and flows to intercourse. To have an enjoyable ride, it does not always have to end in fifth gear.

Some couples have a pattern in which half of their nondemand pleasuring experiences transition past third gear. Of these, 85 percent flow into intercourse. Those that flow into fourth gear have special value. Couples who are aware of and comfortable with the concept that not all erotic activity has to culminate in intercourse have a flexible couple style that helps prevent relapse. The key to successful transition from nondemand pleasuring to intercourse is to not treat this as a dichotomy. Be aware that you have sensual and erotic choices. This prevents you from falling into the "Are we going to have intercourse or not?" trap. Intercourse is a valued option, not a demand. The healthiest way to view intercourse is as a "special pleasuring technique."

Intercourse is a natural extension of pleasuring and eroticism, not a pass–fail test. Cuddling in bed before sleep is an example of nondemand pleasuring. If both partners become erotically responsive and want to transition into intercourse, that is fine. If one becomes aroused and requests intercourse, that is fine, as long as both realize it is a request, not a demand. Sometimes the wife prefers to stay with cuddling. Other times she suggests an erotic, nonintercourse experience (mutual or one-way). Sometimes she wants to create eroticism so that a mutual intercourse experience occurs; other times she goes along for the ride, with sex being more for her spouse. As long as there is a comfortable flow of touching and communication, this is a healthy process. If nondemand pleasuring becomes a sham—that is, if there is a felt or perceived demand for intercourse—it loses its value. In that case, the answer is a couple agreement that nondemand pleasuring *cannot* lead to intercourse. The partners close off a bridge to sexual desire and intercourse, but if the choice is losing the value of nondemand pleasuring, they are better to maintain that.

SYBIL AND MARTIN

Couples faced with chronic or intermittent sexual dysfunction find nondemand pleasuring of particular value in rebuilding their sexual bond. Sybil and Martin had been a sexually active couple for 21 years (which included conceiving three children) until Martin began having erection problems at age 47. Sybil blamed it on work, stress, and drinking. She told Martin not to worry. Martin responded that it was like trying not to think of a 500-pound yellow canary sitting on the side of the bed. After 2 months, Martin felt totally "impotent" and began avoiding sex. Sybil tried to minimize the problem by noting that Martin did obtain erections, but lost them when they tried to have intercourse. Rather than being reassured, Martin stopped getting erections. When faced with a sexual dysfunction that does not spontaneously remit within 6 months, the couple is well-advised to seek sex therapy. The man can consult his internist or family practitioner to do an initial screening for potential physical or medication factors. We suggest seeing a sex therapist before consulting a urologist.

Martin did the opposite of these guidelines. He avoided dealing with the erectile problem for 3 years. Sybil stopped initiating because it was so tense and conflictual; she wanted to lessen pressure. Sybil's intentions were good, but resulted in increased pressure on Martin. He was afraid she had given up and would have an affair. Once a month Martin initiated sex, with the hope for a miraculous cure. Instead, he felt embarrassed and humiliated.

Martin masturbated two to three times a week with good erections, but felt ashamed. After a year, he went to an impotence clinic that was advertised on sports radio. It guaranteed to restore potency or give a full refund. The technique was penile injections with a vasodilator (to increase blood flow). Martin had two injections at the clinic and was taught to do injections at home. He found self-injection awkward and at times painful. Martin felt self-conscious and worried about the clinical nature of the procedure. He told Sybil nothing about the injections. The first time they tried intercourse, Sybil was excited to see him erect. Martin did not want her to stroke him, but went right to intercourse. Sybil lubricated, but her lubrication dried up because she felt that the sex was uninvolving and mechanical. Although Martin was objectively aroused (he had an erection), subjectively he did not feel turned on and was not enjoying intercourse. He did not reach orgasm, and Sybil complained of vaginal irritation. He pulled out and seemed very distressed, but maintained an erection; both knew something was amiss.

Sybil heard the story of the injection from Martin 2 days later. She did not object to consulting a urologist and trying the injection, but was hurt that he did not tell her or say what she could do to help. Sybil's not being allowed to touch Martin's penis and his fear that her stimulation might cause him to lose the erection were very upsetting. This fiasco resulted in Sybil confronting Martin; both sex and marital trust were dissolving. They needed professional help. Martin was very reluctant to see a sex therapist, but Sybil insisted and made the appointment.

Sex therapists see many couples with whom the sexual problem (especially, erectile dysfunction) coexists with inhibited sexual desire. Erectile dysfunction is the most common cause of male inhibited sexual desire. Martin was anxious to find a quick, easy solution. He hated the idea of being in therapy for months or years. Once Martin was in the therapist's office, Sybil wanted to talk about their relationship and focus on emotional issues. The therapist understood this gender split. He reassured Sybil that sexuality would not be dealt with outside of the context of intimacy (the fatal flaw of the injection program). He reassured Martin that the prognosis for restoring erectile comfort and confidence was good. Erectile functioning is best dealt with as a couple issue; both partners needed to realize there is no miracle cure, but that change is possible.

After the assessment and feedback sessions, the therapist started Martin and Sybil with nondemand pleasuring exercises. When erection and intercourse are problematic, the couple reacts by decreasing or ceasing affectionate and sensual touching. Sybil missed touching more than intercourse. Martin associated anything other than kissing and hand-holding with a sexual demand and fear of failure.

Nondemand pleasuring exercises began with a temporary prohibition on genital touch, orgasm, and intercourse. With performance pressure reduced, Martin and Sybil focused on the feelings and sensations of nongenital touching. Sybil's reaction to pleasuring was quite positive. She felt more intimately connected than in the past 2 years. Martin's reaction was positive, but mixed. He obtained erections, but became discouraged when they dissipated. He missed the old days when sex, erection, and intercourse flowed easily and automatically. He enjoyed stroking Sybil, but could not hold the good feelings. Sybil found it easier to initiate pleasuring than did Martin. Although he read and understood the words about pleasuring and broad-based sexuality, he felt ambivalent and self-conscious.

The transition to genital pleasuring and erotic stimulation was easier for Sybil. Her desire, arousal, and orgasm flowed during these exercises. Sybil, like many women, could be orgasmic during manual stimulation, as well as during intercourse. Martin was perplexed as to why he was more aroused when he was stimulating Sybil than when she was stimulating him. Instead of feeling embarrassed and not saying anything, Martin expressed his puzzlement. He told Sybil that when the exercise focused on her, his desire and arousal were high, but when reciprocal, both his desire and his arousal waned. With prodding by the therapist, Martin admitted that during masturbation he predictably experienced desire, erection, and orgasm. Martin feared Sybil's censure and was pleasantly surprised when she reported being hopeful because the "machinery worked." Sybil shared that she, too, masturbated and enjoyed arousal and orgasm. Sybil wanted Martin to understand that although orgasm was easier and more predictable with masturbation, sex was more exciting and fulfilling with him.

The next day Martin suggested that they take a walk and talk about their sexual relationship. He disclosed how self-consciousness and performance anxiety inhibited his pleasure. Previously, he could not understand why he did better during masturbation and when being the pleasurer. Now he realized that it was because there were no distractions or performance worries. He asked that they start nondemand pleasuring over so that he could share pleasure without self-consciousness or performance demands. Martin felt freer emotionally and physically when he kept contact with Sybil, rather than being passive. He was open to experimenting with his waxing and waning of erections. Martin learned to be comfortable with erotic stimulation flowing into arousal, erection, and orgasm during nonintercourse sex. This was a new experience—previously, Martin had been orgasmic only during intercourse. Sybil was open to experimenting and sharing eroticism. Flexible, variable sexuality was good for Sybil, and she wanted it to be good for Martin.

Eventually, Sybil and Martin developed three comfortable sexual patterns:

1. Nondemand pleasuring that focused on sensuality (gears two and three)
2. Pleasuring that evolved into erotic stimulation, leading to orgasm for one or both (gears two, three, and four)
3. Pleasuring that evolved to erotic stimulation, which flowed into intercourse (gears two, three, four, and five)

Martin valued gear five dates the most, but learned to enjoy gears two, three, and four. Sybil found gear four dates most sexually satisfying, although she enjoyed all the sensual and sexual gears. Sexual desire was expressed in a varied, flexible manner. Sex was less predictable, but more intimate, more communicative, and of higher quality. Nondemand pleasuring was the key in revitalizing sexual desire.

how to keep the "demand" out

Nondemand pleasuring is more than a technique to use to recover from sexual dysfunction. It is a core strategy to maintain a vital, intimate bond. For this to continue after you resume intercourse, you have to keep the demand out of the pleasuring. Each spouse is comfortable initiating touching. Each communicates the type of touch he or she wants. One might want sensual touch, but not erotic stimulation; one might want erotic touch, the other says no, but is open to affectionate touch; one wants sensual touch, the other prefers erotic touch; one wants intercourse, the other prefers erotic stimulation. Touching and sexuality are about pleasure and communication. They are about requests, not demands. When you remove prohibitions from orgasm and intercourse, you are opening new options for touching, not creating demands. Keep the focus on awareness, comfort, communication, and pleasure; do not fall into the traps of demands or performance orientation.

closing thoughts

Nondemand pleasuring is a vital component in couple sexuality. Pleasuring can include affection, sensuality, playfulness and eroticism. The essence of sexuality is giving and receiving pleasure-oriented touching. Nondemand pleasuring has value in itself, not just as a bridge to sexual desire. Pleasuring includes touching both inside and outside of the bedroom, with the understanding that touching is not always directed toward intercourse. Intimacy and nondemand pleasuring confront the rigidity of a no-sex or low-sex marriage and help rebuild sexual desire.

CHAPTER 9

The Fifth Step: Just Do It— Challenging Inhibitions

Both women and men have a healthy capacity to experience sexual desire and satisfaction. The essence of sexuality is giving and receiving pleasure-oriented touching. Each person deserves to feel comfortable with and to enjoy touching, sensuality, and sexuality. You positively anticipate being sexual, rather than feel fearful, uncomfortable, or pressured. Awareness, comfort, anticipation, desire, pleasuring, eroticism, intercourse, orgasm, and afterplay can flow as a natural process.

"Inhibited sexual desire" means this natural process is blocked. The couple's task is to increase awareness of and to challenge inhibitions. There are a myriad of possible inhibitions, which can be divided into two broad categories—emotional and sexual. Emotional inhibitions include fear of intimacy, anger, poor communication, not valuing couple time, lack of respect due to job or money problems, disappointment with the spouse or marriage, power struggles, role strain, focus on parenting at the expense of being a couple, too much time and energy spent on work, being overly involved with family of origin so that there is little emotional energy for marriage, being distracted by television or sports, being turned off by a spouse's drinking or eating habits, depression or anxiety, and parenting conflicts. Examples of sexual inhibitions include anticipatory anxiety, performance anxiety, guilt or shame about past sexual experiences, embarrassment about sexual dysfunction, poor sexual communication, history of sexual trauma, aversion to kissing, self-consciousness about giving or receiving oral stimulation, fear of becoming pregnant, history of sexual coercion, masturbation being more valued than couple sex, fear that a sexual secret will be discovered, a compulsive sexual pattern, a poor body image, embarrassment over nudity, not being comfortable making sexual requests, and feeling constrained from letting go and experiencing orgasm.

What is a psychologically healthy way to address your inhibitions? The spouse's inhibitions? The least healthy is to feel guilt and shame about yours and anger and blaming about the spouse's.

A first step is to confront denial. Be honest with yourself about inhibitions and how they interfere with sexual intimacy. Disclosing negative attitudes and feelings is an important step. Sometimes these come from abusive or traumatic childhood experiences, humiliation or rejection during adolescence, disappointment or anger at dating partners during young adulthood, or frustrating or dysfunctional adult sexual experiences. You can discuss these with the spouse, a therapist, a sibling, or your best friend. You learn to trust that the spouse will be empathic and nonjudgmental and will not use this information to blame or belittle you. Self-disclosure is therapeutic. However, if self-disclosure is used against you, it adds to alienation and further inhibits desire.

The next step is assessing whether this inhibition can be overcome, can be lessened significantly, or needs to be accepted and worked around so that it does not control your sexuality. This is a difficult assessment to make without the help of a therapist.

Some inhibitions can be confronted and overcome. For example, the male who could not tolerate cunnilingus finds that he is gradually desensitized to oral sex, and her responsiveness becomes a turn-on for him. Cunnilingus becomes an integral part of their lovemaking. Most inhibitions can be significantly reduced, even if not overcome. The goal is to reduce the negative impact so that desire is not blocked. An example is a woman who did not like deep (French) kissing, which her husband found erotic. She enjoyed lip and neck kissing, which became a regular part of their lovemaking. She became comfortable putting her tongue in his mouth, but did not enjoy reciprocal deep kissing. Some sexual techniques are not comfortable for an individual or couple. This needs to be accepted and worked around. For example, use of lotions is commonly recommended as a way to enhance touching. Couples are encouraged to experiment with different fragrances and smells to discover those they find sensuous. However, some people dislike the feel of lotion on their body. This inhibition is accepted and worked around. Enjoy other aspects of touching, such as varying pleasuring positions, combining manual and oral stimulation, alternating one-way and mutual touching, standing rather than lying, and using erotic touch in the shower or bath.

In deciding whether to try to overcome, modify, or accept an inhibition, assess the severity of the inhibition and how much it interferes with sexual desire. How strong is your motivation for change? How much energy and persistence will it take? Ideally, you view confronting the inhibition as a challenge, enlist the spouse's support, put in the time and energy to succeed, and persevere until the inhibition is overcome. Unfortunately, some inhibitions are chronic and severe, the spouse colludes in maintaining the inhibition, motivation to change is low, there is a significant secondary gain for maintaining the status quo, and the couple has a history of unsuccessful change attempts. In this situation, reducing the harm caused by the inhibition makes more sense. Contrary to the overpromises of "pop psychology," not everything is curable.

Next, choose a change strategy. Good intentions are not enough; you need a plan. The most successful strategy is gradual step-by-step change, reducing the inhibition by engaging in a comfortable, pleasurable alternative. Implementing a change plan requires thought, time, energy and communication. For example, in confronting an inhibition about requesting your husband to stimulate you genitally, begin by seeing him as your intimate friend, talk outside the bedroom, tell him what you want and how he can be supportive, put your hand over his and guide him, say what feels good, acknowledge what he does that you like, make verbal requests, reinforce what is working, and make further requests. When something is awkward or is not working, do not avoid or give up. Overcoming inhibitions takes practice, feedback, and creative problem-solving.

The last step, usually ignored, is maintaining and generalizing gains. Couples make initial changes, only to regress to the old inhibition. Going back to "square one" not only is frustrating, but makes it harder to regain motivation to again confront the inhibition. A major impediment with a long-standing problem is the weight of the chronicity. Failed attempts at change are more demoralizing than the original problem. To avoid that trap, implement a relapse-prevention program. It is normal to have lapses and setbacks, especially when stress interferes. The key is to view this as a lapse and actively problem-solve. Do not give up and allow it to become a relapse.

Benign neglect and avoidance result in the inhibition regaining control. If you have overcome an inhibition about touching yourself during partner sex, continue doing this on a regular basis. Otherwise, self-conscious feelings and thoughts that self-stimulation is wrong regain strength. The most important relapse-prevention strategy is to acknowledge and reinforce healthy sexual attitudes, feelings, and behavior. A second strategy is to anticipate occasional anxieties, inhibitions, or lapses—be prepared to problem-solve and get back on track. Do not allow a lapse to become a relapse.

individual and couple responsibility for changing inhibitions

The best way to change inhibitions is a one-two combination—first, you are responsible for your sexuality and second, you consider yourself part of an intimate team. Take personal responsibility; change for yourself and for the good of the marriage. The spouse cannot coerce you to change or make changes for you. You can influence and support each other in the change process.

It is unusual for spouses to have the same inhibitions. Even when both spouses have inhibitions, these are different. Empathize with and support the spouse in challenging his or her inhibitions. The most destructive role is being the spouse's worst critic, blaming and making the person feel guilty. That is not in your best interest, the best interest of the spouse, or that of the marriage. The person responsible for change is more invested in the process, but the spouse's encouragement and support are vital. Sex is a team sport; you win or lose as a team.

Often, inhibitions involve the spouse. This is particularly true of emotional inhibitions. Rather than the spouse feeling like the "bad guy" and becoming defensive or counterattacking, the team approach allows him to be on the side of growth, challenging inhibitions.

emotional inhibitions

The chief guideline is to deal with emotional inhibitions outside of the bedroom. Sexuality is the wrong context in which to play out emotional disappointments and conflicts. For example, when anger inhibits sexual desire, identify the source of the anger and confront it. Anger, more than anxiety, is the chief emotional inhibitor of sexual desire. The traditional argument is that you cannot feel sexual in the bedroom if you are angry outside of the bedroom. Although sometimes a feeling is so powerful that this is true, it is not the case for the majority of couples. Our suggestion is to recognize that there is a separate anger problem and a separate sexual problem. Ideally, you would address the problems concurrently. You can deal with anger issues over the kitchen table, while rebuilding trust, intimacy, and touching in the bedroom. The traditional belief that when you resolve emotional conflicts, then sex will take care of itself is untrue for most couples.

Once sex has gotten off track, you need to focus on sexual issues in order for change to occur. The question is whether the wife is open to touching and sexuality when she is still angry. If you had to wait for everything to be in sync emotionally before being sexual, there would be a dramatic increase in low-sex marriages. Couples can deal with anger issues while concurrently revitalizing their sexual relationship. A prime function of sexuality is to energize the marital bond. This increases motivation to address difficult issues, including conflict and anger.

Sex is more than genitals, intercourse, and orgasm. Sexuality includes self-esteem, body image, intimacy, touch, and openness to erotic scenarios and techniques. The mind is your main sexual organ. Feeling comfortable, open, and sensual provides the basis for erotic feelings. Emotional inhibitions cause sexual roadblocks, especially those affecting desire. Inhibitions interfere with sexual anticipation. This is particularly true for females, but can be just as inhibiting for males.

Key to overcoming inhibitions are feeling that you deserve sexual pleasure and identifying the value of sexuality for you and your marriage. Is it in your best interest to allow emotional inhibitions to dominate your sexuality? Emotions that had a positive function (to maintain autonomy, express hurt or anger, maintain perspective, or allow you space to regroup) now keep you stuck in a self-defeating sexual pattern.

The relationship between thoughts and emotions is complex. The cognitive therapy approach involves challenging self-defeating thoughts, perceptions, and assumptions. Reinforce thoughts and perceptions that are rational, productive, and congruent with your sexual values and goals. Challenging self-defeating thoughts and assumptions facilitates intimacy and sexuality. For example, if the emotional inhibition involves fears of vulnerability and rejection, identify habitual thoughts such as "If I'm open, I'll be hurt," "The more I care, the more painful the rejection," "I won't let my spouse own me," and "I won't beg for intimacy." Are these thoughts in your best interest? Do they serve a positive function for you or marital sexuality?

The best way to deal with negative thoughts is to replace them with positive, realistic thoughts. Use these each time you are tempted to fall into the inhibited pattern. Self-esteem is strengthened by a healthy marriage. There is a positive, reciprocal relationship between self-esteem and marriage. The healthy cognition is "I can be me in an intimate marriage." Marriage should never contribute to more than one-third of one's self-esteem. A satisfying, stable marriage fulfills needs for intimacy and security better than any other human relationship.

Traditionally, marriages stayed together regardless of quality. Stigma against divorce, family pressure, religious sanction, and community norms supported marginal marriages. Couples stayed married unless there was a major disruption such as physical abuse of the spouse or children, the man stopped working, or the woman abandoned the family. In our culture, low quality marriages do not survive. If you value the marriage, you have to be committed to both quality and stability.

Emotional inhibitions can be challenged. Take the risks necessary to reconnect with the spouse. If the inhibition involves overcommitment to family of origin or stress due to an overwhelming yet unsatisfactory job, it is the person's responsibility to address this. One element of a change plan is to enlist the support of the spouse. For example, if the wife wants to switch jobs, the husband increases his contribution to housework and child care so that she has the time and energy to write inquiry letters and to network. If the decision is to limit family contact, the spouse conveys to relatives the parameters of the time available. It is easier to say "no" to social demands if both partners do it together.

There is great value in confronting emotional inhibitions. Successfully challenging inhibitions improves psychological well-being and increases the feeling that you deserve sexual pleasure. A powerful cognition is pride in seeing yourself as a "survivor, not a victim." Another helpful cognition is "Living well is the best revenge."

challenging sexual inhibitions

This is what the high-desire partner has been waiting for. How to get the spouse to overcome her or his sexual inhibitions. Is the key to be sexually free, with no inhibitions? Is the *Playboy* philosophy correct? No! The focus is on developing a comfortable, functional couple sexual style, not "anything goes." You do not have to prove anything to yourself, the spouse, or anyone else.

Some sexual inhibitions can be totally overcome, others significantly changed, whereas others must be accepted and worked around. Seldom do people have the same sexual inhibitions, so it is hard for the partner to understand and empathize. For example, consider the husband who makes fun of the wife's preoccupation with breast shape or her sensitivity to heavy thighs. Or the wife who cannot understand why he is so concerned about the size of his penis or why he gets anxious when she plays with his buttocks. Accept the spouse's sensitivity; do not put the spouse down or try to talk that person out of it. Listen in a respectful, caring manner to the spouse's feelings and perceptions. Be an intimate friend and supporter, not critical or demanding.

People do not magically overcome sexual inhibitions. Change is a gradual process that occurs over weeks, months, and, yes, even years. Barry recalls a couple where the man had a strong aversion to looking at, much less touching, the wife's vulva. After six months of therapy, taking very small steps, he was able to successfully engage in manual clitoral stimulation, but needed to do so with his eyes closed. Both were pleased with the progress; this inhibition no longer interfered with desire or arousal. Two years later, the man wrote on his follow-up form that he now enjoyed giving manual stimulation and especially seeing the pleasure in his wife's eyes.

It is easiest to change sexual attitudes, next sexual behavior. Feelings do not change until there have been a number of successful experiences. Orgasm is important and a natural culmination of arousal, but is not the best measure of success. The best measure is emotional satisfaction. Women find this easier to accept than men do—women can recall highly satisfying experiences that did not include orgasm. Men rigidly measure sex by intercourse and orgasm. If pressed, the man discloses that on occasion he has ejaculated, but felt little satisfaction. Experiences with pleasuring help identify emotional, sensual, and erotic sources of satisfaction, in addition to intercourse and orgasm.

Throughout this book, we take a pro-sexual attitude. Confronting past abusive or traumatic sexual experiences is a challenge facing many people. Clients ask Barry, if he had their experiences with childhood sexual abuse or had been a victim of incest, been raped, been sexually humiliated, dealt with an unwanted pregnancy, contracted a sexually transmitted disease, been peeped on or exposed to, or been made to feel guilty or shamed, would he have pro-sexual attitudes and feelings? Other people have to deal with present negative experiences that include being harassed at work, receiving obscene phone calls, dealing with infertility caused by an untreated sexually transmitted disease, or feeling psychological stress due to a sexual dysfunction. This is in addition to the stress and stigma of a no-sex or low-sex marriage. With these past and present negative experiences, is it possible to adopt a pro-sexual attitude?

Negative motivation does not promote change; it serves to keep the individual and couple "stuck." Do not feel blamed or blame yourself for negative sexual attitudes and feelings; you just "pile on," which makes the problem worse. Positive motivation, attitudes, and actions promote change. Does any healthy function for you or your marriage derive from maintaining negative sexual attitudes? Very unlikely.

What would be the result of adopting a pro-sexual attitude? It would mean seeing sexuality as a good thing, an integral part of you as a person, and feeling that you deserve to express sexuality in a manner that promotes your intimate relationship. What can you do and what can your spouse do to facilitate this change?

One way to promote pro-sexual attitudes is receiving encouragement from an authority figure. For example, almost all religions are pro-sex in marriage. Barry refers Catholic clients for a consultation with a priest. The husband and wife are amazed when the priest tells them that having intercourse is spiritually a good deed, equivalent to saying a prayer. They say, "That's not what the nuns told me in grade school." You are a married adult and deserve sexuality to be a positive part of your life and relationship. Another source of permission giving is parents. When you were an adolescent, parents were controlled by fear, especially fear of you getting pregnant, contracting an S.T.D. (this generation of parents is afraid of HIV/AIDS), or falling in love with the wrong person and derailing your life. Talking to parents as a married adult is very different. Parents who had disappointing (and even disastrous) marriages and sexual problems are supportive and encourage you to enjoy marital sexuality.

Your spouse is the most important person in helping change your attitudes. The spouse's role is to be genuinely empathic and supportive, not patronizing or coercive. The one-two combination of personal responsibility-intimate team promotes change.

What to do about specific sexual inhibitions? For example, consider the man who is unable to talk during a sexual experience or to touch after orgasm or the woman who is not comfortable giving genital stimulation or can only be sexual in the dark. The couple's task is to build a comfortable, functional sexual style that promotes intimacy and satisfaction. There is *not* "one right way" to be sexual. You do not have to perform to a rigid sexual criterion. The strategy is a gradual step-by-step effort to build comfort, acquire skill, and encourage free expression.

A common sexual inhibition is fear of not maintaining an erection. Rather than panicking when this happens, the couple is encouraged to use a "trust position" to reinforce physical connection. Partners can lie side by side, hold hands, and share feelings. Other couples find it more comfortable for the woman to lie in the man's arms, with minimal movement or verbal communication. Develop a trust position and way of being together that reestablishes comfort and intimacy.

Sometimes you end the experience with the trust position, other times you return to genital stimulation, thus expanding your sensual and erotic repertoire. Manual, oral, or rubbing stimulation to facilitate arousal is of great value in overcoming erection problems. Realizing you can achieve arousal and orgasm with nonintercourse sex rebuilds confidence. Couples who have a flexible sexual repertoire that allows for normal variation in male and female arousal do not remain stuck in self-defeating patterns.

The woman who wants to feel comfortable giving genital stimulation begins by rubbing his penis against her thigh, moves to rubbing her body against his (including genitals), and holds the penis while they are kissing. They might stop at that point or progress to her stimulating his penis with a vibrator, beads, or her hand. Once aroused, she is open to his rubbing the penis between or against her breasts, their engaging in mutual manual stimulation, or her manually stimulating him while he stimulates her orally.

The main change in sexual technique during the last generation is the increased use of oral sex. The "chic" erotic scenario is for the woman to be multiorgasmic with cunnilingus and the man fellated to orgasm, with the woman swallowing the semen. If you are not comfortable with this, does it mean you are inhibited? We urge the couple to develop a comfortable, pleasure-oriented approach to oral sex. You do not have to prove anything to yourself or to the spouse. Some women enjoy cunnilingus as an erotic technique, but not to the point of orgasm. Many women enjoy cunnilingus naturally flowing to orgasm. Some women do not like cunnilingus unless they are very aroused. Other women find mutual oral sex (cunnilingus and fellatio simultaneously) extremely arousing, whereas some find it distracting or a turnoff. Many women prefer manual, rubbing, or intercourse stimulation and choose to not engage in cunnilingus. Some men enjoy fellatio to orgasm; others do not because it means they cannot engage in intercourse. Many men enjoy movement during fellatio; others prefer to lie passively and take in pleasure. Some people genuinely enjoy giving oral sex; others engage in it because it is arousing for the spouse. Like other aspects of sexual expression, the couple's task is to develop a comfortable, pleasurable style of oral sexuality.

EXERCISE—CHALLENGING INHIBITIONS

Each of you should list emotional and sexual inhibitions that subvert your sexual desire. Next to each item, list whether your goal is to overcome, reduce, or accept the inhibition. Your spouse provides insights, perceptions, and feelings, but does not talk you out of or into anything. It is your inhibition and your responsibility. Discuss with your spouse how he or she can be helpful. For example, perhaps a woman's inhibition involves not enjoying sexual touching while semiclothed. The goal is to lower the inhibition so that she can receive and give stimulation freely. Yet the man tries to talk her into mutual stimulation, rather than being supportive of her goals. Her focus should be to develop comfort with receiving kissing and hugging semiclothed, not to feel pushed to do more.

Once you have established mutually acceptable goals, begin the change process. Clearly spell out steps to take and how your spouse can be supportive. A crucial guideline is to move at the change pace that is comfortable for the person with the inhibition. Equally important, the spouse can veto or stop uncomfortable stimulation, but not stop or avoid touching (this reinforces anxiety). If you feel anxious, keep contact and switch to touching that is comfortable. You can use a "trust position"—examples include putting your head on the partner's heart, his lying in your arms, or sitting facing each other while keeping eye contact and placing your hand on his heart.

Do not try to change more than two inhibitions at a time. The trap is being overly ambitious. For instance, if each spouse targets two emotional and two sexual inhibitions, both partners lose focus and become discouraged. A common pattern is making significant progress and then regressing. It is crucial to maintain gains and prevent relapse. It is better to maintain changes in two inhibitions, rather than to experience mixed progress and frustration in six areas.

Be clear and specific about change steps, communicating as an intimate team. One advantage of working with a therapist, as opposed to doing this on your own, is that the therapist helps you process what you learn, deal with frustrations, design and alter exercises, and maintain focus and motivation. The process of changing inhibitions often involves "two steps forward and one step back." It is seldom quick or easy. If change is easy for you, it is a cause for celebration.

The more specific the inhibition, the easier it is to change. Interestingly, sexual inhibitions tend to be easier than emotional inhibitions are. It is simpler to break the cycle of avoidance than to build a comfortable, pleasurable sexual style. Talk about and acknowledge improvements and plan next steps. Talk at least once a month and preferably weekly. If the inhibition has not been resolved within 6 months, we strongly urge seeking professional help.

BETH AND CRAIG

Beth and Craig argued about inhibitions during the entire 8 years they had been in a relationship, the last 4 as a married couple. They met through an "in search of" ad Craig had placed. Beth was intrigued that rather than his writing an upbeat, overpromising ad, Craig admitted to shyness and being a critical person. He was looking for a woman who would tolerate initial hassles and discover the gem of a person underneath.

Beth felt comfortable with the giving/helping role. Beth realized that Craig was more than shy; he suffered from social anxiety. Sex was a particularly sensitive area. Craig had an unusual sexual dysfunction—ejaculatory inhibition. Craig became easily erect and moved quickly into hard thrusting intercourse. Even with an hour of intercourse, he would only occasionally ejaculate—less than one third of the time. Beth found Craig's approach to sex both intriguing and off-putting. She was used to men who were premature ejaculators and who brought her to orgasm manually. Craig's sexual intensity and intercourse pattern presented a different dimension. Beth did not believe she could reach orgasm with intercourse and was pleasantly surprised when she was orgasmic during intercourse with Craig. On the other hand, she tired of Craig's incessant thrusting. After 10 minutes, she stopped lubricating and found sex boring and tedious. If intercourse extended over 20 minutes, it became physically irritating.

Craig and Beth felt that the relationship was emotionally validating and satisfying. Craig enjoyed Beth's warmth and giving. Beth was able to disarm his criticalness through humor. She realized that Craig longed for trust and acceptance.

Craig was more successful professionally than personally. His background was in accounting and computers; he was a consultant specializing in streamlining financial systems This was a good professional match with his personality; he enjoyed detail work and problem-solving. They took advantage of the perks of Craig's consulting. Beth was the first woman who had the professional flexibility (she was a successful freelance editor) to accompany him on trips, taking advantage of frequent flyer miles and free accommodations. They admired each other's professional expertise.

Beth had one sexual inhibition—she was not comfortable lying in bed nude after sex. She put on her granny gown, which Craig found antierotic. Beth had two emotional inhibitions—she was wary of the institution of marriage and did not trust men (including Craig) to be sexually faithful. This resulted in a paradox—Beth could be loving, giving, and humorous, which enhanced the quality of their relationship. However, she was tentative and unwilling to commit. Craig offered stability and security, but Beth was not buying. This worked on his insecurity—fear that Beth would leave because of the ejaculatory inhibition. Beth assured Craig that the problem was not whether he ejaculated, but his frustration, anger, and emotional distance when he did not.

Craig wanted to marry a year after meeting, but it took 2 years of his lobbying, her parents' and friends' urging, and Beth's desire for children to convince her. Craig believed that a marital commitment would eliminate Beth's emotional inhibitions. He was upset when that did not occur and blamed her, which infuriated Beth. She hoped that the marriage would help Craig's ejaculatory inhibition. She never said it to Craig, but worried about their ability to get pregnant. Beth had ambivalence about a lifelong marriage commitment, but no ambivalence about parenting. She was thrilled that after 19 months of marriage (and only 3 months of trying), they became pregnant. Craig was just as pleased—he silently had feared they would not be able to conceive. They did not share these fears until after the pregnancy.

Beth and Craig enjoyed parenting, but with less time and energy, conflicts over sexual and emotional inhibitions increased. Beth resented prolonged intercourse and had neither the time nor the patience to lie in bed afterward. As Beth became less sexually desirous, her fear that Craig would have an affair increased. Craig felt defensive and blamed for something he had not done and had no intention of doing. Craig kept it secret that he masturbated daily and was orgasmic 100 percent of the time. Craig found masturbation easier and more satisfying than partner sex.

The stimulus for entering couple therapy was an emotionally charged incident. Beth was holding the baby and needed to tell Craig something, so she interrupted while he was showering. Then Beth realized that he was masturbating. Craig was mortified; Beth was apologetic, but later angry. She felt betrayed by his masturbating—it was as if masturbation was his way of having an affair. Beth did not oppose masturbation; she had masturbated since age 19. Beth felt free to masturbate when Craig was out of town. However, Craig's masturbation was a compulsive activity that took place when she was available. She was devastated to learn that he was easily orgasmic by himself. During couple sex, he was orgasmic only once a month. Beth was not sure whether to blame herself or Craig. Interestingly, it was Craig who made the call to the therapist. It is sad that it took this crisis to initiate their seeking help because Beth and Craig were excellent candidates for sex therapy.

Although Craig and Beth argued and blamed concerning inhibitions, they had not honestly and objectively assessed what the inhibitions were and disclosed them to the spouse. Craig became easily erect, but his level of subjective arousal was low. Because he had an erection, he felt silly asking for additional stimulation. Craig did not find intercourse stimulating (but thought he was supposed to). The concept of subjective arousal (i.e., feeling turned on) was new to Craig, although not to Beth. Beth was aware that her subjective arousal was usually greater than her objective arousal (i.e., vaginal lubrication) and just assumed this was true for Craig. Realizing that he became erect at a low level of arousal was a revelation. Beth was eager to give manual and oral stimulation to build subjective arousal. This increased involvement and eroticism for both. It was Beth's idea to continue erotic (multiple) stimulation during intercourse. Craig was especially responsive to testicle stimulation while thrusting. Giving breast stimulation increased his erotic involvement. As subjective arousal increased, so did his pleasure at being orgasmic. Craig valued marital sex and agreed to masturbate only when Beth was not available.

The therapist took a different tack with Beth's inhibitions. These were conceptualized as an inability to accept intimacy and security. Beth's parents divorced when she was 3. Her mother chose not to remarry; her father was divorced an additional two times. Two of Beth's siblings were divorced (one successfully remarried), and the sibling in a first marriage was very unhappy. Beth's best friend had been abandoned when the husband left her for his business partner. Last, but not least, Beth was an avid fiction reader and moviegoer—affairs are a major theme in the media. Her favorite movie, which she watched at least three times a year, was *An Unmarried Women*, about the strength a woman needs to deal with the husband leaving for a younger woman. Beth loved being emotionally giving, but hated to be emotionally vulnerable.

Traditionally, religious, family, and community pressure ensured that marriages remained intact. Men having affairs or mistresses was frowned upon, but accepted as long as the man did not disgrace or abandon the wife. The double standard is not culturally acceptable now and was totally unacceptable to Beth. Yet she felt vulnerable and helpless in dealing with her fear of Craig having an affair. The therapist suggested five things: (1) an upfront commitment on both Beth's and Craig's part to remain faithful and not have affairs; (2) an agreement to disclose any potential risk situation and talk about it before acting on it (an excellent technique to confront the secrecy that affairs thrive on); (3) if there was a sexual incident with another person, the spouse would be told within 24 hours; (4) putting time and energy into enhancing sexual intimacy; and (5) after a sexual experience, Beth put on underpants, lay in bed, and talked about intimate feelings. Beth was pleased that Craig would have a positive role, rather than just complaining about her inhibitions. As inhibitions decreased, what had been a good marriage turned into an excellent marriage. Intimacy and sexuality thrived in a secure milieu.

the importance of freely flowing emotional and sexual intimacy

Inhibitions block the flow of intimacy and sexuality. This drains the marital bond of energy and good feelings. Decreasing inhibitions frees emotional and sexual energy. Couples report a romantic love surge. A favorite analogy is that the couple is operating on all six cylinders, instead of limping along on four. It is difficult to gauge the negative impact of inhibitions until you are free of them.

Inhibitions, whether personal or relational, emotional or sexual, block sexual desire. Some inhibitions can be totally overcome, others significantly reduced, whereas others need to be accepted and worked around so that they do not control the person or relationship. Inhibitions function as a means of withholding, although this is seldom intentional. Blame/guilt struggles concerning inhibitions result in marital alienation. Taking personal responsibility and working as an intimate team free you and the marriage from the tyranny of inhibitions.

CHAPTER 10

The Sixth Step: Making It Special—Creating Erotic Scenarios

INTIMACY AND NONDEMAND pleasuring are necessary for sexual satisfaction, but are not sufficient. For arousal and orgasm, you need erotic scenarios and techniques.

When people think of erotic sex, they recall movies featuring passion, romance, youthful couples, or extramarital affairs. Have you ever seen erotic marital sex in the movies? Is there eroticism after marriage? You can create eroticism in your marriage and revitalize sexual desire. Arousal, intercourse, and orgasm are not the core of a sexual relationship, but are integral components. The prescription for a vital sexual relationship is integrating intimacy, nondemand pleasuring, and erotic stimulation.

Couples plagued by inhibited sexual desire and a no-sex or low-sex marriage do not have erotic scenarios. Premarital sex was good because of newness, romantic love, and wanting to please the partner. Yet these couples did not have the comfort, communication, or freedom to share special turn-ons and erotic scenarios. Young couples, especially males, find that sexual functioning is easy and predictable. However, the quality is often mediocre or worse. If sex remains poor quality, then anticipation declines and frustration increases. Do not treat your sexual relationship with benign neglect. This leads to resentment, alienation, and

147

avoidance. Eventually, one or both spouses develop inhibited sexual desire. Unless one pushes to maintain contact, you fall into a low-sex or no-sex marriage.

Couples with primary sexual dysfunction are open to a new approach. Building a vital sexuality is easier because the concept of developing bridges to desire and erotic scenarios is new and inviting. Optimism is high. Awareness, comfort, being an intimate team, nondemand pleasuring, and erotic scenarios and techniques facilitate desire.

A significant number of couples had good-quality sex and then lost desire and eroticism. For some, good sex ended with the birth of the first child. For others, a sexual conflict (an affair, dysfunction, or an unplanned pregnancy), a practical conflict involving jobs or living conditions, or an emotional conflict destroyed sexual intimacy. When the couple avoids, communication and sexual skills atrophy. What had been easy and flowing becomes awkward, self-conscious, and difficult. It is reassuring for partners to know they have experienced eroticism so they can again in the future. It is hard to accept that you cannot magically turn back the clock. You can build bridges for desire and create erotic scenarios. Knowing that you have the potential for eroticism is helpful, but you have to be open to experiment, communicate, and play.

sexual desire and eroticism

It is possible to maintain sexual desire with minimal eroticism. Some couples have a pattern where one spouse (usually the male) initiates sex once a week. Sex is functional, even if not particularly fun. For other couples, sex is tied to becoming pregnant, is viewed as a duty, or is part of the commitment to the marriage.

Anticipating erotic, arousing sex is a major motivator in revitalizing sexual desire. Sharing high levels of arousal and letting go and being orgasmic are energizing. The essence of eroticism is using scenarios and techniques to increase involvement and arousal. This includes, but is not limited to, intercourse. Ideally, each spouse's arousal plays off the other's. The "give to get" pleasure guideline is generalized to giving and getting erotic stimulation. The main aphrodisiac is an involved, aroused partner. Couples find that giving and receiving multiple stimulation enhance arousal. The more you turn your partner on, the more turned on you feel. Mutual arousal and multiple stimulation build high levels of eroticism.

Feeling open and receptive is the underpinning of eroticism. If you think of arousal as being a 10-point scale, where 0 is feeling neutral and 10 is being orgasmic, you cannot jump from 0 to 8 with erotic scenarios. Erotic techniques and scenarios assume your openness and receptivity to touching and genital stimulation—your being at least 3 and preferably 5 on the arousal scale before transitioning to erotic stimulation. Erotic techniques during the pleasuring/foreplay phase include mutual manual stimulation; his doing oral breast stimulation and manual vulva stimulation, while she caresses his penis; her giving fellatio, while he does breast stimulation and utilizes fantasy; kneeling, kissing, and engaging in mutual genital stimulation; watching a sexy movie, undressing each other, and erotically touching; verbalizing or playing out a sexual fantasy; standing in front of a mirror so that you have visual feedback while doing manual and oral stimulation. There are a variety of pleasuring positions, variations in stimulation, and uses of fantasy, lotions, music, movement, and scenarios to enhance erotic feelings.

Multiple stimulation can and should be integrated with intercourse. Why cease multiple stimulation because the penis is in the vagina? Many couples find that multiple stimulation is most erotic during intercourse. This includes switching intercourse positions two or three times; enjoying kissing or breast stimulation; using the man's hand, woman's hand, or vibrator for additional clitoral stimulation; the woman giving testicle stimulation; fantasizing during intercourse; enjoying buttock or anal stimulation; using intercourse positions (like side-by-side) that facilitate body contact; and taking a break for manual or oral stimulation, then resuming intercourse.

Arousal and orgasm are important, but are not the core of sexuality. Desire and emotional satisfaction are the critical elements of a vital sexual relationship. Unless you experience anticipation, receptivity, and involvement, even the most erotic scenarios and techniques will not elicit arousal.

creative and erotic sex

When people think passion, excitement, and eroticism, they focus on premarital or extramarital affairs. Why are people willing to take sexual risks with a new person, but not with the spouse? Erotic sex connotes new, illicit, swept away, "fun but dirty." Can couples with chronic desire problems learn to enjoy sex that is intimate, exciting, erotic, and satisfying? Yes!

It is not technique alone, or even primarily, that serves to eroticize sex. Sexuality is enhanced by anticipation, playfulness, and experimentation, but, above all, awareness of feelings and openness to creative expression. Sexual creativity emanates from three sources: awareness of feelings, thoughts, and fantasies; a dynamic process between you and the spouse that includes touching, teasing, and nonverbal cues; and openness to experimenting with erotic scenarios and techniques. Eroticism need not reach a Hollywood-level lustful performance. Critical components are multiple stimulation, creativity, and letting go. Arousing, erotic sex can and does exist in the context of a marital bond. Intimacy and eroticism complement each other. Erotic sex energizes the couple bond and adds a special dimension to your marriage.

guidelines for erotic experiences

Creative sexuality is a voluntary, pleasure-oriented, mutual experience. A major poison for desire is intimate coercion. This involves sexual demands where the stated or implied threat is that if one person does not give the other what the other wants, there will be a negative consequence. Sex is then neither intimate nor voluntary; it is a demand performance under threat of punishment. Intimate coercion includes the threat of an affair if the spouse does not have sex, withholding love or money if a specific sex act does not occur, being distant or angry if there is no sex, or using sex as a bribe.

What is erotic for one spouse might feel "kinky" or distasteful to the other. Experimentation should *not* be to prove anything to anyone, involve performance demands, or be manipulative or coercive. Focus on eroticism, not performance; on requests, not demands; on honesty, not manipulation. Remember, you are trying to revitalize sex with your intimate friend, not coerce that person to have sex your way.

EXERCISE—CREATING EROTIC
COUPLE SCENARIOS

One of the most fascinating aspects of sexuality is the differences in what people find erotic. When exploring turn-ons, you do not have to prove anything to yourself, your spouse, or anyone else. Request and share scenarios and techniques that heighten your desire and arousal.

The husband takes the first initiation. From a smorgasbord of erotic turn-ons, he chooses what he would like to try or designs something of his own. Erotic couple scenarios include slow, mutual kissing and touching, followed by rapid, intense intercourse; making love while watching a favorite R-rated video; being sexual in the shower or right after, so that both partners are fresh for oral sex; reading a sexual fantasy aloud or playing out the fantasy; using a favorite lotion to heighten erotic sensations as the partners stimulate each other to orgasm; a quick, intense intercourse followed by afterplay, where he gives her as many orgasms as she wants; having intercourse standing up or with her sitting on the bed and him kneeling; and mixing manual and oral sex until both partners are highly aroused, with intercourse in the woman-on-top position, where he engages in manual clitoral stimulation and she strokes her breasts. The man creates scenarios that are personally inviting and a turn-on. The woman is open to his requests and desires. They share turn-ons that heighten eroticism and arousal.

The wife designs her creative erotic scenario. This is a sharing, not a competition. She can explore external turn-ons and use milieu and special techniques to heighten eroticism. The husband can veto anything he finds negative, but is encouraged to be open and experimental. Examples include being sexual in front of a mirror and enjoying visual feedback; watching an erotic or X-rated video; being sexual in the guest room, living room, or family room; using vibrator stimulation; being sexual on a deserted beach; sex in a shower or jacuzzi; using play aids (a feather, silk sheets, mittens); being sexual in the back seat of the car in remembrance of adolescence; using "toys" like loosely tied ropes or a paddle for spanking; being sexual at a bed-and-breakfast, upscale hotel, or funky inn; lighting a scented candle and putting on their favorite music; and being sexual under the stars during a camping trip.

Whether creating scenarios individually or mutually, partners should be open to their spouses' feelings and requests. They should not set artificial barriers between sex play and intercourse. They can experiment with positions, multiple stimulation, expressing feelings—and enjoy creative, flowing, erotic sexuality. Creative sexuality does not end with orgasm. Parners can stay connected and enjoy afterplay.

Intimacy and eroticism can be successfully integrated. Eroticism builds anticipation and desire.

realistic sexual expectations

Couples envy friends in a new relationship who feel in love, are lustful, and brag about fantastic sex. Instead of going for ice cream after a movie, they rush home to have sex. It is hard not to be envious. The romantic love, passionate sex phase is great, but is precarious and time-limited. Unfortunately, "hot sex" couples have high rates of dysfunction and low-sex or no-sex marriages. Part of that is the natural transition of time and experience, but a prime cause is unrealistic expectations. Passionate, driven sex does not last. It needs to be replaced by mature, intimate sexuality that integrates eroticism to energize the marital bond. That is a positive, realistic expectation. Striving to return to the lustful, passionate, super-charged sex of the first few months is unrealistic and crazy-making.

Empirical studies of sexually well-functioning, happily married couples present a very different view than the media hype. The average married couple has sex one or two times a week. The normal range of sexual frequency is between three times a week to once every 2 weeks. In 40 to 50 percent of sexual experiences both partners feel desirous, aroused, orgasmic, and satisfied. So the ideal sexual scenario occurs less than half the time, even with well-functioning couples. Other patterns include one spouse being highly satisfied while the other is satisfied, one spouse being satisfied while the other finds it okay, and one feels satisfied, whereas the other went along for the ride. These are acceptable and realistic, but quite different from the sex portrayed in movies and novels. Of particular interest is that 5 to 15 percent of sexual experiences are mediocre, disappointments, or failures. That, too, is a realistic part of marital sexuality. You know that partners are cured when they are able to laugh or shrug off a negative experience. They look forward to getting together in the next day or two when they are feeling desirous, receptive, and responsive.

What is a realistic expectation regarding creative, erotic scenarios? If you have one or two special sexual experiences a month, count yourselves lucky. You cannot expect each encounter to be special nor can you expect each erotic scenario to be fabulous. Erotic scenarios sometimes turn out to be duds. This is not to discourage you, but to emphasize realistic expectations. If 85 percent of erotic scenarios are successful, you can feel very good about yourselves as a sexual couple.

DANIELLE AND JACOB

Danielle was 34 and in her first marriage to 47-year-old Jacob, for whom this was a second marriage. Jacob has two adolescent children from his first marriage.

Danielle met Jacob through work. They were friends for 2 years before becoming sexually involved. Danielle's premarital pattern was that she always had a boyfriend and sex went fine, although as the relationship progressed, sex became less important. She was 29 when she became involved with Jacob; they had been married 4 years.

Jacob was sexually active before his first marriage at 26. He was disappointed when sex slipped into a once-a-week Saturday night routine, functional but unexciting. Divorce had been difficult. The wife left, saying that he was more interested in his job and hobbies than in being a husband. The years between marriages were stressful. Jacob did not enjoy the dating scene.

Jacob had been a professional mentor for Danielle. He was attracted to her intelligence and enthusiasm, which combated Jacob's dour life outlook. Jacob felt attracted, but it was a safe attraction. He enjoyed hearing stories of the ups and downs of Danielle's relationships. Then they attended a convention in Boca Raton, Florida—a romantic milieu. After the inaugural speech, they went with a group for dinner, which evolved into drinking and dancing. Jacob was acutely aware of how attractive Danielle looked and what a sexy dancer she was. Jacob felt awkward and resisted dancing, but impulsively suggested that they have a drink at the bar on the beach. After two drinks, Danielle suggested dancing on the sand where no one could see them. They still argue about who seduced whom.

The first 6 months were a very exciting time. They kept the fact they were a couple from work colleagues, which added to the sense of intrigue. Jacob felt sexually revitalized, as if he were 25 again. Danielle felt totally in love and amazed at having a relationship with a man of Jacob's maturity and professional status. Especially exciting were their weekends away. They forgot about work and really cut loose. Danielle had never been involved with an older man and was pleased to find that the stories and jokes her girlfriends told were not true of Jacob. He was desirous and sophisticated and had excellent ejaculatory control (this had been a problem in Danielle's prior relationships).

Romantic love and passionate sex are great at the beginning of a relationship, but set a couple up for frustration and resentment later. Unfortunately, this was the outcome for Danielle and Jacob. Nonsexual factors interfered first. Danielle expected to win over his children (which she did years later), but the initial meetings were tension-filled competitions for Jacob's attention. When the relationship became a source of office gossip, the management urged Danielle to find another job as soon as possible. Jacob tried to facilitate placing her with a prestigious organization, but was unsuccessful. Danielle felt increasingly uncomfortable and took a less-than-satisfactory job offer.

The romantic bubble had burst. However, they vowed to maintain the relationship. The decision to marry was with the hope that marriage would revitalize the relationship. Sex was strained, but functional. Frequency decreased to once or twice a month. Both were tentative in initiating and wished the other would take the lead—a common pattern. Marriage seldom revitalizes sexuality, nor does the honeymoon. They were sexual three times during their 2-week honeymoon, but it was not free-flowing sex. The constant comparison to their 6-month romantic, passionate sex phase depressed and devitalized them. They could not live up to that magical comparison. Four years later, when they consulted a sex therapist, he advised them to remember those 6 months fondly as a symbol of attraction and desire, but to stop using this as a comparison and not try to replicate it. They needed to build a comfortable, intimate couple style in the present.

Danielle and Jacob were a demoralized couple in a low-sex marriage. To make matters worse, Jacob was experiencing performance anxiety and erection problems. Danielle was turned off by Jacob's tentativeness and apologizing—these qualities were not sexually appealing.

Danielle wanted a baby. Her hope was that their trying to get pregnant would revitalize sex. Although sex with the intention of becoming pregnant can be a positive motivator, that is not how it worked for Jacob. He worried about the pressure of intercourse on a fertility timetable. He was ambivalent about starting a second family in his late 40s, although he felt guilty about cheating Danielle of the opportunity to have a child. It was a depressing impasse. Danielle's gynecologist was not helpful, but instead was judgmental. After 3 stressful months, Danielle's friend suggested they consult a sex therapist.

The therapist was respectful and empathic. Danielle and Jacob felt relieved to hear that pregnancy was not a quick fix for sexual problems. The concept of working as an intimate team was particularly attractive for Jacob, who felt overwhelmed by guilt, self-blame, performance anxiety, and ambivalence. Each spouse came for an individual sexual history session. Danielle felt bewildered, betrayed, and cheated by Jacob and the marriage. Although she did not voice it, she was angry that her career plans had been derailed. She resented that she, rather than Jacob, had been forced to leave the organization. Danielle blamed herself for the erection problem, feeling that her attractiveness and seductiveness had failed. She feared a marriage where both sex and children were missing. Danielle felt that she had lost sexual creativity and eroticism. Jacob felt defeated by sex, marriage, and life. He was more depressed than ever. He felt shame over letting down Danielle personally, maritally, sexually, in her career, and in keeping her from having a child. These emotions negated Jacob's desire for couple sex. He masturbated one to two times a week. He was able to get an erection and ejaculate, so he knew "it still worked."

In the couple feedback session, the therapist confronted these negative emotions. He proposed a plan to revitalize intimacy and introduce nondemand pleasuring. The feedback session provided a mirror where Danielle and Jacob could identify the "poisons" of guilt, anger, shame, and withdrawal, which drained sexual desire and marital vitality. Performance orientation, inhibitions, and avoidance dominated sexuality. Depression and demoralization characterized their relationship. This feedback put the pieces of the puzzle together for Danielle and Jacob. No wonder they had a low-sex marriage. Confronting inhibitions and traps and building bridges to desire had a strong appeal.

It was not until the 10th week of therapy that they began discussing erotic scenarios. The therapy process and nondemand pleasuring exercises resulted in gradual, but sure, improvement. There were frustrations and setbacks, but they stayed on the same team and felt that touching was back on track. Pleasuring served as a way to connect and build intimacy. Danielle's anger was acknowledged and dealt with, which freed sexual energy. Danielle realized that Jacob was still attracted to her. Once Jacob stopped apologizing, his attractiveness quadrupled. Danielle enjoyed pleasuring, and her arousal was arousing for Jacob. Performance anxiety was greatly reduced when Danielle agreed to initiate sexual encounters. However, Jacob's desire and arousal lagged behind Danielle's, who was enthusiastic about manual and oral stimulation. Jacob's obsession about whether intercourse would succeed or fail dampened his sexual pleasure.

The therapist suggested that Jacob take the lead in designing and playing out a nonintercourse erotic scenario. He provided Jacob with a smorgasbord of choices—discussing them in the session and referring him to the chapter on special turn-ons in the *Sexual Awareness* book (listed in appendix 2). Jacob was hesitant, but Danielle assured him that she was open to his erotic requests. The following week included pleasurable experiences, but Jacob did not make an erotic initiation. He came to the session depressed and expecting to be censured. Jacob easily fell into the trap of feeling guilty and defensive, which was sexually paralyzing. This was in no one's interest. Jacob needed encouragement and a positive impetus, not punishment. The therapist loaned them a psychoeducational erotic videotape, suggesting that they watch it and discuss scenarios and techniques they would be open to trying. Jacob found the tape freeing and a turn-on. It gave him permission to be sexually selfish. Realizing that Danielle became aroused by arousing him was a great impetus. Jacob requested that Danielle be totally passive while he teasingly turned her on. When she was highly aroused, he requested that she orally stimulate him while he lay on his back and she knelt (which allowed him to continue stimulating her). She put him inside her from the female-on-top position and stroked her breasts as they engaged in rapid in-out thrusting. This scenario was almost as arousing for Danielle as for Jacob.

Danielle's erotic scenario was quite different, which was fine because this was not a competition. Danielle found milieu and accouterments key for her sexual desire. She took the opportunity to experiment with creative lighting. She loved different colors and fragrances of candles—she put five in the bathroom when they took a sensual bath and five different ones in the guest bedroom for later. In her scenario, Danielle luxuriated in the bath, enjoying the smells and colors of candles reflecting off the walls. She stood while Jacob orally stimulated her. She allowed herself to let go and have a series of orgasms. As a side effect of sex therapy, Danielle developed a multiorgasmic response pattern.

Danielle returned to the bath and had a glass of wine. Jacob told wonderful fantasy stories. It was one of her favorite things about him.

They went into the guest room, and Danielle tied Jacob's hands over his head. This allowed him to be passive—something she liked, but Jacob found hard to do, because he was always trying to stimulate her. Danielle found it arousing to stimulate Jacob when he was passive, especially playing with his penis around her breasts. She was orgasmic rubbing against him and then had intercourse with her on top and moving her hips in a circular rhythm. Danielle designed a creative afterplay. They lay on their backs, watching the candles play off the ceiling, and talked about dream vacations. This was a symbolic affirmation of their intention to remain a vital couple.

At therapy termination, Danielle and Jacob knew that their marital bond and marital sexuality were solid. Sex was less frequent than in their first 6 months, but was based on a genuine sexual attraction and openness to each other's needs. They trusted that desire and eroticism would remain vital. Their decision to become pregnant was a further sexual incentive.

Danielle and Jacob were committed to maintaining a vital sexual bond; they would not allow themselves to regress. They adopted three relapse-prevention strategies: (1) setting monthly intimacy dates that focused on sharing feelings and nondemand pleasuring; (2) if there were a failure experience or they had not been sexual for 2 weeks, setting a nonintercourse erotic date; and (3) introducing an erotic technique into their sexual repertoire every 6 months to keep sexuality vital.

creative sex and desire

You look forward to going to movies; each movie is different. Some will be Academy-Award quality, others okay, some disappointing. A few movies are so good, you rent them on video two or three times. Creative sex is like anticipating a really good movie—you hope it turns out special, but nothing is guaranteed. Even so, the anticipation enhances desire.

The essence of creative sexuality is not technique, but awareness of sexual feelings and willingness to take a risk and play these out. Creative sex can be planned or spontaneous. A healthy sexual relationship mixes spontaneous and intentional erotic experiences.

Creative sex can be experimental, using external turn-ons. Creative sex also involves tuning into internal feelings and sharing them in an open, erotic manner. The most powerful aphrodisiac is not an esoteric technique; it is an involved, aroused spouse.

The most popular erotic technique is oral sex. There are a variety of positions, stimulation techniques, sequences, uses of fruit or flavored lotions, whether one-way or mutual. People differ in their preferences and turn-ons. Some prefer oral sex as a pleasuring technique, others as a means of reaching orgasm. Some prefer whole body and visual contact; others want a sole focus on receiving with eyes closed. For some, multiple stimulation is the key to arousal; for others, it is one thing at a time. Some prefer slow, tender stimulation, others fast and lustful. It is not a right–wrong question, but a matter of personal preference and sequencing. Creative sex means awareness of feelings and desires and freedom to express these in the context of an intimate, erotic marriage.

individual and couple scenarios

Individual scenarios are easier to design and introduce—it is a matter of taking a risk and making requests. The partner is open to playing out the erotic scenario, knowing that he or she can veto or alter any element. Although people worry about being coerced into doing something they find aversive, the typical situation is that shyness or inhibition blocks the spouse from requesting erotic scenarios.

Creative couple scenarios require communication and mutuality. Instead of taking turns, allow sex play to be mutual. When feelings, touches, and sexual expression flow, your feelings of arousal enhance each other's. Couple scenarios are an erotic extension of the "give to get" pleasure guideline. Choose your favorite place to be sexual (the den, dining room, guest room, outside on the secluded porch). You need not plan a detailed scenario; be open to feelings and requests—let sexuality flow. Have favorite external turn-ons readily available if you decide to introduce them—lotions, a mirror, a sexy story, beads or feathers, a vibrator, an erotic video, or scented candles. Be free and playful. Be open to positions: standing, lying, kneeling, sitting. Have your favorite music on—dance, touch, be seductive. Do not place an artificial barrier between sex play and intercourse. Communicate what you feel and want through touch, words, and movement. Allow touching to flow into intercourse. Experiment with positions and multiple stimulation during intercourse. Express feelings; allow sexuality to flow.

Creative sexuality does not end with orgasm. Stay together and enjoy afterplay. Express affectionate, sensual, romantic, and playful feelings verbally, as well as through touch.

enhancing your erotic relationship

If companies put as little time and energy into their business as couples put into their marriages, we would have a bankrupt country. A chief guideline in maintaining an erotic relationship is to place a priority on couple time. Valuing your intimate relationship is the foundation for eroticism.

You can spot people who are having an affair. They are attentive, aware of each other, playful, and seductive. When people think of eroticism, they think of youthful couples, extramarital affairs, or the jet set, not of themselves. Can married couples fan the flames of eroticism?

An important sexual enhancer is a couple weekend without the kids. This gives you the time and freedom to be an expressive couple and do things you enjoy—hiking, antiquing, shopping, sleeping late, or biking. Enjoy a bed and breakfast, luxury resort, rustic inn, or camping—choose what fits you. Sexuality becomes an integral part of the weekend, instead of sex being the last thing at night when you are both exhausted. You can be sexual when you awake; take a shower and come back to bed; have sex after a walk; indulge in a nooner; or have sex before or after lunch, after a golf game or hike, before or after a nap, before dinner, as dessert, or during an early evening sex date, then sit on the porch and have a drink as afterplay.

Another way to enhance your erotic relationship is by sharing fantasies. Sexual fantasies are the most common form of multiple stimulation. People associate fantasies with masturbation, but 75 percent of married men and 50 percent of married women utilize fantasies during partner sex. It is a natural, healthy bridge to desire and arousal. What makes sharing difficult is that fantasies are the most private and idiosyncratic sexual behavior. Sharing a fantasy reveals a very private part of yourself, increasing your personal vulnerability. Most sexual fantasies are about unusual or unacceptable people, behaviors, or situations, and many are bizarre. Common fantasy themes include sex with an unattainable or inappropriate partner, forced sex, group sex, watching people being sexual, gay sex, and illicit sexual activities. What gives fantasies their erotic charge is that they are different from who you really are.

It is hard enough to accept your fantasies, much less share them with the spouse. Although many sex books advise acting out fantasies, we believe that it is unwise to act out fantasies unless both partners are genuinely comfortable with this. Fantasy and behavior are separate realms. What is exciting and erotic as a fantasy can become destructive and self-defeating when acted out. Being turned on by a fantasy is not the same thing as desiring to experience it. Most fantasies are best kept as fantasies. For most couples, verbally sharing a fantasy is better than acting it out.

If you decide to play out fantasies, we suggest these guidelines: Only involve the two of you, do not be physically or psychologically coercive, and do not humiliate or intimidate the spouse. Either person can call a time-out or veto a technique. Remember, there is no place for intimate coercion in your marriage.

closing thoughts

Breaking the pattern of a low-sex or no-sex marriage requires communication, effort, and courage. Erotic scenarios elicit and maintain sexual desire and vitality. Creative scenarios enliven your relationship and prevent relapse. Erotic scenarios and techniques enhance intimate sexuality.

PART 3

Preventing
Relapse

CHAPTER 11

The Seventh Step: Keeping It Vital—Preventing Relapse

YOU HAVE BROKEN the pattern of inhibited sexual desire and a no-sex or low-sex marriage. Congratulations! However, you cannot rest on your laurels and take marital sexuality for granted. Maintaining and generalizing healthy marital sexuality are crucial. You have come a long way—you owe it to yourself, your spouse, and your marital bond to not allow a relapse.

It is unrealistic and self-defeating to believe that each sexual encounter will involve equal desire, arousal, orgasm, and satisfaction. It is equally unrealistic to believe that touching and intimacy will always flow easily. Setting nonperfectionist goals is crucial. A positive, realistic expectation is that sexuality will nurture your intimate bond. Sexuality is a positive, integral part of your lives and your marriage. By reinforcing healthy sexual attitudes, behavior, and feelings, you are inoculated against future problems. Whether the sexual experience is joyful, satisfying, mediocre, or unsuccessful, the couple remains an intimate team. Both spouses are committed to maintaining intimacy and to not falling into the avoidance trap. Giving and receiving pleasure-oriented touching are the essence of intimate sexuality.

The core of relapse prevention is awareness that intimacy and sexuality need continual time and energy. Sexuality cannot be taken for granted. When there are mediocre or negative experiences, you treat this as a lapse and ensure it does not relapse into inhibited sexual desire. Relapse prevention is an active process.

specific strategies and techniques

When couple sex therapy is about to end, Barry suggests 10 guidelines to ensure that gains are maintained and generalized. The partners agree to utilize three or four personally relevant guidelines to ensure that their hard-won gains continue.

1. As a couple, you continue to meet on a regular basis. One advantage of therapy is that on a weekly or biweekly basis, you both engage in serious communication about your relationship. Instead of going to the therapist's office (you have both cleared your schedules and are used to regular meetings), keep the time for yourselves. You can go for a walk, have a sexual date, go to dinner, problem-solve a difficult issue, or have an intimate talk. Devote time and energy to maintaining your intimate bond.

2. Schedule a 6-month follow-up therapy session. This ensures that you remain accountable to each other and to the therapist. Intimacy and sexuality cannot rest on their laurels. Commitment and accountability prevent relapse.

3. Schedule a nondemand pleasuring session at least once every 2 months, preferably monthly. Setting aside time for a pleasuring session (with a prohibition on intercourse) reinforces communication, sensuality, and playfulness. This allows you to experience sensuality and experiment with new stimuli—an alternative pleasuring position, body lotion, a new setting or milieu. Maintaining a vital pleasuring and sensuality combats relapse.

4. When a problem occurs, treat it as a lapse, a mistake to learn from. Do not permit it to become a relapse. Even among happily married couples with no history of sexual dysfunction, 5 to 15 percent of sexual interactions are mediocre, unsatisfying, or failures. People are not perfectly functioning sexual machines. There is an inherent variability and flexibil-

ity to couple sexuality. Do not panic or overreact to a mediocre or negative experience. Rather than hoping it will never happen (an unrealistic expectation), learn coping techniques to ensure that a lapse does not become a relapse. Whether it occurs once a week, once a month, or once a year that the man does not get an erection, the woman experiences pain during intercourse, or one or both do not feel sexual desire, this is not a cause for panic or blame. Accept this as disappointing, not as a tragedy or being back at square one. You can laugh or shrug off the experience, and make a date within a day or two when you both feel desirous, receptive, and sexier. Better yet, you can find pleasure in a sensual massage or an erotic nonintercourse scenario. A negative experience can turn into a pleasurable one.

5. Establish positive, realistic expectations about marital sex. In movies (where healthy marital sexuality is almost never portrayed), sex is spontaneous, intense, nonverbal, passionate, and perfect. The reality for married couples is that less than half the time is there equal desire, arousal, orgasm, and satisfaction. If you experience movie-quality sex once or twice a month, you are a lucky couple. If sexuality is to remain positive and to nurture your intimate bond, you need to accept flexibility and variability. Adopt a broad-based approach to touching and eroticism. Sexuality meets a variety of individual and couple needs. Sometimes sex is a tension-reducer, sometimes a way to share closeness, at other times a passionate experience, a way to heal an argument, or a bridge to reduce emotional distance. Often, it is better for one spouse than the other—that, too, is a realistic expectation.

6. Plan intimacy dates, weekends, or both without children. Sex therapy confronts the rigidity of the male always initiating and the expectation that all touching should end in intercourse. Both spouses feel free to initiate intimacy and sexuality. Especially valuable is a weekend away (without children) at least once a year. Couples report better sex on vacation.

7. Generalize and expand your sexual repertoire. There is not "one right way" to be sexual. Each couple develops its unique style of initiation, pleasuring, erotic stimulation, intercourse,

and afterplay. The more flexible the couple sexual style and acceptance of the multiple functions of touching and sexuality, the greater the resistance to relapse. Develop a comfortable, functional, and satisfying sexual style that meets the needs of both of you and that energizes your marital bond.

8. You can cope with mediocre or negative sexual experiences. The single most important technique in relapse prevention is the ability to accept and not overreact to experiences that are mediocre, unsatisfying, or dysfunctional. Any partners can get along if everything goes well. The challenge is to accept disappointing or dysfunctional experiences without panicking or blaming. Whether a miscommunication about a sexual date, a minimally arousing sexual interaction, or an erectile or orgasmic failure, these happen to all couples. Intimate couples accept occasional mediocre or failure experiences and take pride in having a resilient sexual style.

9. Develop intimate and erotic ways to connect and reconnect. Intimacy includes sexuality, but is much more than sexuality. You need a variety of ways to connect, reconnect, and maintain connection. These include five gears of connection—affectionate touch, nongenital pleasuring, playful touch, erotic touch, and intercourse. In traditional sex role socialization, females emphasized emotional connection and males emphasized sexual connection. It is hoped that now both the wife and husband are comfortable initiating intimacy and eroticism. This promotes a variety of ways to remain connected and build bridges to sexual desire. The more ways you have to maintain intimate and sexual connection, the easier it is to avoid relapse.

10. Each of you makes sexual requests, and as a couple, you develop special erotic scenarios. The importance of having a variety of sexual alternatives and scenarios cannot be overemphasized. Couples who express intimacy through massage, taking walks, bathing, and engaging in semiclothed or nude sensual touch have a flexible repertoire. Couples who are open to "quickies," prolonged and varied erotic stimulation, various intercourse positions, multiple stimulation during intercourse, and planned, as well as spontaneous, sexual

encounters have a robust sexual relationship. A flexible, variable sexual repertoire is a major antidote to relapse. Sexuality that meets a range of needs, feelings, and situations will serve you both well in maintaining gains and preventing relapse.

assumptions behind relapse prevention

The best strategy for relapse prevention is a broad-based couple sexual style that is comfortable, intimate, and satisfying. Emotional intimacy, nondemand pleasuring, and erotic stimulation, combined with realistic expectations, ensure healthy sexuality. This inoculates the couple against sexual problems, especially with aging of the partners and the marriage.

Partners who trust each other to deal with problems are in a much better position than those who magically hope that nothing goes wrong. Resilient couples are confident in their ability to deal with difficulties and lapses. Relapse prevention is more than luck—it is confidence in yourself, your spouse, and your relationship. You can deal with stress and disappointment while remaining an intimate couple. Affectionate, sensual, playful, erotic, and intercourse experiences are flexible and can withstand occasional problems, dysfunction, or disappointments. The most important component is motivation. You feel like an intimate team that is committed to maintaining a vital sexual relationship.

TRACY AND SEAN

Two years after the completion of couple sex therapy, Tracy and Sean felt secure in their marriage. Intimacy was a forté. Sexuality was functional and satisfying. They felt proud that the marriage had survived a stressful crisis and no-sex period.

At the time of starting treatment, Tracy and Sean had been married 3 years, had a 1-year-old daughter, and had not been sexual since she was born. Unbeknownst to Tracy, Sean began an affair with a divorced woman from his office when Tracy was 4 months pregnant. Sean used the pregnancy as a justification for the affair, rationalizing that Tracy did not enjoy sex when pregnant. Sean was an example of the adage "Affairs are easier to get into than out of." The stress of a double life caused by the affair, plus adapting to a new baby, resulted in marital alienation.

Tracy suggested marital therapy. Sean was resistant, afraid that the affair would be revealed. When Tracy found a therapist who specialized in marital and sex therapy, Sean relented and agreed to go. Consulting a professional confronts partners with the seriousness of their problems. Tracy was sad and angry over the lack of intimacy and sexuality. She alternated between blaming herself and blaming Sean.

Sean minimized the impact of the affair, although he realized the precarious state of the marriage. In the individual session Sean told the therapist about the affair, feeling relieved to disclose this secret. After the first few months the affair was no longer exciting or satisfying, but he could not extricate himself. The affair was becoming increasingly destructive. Sean could not devote the time and energy needed to revitalize the marriage while distracted by the affair.

In their conjoint session, the therapist asked Tracy whether she was willing to help Sean terminate the affair. This was a novel strategy, but the more they discussed it, Sean felt that this was what he needed. Tracy said she would not tell the other woman for him, but agreed to actively support Sean in confronting her.

Tracy was hurt at learning that Sean was having an affair, but felt validated that her intuition had been right—there was a specific cause for their feelings of alienation. They invited the woman to their home for lunch. To be sure that emotions remained in check, no alcohol was served. Sean showed her the baby and said that he and Tracy were recommitted to the marriage and they needed to devote time and energy to rebuilding their marital and family bond. He hoped this would not interfere with the professional work relationship, but there could not be a personal relationship. The woman was upset and it was an awkward, uncomfortable lunch, but the message was clear and unequivocally communicated. Tracy and Sean agreed to a 5-minute check-in weekly to ensure that there would be no secrets. Sean agreed that if a high-risk situation arose, he would tell Tracy within 24 hours. This agreement freed Sean and Tracy to focus on revitalizing their sexual bond.

Realizing how much work it takes to rebuild trust and intimacy increased their motivation to not allow an affair or another crisis to destabilize their marriage. Six months after they resumed being a sexual couple, Tracy unexpectedly broke into tears—this occurred after being orgasmic and feeling close to Sean. At first, Sean was defensive and wondered if Tracy was doing this as a guilt-inducing manipulation. Tracy was clear that it was neither manipulative nor to punish Sean, but a genuine feeling of sadness. You cannot change the past, nor does guilt help rebuild intimacy.

Renewing intimacy is a joint venture. Trust is not a simple process—it requires talking and supporting each other emotionally through stresses and disappointments. When Tracy cried or Sean was frustrated, rather than go their separate ways, they used their trust position (Tracy put her head on his heart and he stroked her hair). They found that being quiet, yet together, was better than trying to talk the problem to death.

The strategy that was most helpful was thinking of themselves as an intimate team fighting against the common enemy of inhibited sexual desire. The most helpful technique was building bridges to desire. Before a sexual date, Tracy took time for herself while Sean watched the child. Tracy became comfortable using a vibrator during partner sex, and Sean integrated loving and erotic feelings. Sean's favorite bridge was taking a shower while Tracy was putting the baby down and then their getting together. Tracy's favorite bridge was being sexual when the child was out of the house (mother's day out or eating at another family's house).

The therapist encouraged them to develop a specific relapse-prevention plan. Tracy worried that this was overkill because they were doing well, but Sean was insistent. He felt responsible for the intimacy and trust problems and was committed to doing everything he could to ensure that the marriage remained satisfying and secure. Sean suggested that they go for coffee and a serious conversation once a month to ensure that there would be no relapse. The quality of their sex was much improved. Sean became comfortable with showering before sex (which facilitates fellatio). Tracy committed to initiating sex at least once a week. She wanted marital sexuality to continue to be vital, integrating intimacy and eroticism.

Sex with the intention of becoming pregnant enhanced desire. They remained emotionally and sexually connected throughout the pregnancy. By the 5th month, Tracy preferred erotic sex to intercourse. Sometimes it was mutual and sometimes one-way. Although he preferred intercourse, Sean was open to whatever was comfortable for Tracy. Neither Tracy nor Sean were hypervigilant about an affair. They were confident the spouse would discuss a high-risk situation rather than act out.

Tracy and Sean valued an intimate, erotic, secure marriage. They did not take each other for granted. Sexuality was a positive, integral part of the marriage and they were committed to keeping it that way.

relapse prevention versus crisis intervention

In movies and novels, once the problem is resolved, people expect to live happily ever after. Yet neither marriage nor sexuality can rest on its laurels. Prevention is superior to a crisis and the need for crisis intervention. Sadly, a significant number of couples fall into the trap of a second sexual crisis, caused in part by "magical thinking." The partners hope that if they do not worry or talk about sex, it will not be a problem. We do not promote fear or obsessing. However, we do advocate a preventative approach and, if sexuality gets off track, a problem-solving approach.

The best example of relapse prevention involves inhibited desire as an overreaction to an erection problem. The goal of sex therapy is to regain comfort and confidence with erections, resulting in renewed desire. Not maintaining an erection that is sufficient for intercourse might occur once a month or once a year. This is a normal part of male sexuality, especially after age 40. When an erectile difficulty causes the husband (or wife) to overreact and avoid sex, marital sexuality is vulnerable. The answer is not guaranteed erections, but comfortable, pleasurable alternative scenarios for intimate connection. These include manual or oral stimulation to orgasm, lying together and holding each other, stimulating her to orgasm, engaging in sensual pleasuring, or setting a date in the next day or two when you are desirous, receptive, and responsive. Most couples, especially men, would rather not think or talk about this. They fear "jinxing" the erectile success and sensitizing performance anxiety.

The man and the couple confidently anticipate touching, eroticism naturally flowing to erection, and arousal evolving into intercourse. Distraction, anxiety, or spectatoring distracts and disrupts the erotic flow. The way to counter anxieties and distractions is not by "magical thinking," wishing there would never be another sexual problem. The healthy coping strategy is to nurture desire through anticipation and bridges to desire. Be open to the natural flow of sexuality—comfort, pleasure, eroticism, arousal, erections, intercourse, orgasm, and afterplay. Equally important is having comfort and confidence in back-up sensual and erotic scenarios when you are not able to have intercourse. This inoculates you against regression to erectile problems and inhibited desire. Both spouses being open to nondemand pleasuring, erotic stimulation, and orgasm with nonintercourse sex allows a varied, flexible, and robust sexual repertoire. These attitudes and coping skills prevent relapse. A broad-based sexual repertoire is healthier than a pass–fail approach to intercourse. The narrow-based sexual repertoire of both spouses needing to be desirous and orgasmic each time makes relapse likely.

Couples need to be able to deal with emotional and sexual difficulties when these occur, but prevention is easier and more effective. Why create an unnecessary crisis? Why waste psychological energy dealing with a crisis when you can more efficiently and happily prevent the problem? Maintaining his, hers, and our bridges for sexual desire is one way to prevent relapse. Another is having a variety of sensual, erotic, and nonintercourse techniques when sex does not flow. A positive, realistic expectation is that not all experiences will be mutual or satisfying. Realistic expectations are an important ingredient in sexual satisfaction. You can tolerate occasional mediocre, disappointing, or failure experiences. The more your sexual relationship is broad-based, with an emphasis on sharing desire, pleasure, and eroticism, the greater the likelihood you will maintain gains and prevent relapse.

EXERCISE: YOUR PERSONAL PLAN FOR PREVENTING RELAPSE

Take the theory and good intentions of relapse prevention and make them personal and concrete. Each spouse needs to be aware of vulnerabilities and traps. What can you do to ensure that you will not fall into these traps? How can your spouse be helpful and supportive? Individually and as a couple, commit to doing what is necessary to ensure that your sexual bond remains vital.

This exercise involves two phases. First, write down personal and couple traps. Writing facilitates clarity and specificity. Then, discuss how to prevent falling into these traps. An example of a trap for the husband is becoming discouraged and obsessed with career disappointments, which depresses sexual desire. The coping mechanism is to share career perceptions, feelings, and alternatives with the wife, professional colleagues, or both. Your career should be only one factor, at most one-third, in your measurement of self-esteem. If career problems are not changeable, it is crucial to find other sources of self-esteem and satisfaction. One source is marital and sexual intimacy. Your spouse can initiate both supportive hugs and sexual encounters.

An example of a trap for the wife is that orgasms are not as easy as in the past, but she is reticent to request additional erotic stimulation. As sex becomes lower quality and less satisfying, her anticipation and desire decrease. She is more irritated by, than receptive to, his sexual initiations. To counter this, she introduces personal and external turn-ons to enhance sexual quality. She requests additional erotic stimulation; her satisfaction is as important as his. His role is to be a giving spouse, not to pressure her or make her orgasm his responsibility. Bother partners must be open to erotic scenarios and techniques that enhance quality and facilitate desire.

The most common couple trap is self-consciousness about sexual initiation. Exercises can increase awareness and comfort, without the side effects of self-consciousness. Sexual initiations become personal and easier. Each spouse identifies what he or she can do to make initiations inviting.

The second phase of the exercise is to explore strategies and techniques to keep marital sexuality vital. Discuss intimacy and sexuality in a clear, positive, realistic manner. The answer is not to quit your job so that you are stress-free or to send the children to their grandparents for a month. Examples of realistic plans are that each of you initiates an intimate experience once a week and a couple weekend without children every 6 months; if there has been no sexual contact for 2 weeks, you both agree that the husband will initiate a nondemand pleasuring experience on Sunday afternoon; on Friday night after the kids are asleep you rent an R- or X-rated video; you plan an erotic date at least every 2 months, with the understanding that you will not proceed to intercourse; every 6 months you shop for a new sensual lotion or a sexy outfit; or each of you initiates a favorite erotic scenario once a month.

Commit to developing at least one individual scenario and one couple scenario that reenergizes marital sexuality.

Repeat this exercise in 6 months.

ensure that a lapse does not become a relapse

For some behaviors, a lapse (returning to a destructive behavior) is serious and unacceptable—spouse abuse, using heroin, driving while intoxicated, exhibiting yourself, or setting fires. You do not want a lapse, but for the majority of behaviors lapses do occur—examples include fear and avoidance, obsessive-compulsive behavior, and depressive thinking. Behaviors that are a continuous part of the person's life (mood, anxiety, eating) are more likely to involve lapses than are behaviors that are dichotomous and can be abstained from (cigarettes, stealing, drug use). With sexual functioning—specifically, desire—occasional or intermittent lapses are likely.

Lapses in marital and sexual behavior are normal. How can you ensure that a lapse does not turn into a relapse? A lapse involves a temporary situation, a specific regression. Examples include pushing sex when the spouse is not receptive; reacting to a mediocre or negative experience with blame; miscommunication when one spouse wants intercourse and the other wants a sensual experience; the man loses his erection or the woman is not orgasmic and they overreact; one spouse goes along with a sexual initiation, even though he or she is not receptive; they have sex in the middle of the night, which they agreed was not acceptable; or a spouse tries to have sex after an argument when the partner is still alienated. These are normal occurrences. Among couples with no sexual problems, 5 to 15 percent of sexual experiences are mediocre, disappointments, or failures. The key is to ensure that occasional lapses do not become a full-blown relapse.

What is a relapse? A relapse is a regression to sexually dysfunctional ways of thinking, behaving, and feeling. It is a return to infrequent sex (less than once every 2 weeks), inhibited desire, and avoidance. Anticipatory anxiety replaces positive anticipation; the partners no longer feel they deserve sexual pleasure, they revert to guilt and blaming, and they stop acting and feeling like an intimate team. Do not allow yourselves to regress to the cycle of anticipatory anxiety, tension-filled sex, and avoidance.

A relapse is more distressing than the original sexual problem was because it is more difficult to regain motivation. The first time you confront inhibited sexual desire and the no-sex or low-sex marriage, you learn new concepts, skills, exercises, and experiences that challenge this problem. Sexual pleasure and sharing intimacy are powerful reinforcers. Dealing with a relapse (whether for the first or eighth time) is more difficult. There is no new dramatic strategy; rather, you must implement and reinforce techniques that you know are helpful in rebuilding sexual intimacy and desire.

It is crucial to address and recover from a lapse. Feelings of intimacy, pleasure, eroticism, and being a team become stronger and more resilient. It is easier to deal with issues and problems early and not to allow the avoidance that results in a full-blown relapse.

How to prevent relapse? When a lapse or negative experience occurs, you need to acknowledge this, rather than deny that it happened or magically wish it would never happen again. Recognize the lapse and actively deal with it, rather than avoid, pretend, or overreact. Learn from mistakes. Intimacy and sexual self-esteem need not be controlled by problems. A healthy strategy is to set an intimacy date for the next day or two. Some couples choose a pleasuring experience, with an explicit ban on intercourse; others prefer to go with the flow. It is crucial to challenge avoidance. Some couples choose a nongenital pleasuring date to reintroduce touching and sensuality, confronting avoidance in a sensual, as opposed to erotic, manner. Continuing to share intimacy and pleasure is a powerful strategy to prevent relapse.

Couples do not decide they are going to regress to a no-sex or low-sex marriage. It is a result of benign neglect. It is easy to procrastinate, be diverted by other things, and fall into old habits. Sexuality does not remain a priority. Sexuality should not be the top priority in marriage, but should be a positive, integral component. Resting on your laurels or treating sexuality with benign neglect does not work. Sexual desire is like any other activity; if you ignore or avoid, sexuality becomes self-conscious and uncomfortable. The positive feedback loop of anticipation, pleasurable experiences, and a regular sexual rhythm gives way to the negative feedback loop of anticipatory anxiety, tense and failed performances, and sexual avoidance. Anxiety and avoidance feed on themselves. Inhibition and avoidance need to be confronted and replaced by a regular rhythm of anticipation, emotional intimacy, nondemand pleasuring, and erotic scenarios and techniques (including intercourse).

closing thoughts

You have come too far to relapse to a no-sex or low-sex marriage. Confronting the sexual problem was a team effort. Maintaining and generalizing intimacy and sexual pleasure likewise are team processes. Reinforce intimacy and sexual desire, recognize and avoid personal and couple traps, and ensure that a lapse does not become a relapse.

CHAPTER 12

The Eighth Step: Enhancing
the Bond—Intimacy Dates

INTIMACY DATES ARE the single most important technique in maintaining a vital sexual bond. We have emphasized the importance of intimacy in overcoming sexual avoidance and the no-sex or low-sex marriage. Intimacy dates are a powerful resource in preventing relapse and reinforcing marital satisfaction.

Both planned and spontaneous experiences are valuable. Most intimacy dates are planned and anticipated. Couples with children and jobs find that if they do not set aside couple time, it does not happen. Enjoy spontaneous intimacy dates—they are special. However, do not put your marriage in jeopardy by being the romantic who devalues planned dates because you idealize spontaneity and natural feelings.

Emotional and sexual intimacy is like a garden—it requires consistent attention, planning, and tending. Gardens also require pulling weeds; likewise, intimacy requires the couple to deal with negative emotions and difficult issues. Intimacy is so much more than a "feel good" concept. Intimate couples share hurt and angry feelings, as well as close and loving feelings. They deal with disappointments and problems, as well as hopes and successes. Intimacy involves sharing a range of feelings and experiences, sexual and nonsexual. If sexual intimacy were dependent on each person always feeling positive, most couples would have a no-sex marriage. Emotional and sexual intimacy is anchored in knowing and accepting the spouse, with that person's strengths and weaknesses, loving and disappointing characteristics. A great advantage of an intimate marriage is that you feel loved and accepted for who you really are, with strengths and vulnerabilities.

Intimacy dates range from a half hour talk on the porch over a beer, to a night out dancing or to a movie, a weekend at home without the children, or a couple trip to a resort for a week. Each couple has preferences for types of activities and places to stay. The core of intimate time is feeling close and involved, not the activities or places.

What is the relationship between intimacy dates and sexual dates? Intimacy dates can lead to intercourse, but is not their chief reason. Intimate dates always involve emotional connection, usually involve affection, might involve sensual activity, might involve erotic feelings, and might involve intercourse and orgasm. Intimacy dates must not fall into a predictable, mechanical routine that always leads to sex.

Intimacy dates are inviting and facilitate anticipation as long as there is a range of ways to express feelings and a variety of potential outcomes. Closeness builds desire as long as there is not a spoken or unspoken expectation that it must lead to sex. Traditionally, this is a request of women, but, increasingly, men (especially over 40) appreciate the benefits of a nondemand approach to touching. It is possible (and desirable) to share intimacy without sexual intercourse. It is also possible (and sometimes particularly exciting) to share sexuality without feeling emotionally intimate. Passionate, lustful sex adds spice to the marriage.

Couples prefer an intimate basis for marital sex. The prescription for maintaining sexual desire is integrating emotional intimacy, nondemand pleasuring, and erotic stimulation. Marital sex works best when each spouse values both intimacy and eroticism.

We encourage weekly intimacy dates. If a couple go more than 2 weeks without an intimate experience, that is a cue to reconnect. The risk of self-consciousness and avoidance grows and leads to inhibited sexual desire. You cannot make up for lack of intimacy by having an intimate weekend every 3 months, any more than you can make up for not regularly watering the garden by soaking it on occasion. Maintaining a regular rhythm of connection, emotionally and physically, promotes sexual desire.

valuing marital intimacy

Traditionally, very different gender learnings and values were placed on intimacy. In the 1990s, pop psychology books and talk shows focused on differences between women and men, treating them as if they were totally different species. Scientific studies found just the opposite; there are many more similarities than differences between women and men, including desire for intimacy and sexual satisfaction.

What distinguishes women and men is not their needs, but their fears. Women and men have a need for both intimacy and sexuality. Men fear intimacy for two reasons. One is having to sacrifice autonomy, especially in regard to time and career. Second is fear that intimacy is a ruse to criticize the man and coerce him to change. The fear women have about intimacy is giving up their sense of self to serve and protect the man. Too much of female self-esteem is tied to the nurturer role. You are a healthier person and a better nurturer if you balance personal needs with the needs of others. Intimacy does not mean giving up yourself. Autonomy facilitates genuine intimacy.

Intimacy involves openness in sharing positives and negatives, not a hidden agenda to manipulate the spouse. Genuine intimacy allows both the man and the woman to value individuality and maintain self-esteem. Change is based on a positive influence model, not on coercion or threats of abandonment.

Intimacy is key in maintaining emotional connection; this serves as a bridge for sexual desire. Partners who care about each other will not allow sexuality to fade. Caring and trust set the stage for sexual risks—whether this is initiating sex in a new way, trying a different pleasuring scenario, experimenting with an intercourse variation, or integrating fantasies into an erotic scenario. Intimacy facilitates desire and satisfaction, which are more important than arousal or orgasm in maintaining a vital sexual bond.

intimacy dates at home

When couples think of dates, they think of going to dinner, a sporting event, a concert, or a weekend jaunt. These are fine, but the core of intimacy is expressing emotion and sexuality in everyday life where you live—at home. It costs less money, but does not require less time, thought, or planning. It means having privacy—children are asleep or at someone's house, the answering machine is on or the phone is off the hook, and you agree to not answer the door. A crucial variable is being aware and alert. Too often, couples relegate intimacy to bedtime—when they are tired and emotionally drained. Minimal contact cannot pass for quality couple time. Because you sleep with the spouse seven nights a week does not mean that you share intimacy. Minimal contact deadens sexual desire. You are only half there. Boredom and routine subvert intimacy and anticipation, decreasing desire.

Intimacy dates can occur in the morning, afternoon, or early evening. They might involve a walk, sitting on the porch, having a drink and an appetizer, luxuriating in a sensuous bath surrounded by candles, sitting at the kitchen table planning a couple or family vacation, or putting on your favorite music and dancing in the living room (with or without clothes). The date might focus on plans and hopes, sharing feelings, a sensual massage with a new lotion, disclosing a sensitive topic from the past, discussing an important issue, problem-solving a financial difficulty that is interfering with intimate feelings, or having fun playing a board or card game. It might be a time to be emotionally and physically close, or a playful scenario you hope will evolve into a sexual encounter. Intimacy dates are different from the nitty-gritty interactions about kids, chores, money, house, and work. This is a special time for emotional and physical connection.

intimacy dates outside the home

Emily is the one who enjoys being at home. Barry loves to go for day trips, to a play and dinner, and especially on a couple weekend. Intimacy dates outside the house are worthwhile to plan and anticipate. Emily's joke is that half the fun of a weekend trip for Barry is anticipating, which he begins a month before. Although it is important to have activities with children, other couples, and families, intimacy dates are a one-on-one activity.

Intimacy dates can be elaborate, like a week couple vacation, but more commonly they entail an evening date or a half-day outing. Although spontaneous dates are a special treat, most intimacy dates outside the house are planned. The key is not to fall into a predictable routine of doing the same thing, going to the same place, or talking about the same stuff. We both love movies, but if every date involved a movie, it would become stale. What about bowling or exploring a small town? Eating at an ethnic restaurant or attending a community theater? Trying canoeing or horseback riding? Taking a hike in the mountains or a picnic along the river? Sharing a story from childhood you have never told the spouse? Rereading love letters you have not looked at in 10 years? If you usually stay at hotels, what about going to a rustic inn or a romantic bed and breakfast? What about the children staying overnight with friends, while you go dancing and then come home for a sexual evening in the living room (a combination of an inside and outside date)?

One factor that makes an intimate marriage special is that you trust that your spouse will not make fun of you when you take a risk that does not work. We urge you to take psychological risks and try new things—a new restaurant, a new activity, disclosing a hope or dream, a new sexual scenario. If the food is a disaster, the activity is boring, the new idea terrible, the sexual scenario a dud, accept this. Your spouse will not blame or make fun of you. Intimacy is not just sharing close and good feelings, it is sharing disappointing and frustrating experiences.

RITA AND TONY

Sex was a problem throughout Rita and Tony's relationship. The best sex had been in the 8 months prior to marriage, even though premarital sex had never been more frequent than twice a week and always at Tony's initiation. Rita had low desire and was minimally involved, only occasionally aroused, and nonorgasmic. Tony was angry and punishing when Rita said no to sexual overtures. The cycle of his anger and her avoidance was strongly ingrained. The only time they had frequent sex was when trying to get pregnant.

Rita and Tony were professionally and financially successful and enjoyed their two children. Nine years into the marriage, sexual frequency was four to six times per year. Sex was functional for Tony and not unpleasant for Rita. Tony's anger over lack of sexual frequency was a source of great marital stress. Rita's resentment of Tony's blaming escalated, as did her emotional alienation.

Couple sex therapy was not an easy process, but was successful. Talking about the problem as a couple issue was critical. Tony's backing off from sexual demands and anger allowed them the space to develop a comfortable couple sexual style. Tony established himself as Rita's intimate friend, not her punishing critic. Rita developed an arousal-orgasm pattern that was different from those described in female sexuality books. Her response to sexual stimulation was rapid; slow pleasuring was counterproductive. Rita used a vibrator to enhance arousal, which quickly resulted in orgasm. Tony was supportive, rather than feeling threatened or judgmental.

A major breakthrough for Rita was making initiations and sharing her emotional and sexual conditions for a satisfying experience. Rita enjoyed being orgasmic, but orgasm was not her top factor for a fulfilling sexual life. What mattered was emotional dimensions—she needed to feel close to and open with Tony, without the hovering demand that touching culminate in intercourse. Rita needed to feel turned on before stimulating Tony. She preferred to be orgasmic with Tony's manual stimulation or vibrator stimulation before beginning intercourse. Tony enjoyed afterplay (most males tune out sexually after reaching orgasm). Although Rita appreciated this, afterplay with a focus on orgasm did not fit her sexual style. For Rita, afterplay was for closeness, not orgasm. They developed afterplay scenarios that were playful and intimate, a crucial element in Rita's sense of sexual satisfaction.

Rita and Tony had established a vital, satisfying sexual bond and were committed to maintaining it. They had come too far and wanted to ensure there would not be a relapse. A prime component of their relapse-prevention program was intimacy dates. The agreement was that one week Tony would initiate, the next week Rita would. This ping-pong system of initiation worked well.

Interestingly, Rita and Tony initiated very different intimacy dates. Almost all of Rita's initiations involved dates at home. Rita did not value pleasuring, but did value emotional and affectionate connection. Rita loved sitting on the screened-in porch with a glass of wine while Tony gave her a foot massage. She shared feelings about their lives and relationship with an understanding that they would not talk about children or finances during an intimacy date. Rita could spend up to 2 hours on the porch. She cared as much about listening to Tony's feelings and perceptions as about sharing her own. She enjoyed affectionate contact while talking, which facilitated closeness and connection. Usually, the intimacy date would end with a kiss and getting on with their tasks.

Often, Rita would suggest they go upstairs and make love. Tony was intrigued by how quickly Rita would get aroused, a very different pattern than before sex therapy. Talking and affection on the porch were Rita's foreplay. Once Rita was aroused she enjoyed stimulating Tony.

Tony's initiations were more varied. Most of his intimacy dates occurred out of the house. Tony loves going to clubs to listen to jazz. Other romantic activities included going canoeing and having a champagne picnic on the banks of the river or hiking up a hill and watching the sunset. Tony prefers a different style of touching. He is big on holding hands, playful touching, and kisses on the neck and ears. Tony loves to tell stories and construct fantasies (both about the ideal life and erotic fantasies). Rita finds this entertaining and will weave her fantasies with his. Tony likes to play sexually in the car, which Rita finds a turn-on as long as he remains attentive to driving. Tony will initiate sex 75 to 80 percent of the time, and usually, Rita is open to it. If she is not, Tony accepts this and does not pout or punish, a dramatic improvement over the prior pattern.

Tony and Rita place high value on spontaneous intimacy dates. Between two careers and two children, the opportunity is seldom there, but when possible it is special. The last spontaneous date was 5 weeks ago. Tony came home early from work to take care of their ill son. An hour after he was home and the child was sleeping, Rita called, saying that her meeting was canceled. Tony suggested that she come home, he would fix a salad, and they could have a glass of wine. It is fun playing hooky from work and responsibility. It was a relaxed, engaging hour— talking, being silly, and having sex before the child awoke. The boy enjoyed seeing his parents together in the middle of the afternoon.

Rita emphasized the importance of intimacy for her sexual desire. Tony accepted that emotional intimacy was valuable for him and the marriage. Closeness was key for Rita; playful touching was key for Tony. For some couples, intimate time is a good opportunity to discuss tough issues and sad situations and to resolve conflicts. This was not how Rita and Tony used intimacy dates. They focused on positive feelings, touching, and feeling connected. Difficult issues and conflict resolution were dealt with in a different milieu, outside of the bedroom.

Tony did not need intimacy for sexual desire, but accepted this need in Rita. An important component of a viable marriage is awareness of individual preferences for intimacy, touching, and eroticism.

Accept this, rather than engaging in a "right–wrong" power struggle. Accepting and appreciating differences reinforces couple intimacy. Conflicts over differences no longer interfered with their sexual intimacy. Trust that Tony was her intimate spouse was a powerful underpinning for Rita's sexual desire.

blocks to intimacy

Factors blocking intimate communication are based in gender socialization and misunderstanding. A major male fear is that the wife will use intimacy as a cover to criticize and coerce him to change. A major female fear is that the man will withhold intimacy as a way to punish her for sexual difficulties or for saying no to sex. This reflects the traditional gender socialization that males value sex and devalue feelings, and women value feelings and devalue sex. This simplistic dichotomy is reinforced by the media, pop psychology books, and friends. Gender wars interfere with all kinds of male–female relationships, especially marriage. The closer the relationship, the more destructive the rigid stereotypes.

Be aware of differences and vulnerabilities, but do not turn these into stereotypes and prejudices. Respect the spouse's individuality. How can you work as an intimate team to confront and reduce blocks, inhibitions, and anxieties?

"Pop psychology" books advocate greater intimacy, the more the better. This is a new psychological myth. Empirical research has identified four viable couple styles:

1. Best friend style—this is the most intimate;
2. Emotionally expressive style;
3. Complementary couple style; and
4. Conflict-minimizing style—the least intimate.

Which do you think is the most common couple style? It is the complementary couple that balances individual autonomy with moderate amounts of intimacy. Who are the most stable (least likely to divorce)? Conflict-minimizing couples. Our marriage is based on the best friend couple style. However, this is not the right fit for the majority of couples. The key for a satisfying, secure marriage is to establish a level of intimacy that is comfortable and functional for both individuals. Intimacy problems include extremes of too much intimacy (stifling individuality and causing enmeshment) or too little intimacy (causing a lack of connection and resulting in alienation). Find a level of intimacy that promotes sexual desire.

As intimacy increases, so does vulnerability. How vulnerable is each spouse comfortable being? For some people, intimacy means giving up emotional control. How does each person feel about control? Can you share control with the spouse? What level of intimacy fits best for you? How can intimacy facilitate sexual desire? Some couples feel so emotionally close, they lose erotic feelings. Too much intimacy can smother desire. One of the most important balances in marriage is maintaining individual autonomy while sharing couple intimacy. Eroticism and intimacy are not only compatible, but complementary.

Intimacy is only one bridge to desire. Playfulness, fantasy, erotic movies, tension release, teasing touching, and lust are other bridges. Most (not all) couples find that intimacy dates are a vital link in sexual desire.

EXERCISE—INTIMACY DATES

Theory is one thing, implementation and practice another. In this exercise, use the ping-pong system of initiation to establish a pattern of intimacy dates that facilitates sexual desire.

For a 2-month period (enough to experiment and form an intimate pattern), the husband initiates an intimacy date during his week and the wife initiates one during her week. Each person explores his or her preferred style of expressing intimacy. Experiment with in-house or going-out dates; formal, well-planned dates or informal, spontaneous dates; dates that involve sexuality or dates that focus on feelings and affection; half hour dates or a day date; activity dates or talking dates. Develop a comfortable, inviting pattern. Be aware that there is a his, her, and our style. It is unusual for both people to have the exact same intimacy preferences. Yet, by definition, intimacy is a shared experience. Intimate couples accept and enjoy differences in styles and preferences. They do not insist that their style is superior.

After 2 months, share with your spouse aspects of intimacy dates that you appreciate and want to continue. If there is something about intimacy dates you find off-putting or counterproductive, disclose that along with a specific suggestion of how to make the date comfortable and inviting. How do you integrate intimacy so that sexual desire is enhanced? Being an intimate couple promotes desire, sexual satisfaction, and marital happiness.

for better or worse

The United States has the highest divorce rate among developed countries. Traditionally, stability was taken for granted, no matter what the quality of the marriage. People tolerated physically abusive, alcoholic, incestuous, emotionally alienated, and dysfunctional marriages because of family, cultural, economic, and religious pressures to stay together. Destructive marriages continued "for the sake of the children" or the vow "for better or worse." No-sex marriages, low-sex marriages, sexually dysfunctional marriages, or marriages where intimacy needs were negated were tolerated. We are in favor of revitalizing marriages and reducing the divorce rate, but the pendulum should not swing back to the self-defeating ideology of staying in a destructive or fatally flawed marriage.

A healthy marriage involves both satisfaction and stability. Successful marriages that survive a no-sex phase (whether for 8 months or a marriage that was not consummated for 8 years) possess healthy sources of motivation. These include supporting each other through difficult times, being good parents, sharing a dream of a house or a business, dealing with a chronic problem in a supportive manner, overcoming poverty or alcoholism, receiving care and support from extended family, and having a religious or spiritual commitment to the marriage. There is a sense of pride in having survived and triumphed.

Often, the couple maintained a genuinely intimate, if not sexual, bond. Affection and physical closeness were a healthy resource. Couples who value emotional closeness and maintain respect and trust have a solid base from which to revitalize sexual intimacy. Religious or spiritual beliefs anchor the marital bond for many couples. These are positive prognostic signs for overcoming a no-sex or low-sex marriage. They persevered through better or worse, and it is for the better.

How can intimacy reinforce good experiences and feelings, while buffering the couple when problems recur? A prime function of intimacy is to generate special feelings. This is very different from "romantic love" feelings that are celebrated in songs, movies, and novels. The promise of romantic love is that there will be only better, not worse. Romantic love couples do not survive a no-sex or low-sex period.

Intimate couples have a special feeling about surviving a painful time. A sign of a viable marriage is the ability to cope with crisis and loss without destroying the bond of respect, trust, and intimacy. Intimate feelings are badly stressed by inhibited sexual desire and a no-sex marriage. As long as a sense of intimacy remains, sexual desire can be revitalized.

You do not want to again stress your marital bond. Intimacy dates are a powerful strategy to prevent relapse. When you value the spouse and marriage, it is hard to deny and avoid sexual issues. The function of intimacy is to energize the marital bond, generating special feelings about the spouse and marriage. Intimacy has the protective function of not allowing the couple to ignore or avoid critical issues.

Intimacy dates are not sufficient to promote sexual desire, but do establish a base for physical connection. For many couples, intimacy dates are the easiest bridge to sexual desire. For example, the couple talks over a cup of coffee or while gardening—a special time together. Later that day it is easier to initiate sex. You can have a drink on the deck or put on music and dance—an intimate way of being together that flows into a sexual encounter.

Couples who are separated by business travel find intimacy dates a more successful way to reconnect than having intercourse. It is harder to turn on sexually when you feel emotionally unconnected. Passionate coming together works better for unmarried (or maybe it is just in the movies) than for married couples. Intimacy dates provide a means to feel emotionally connected and enjoy affectionate touch. This leads to a sexual encounter that day or the next. Both emotionally and physically, intimacy serves a bridging function. When Barry returns from a trip, it is rare for us to be sexual that night. Typically, the next morning we have an intimacy date—go for a walk or bike ride and then out to breakfast. This serves as a bridge to being sexual later that day.

closing thoughts

Overcoming a no-sex or low-sex marriage and revitalizing sexual desire almost invariably include increased intimacy. One of the best ways to ensure that you will maintain and generalize sexual gains is to recognize and reinforce the vital role of emotional and sexual intimacy. A key is to recognize that not all intimacy can or should result in intercourse. Intimacy is a prime bridge for sexual desire, but not its major function. Time to emotionally share, touch, enjoy, and experience sensuality is crucial in maintaining a vital marriage. Intimacy is not the sole bridge to sexual desire, but is an important bridge. Intimacy dates can be planned or spontaneous, at home or going out, initiated by one spouse or mutual, and involve half an hour or a whole weekend. Some intimacy dates will be nonphysical, some affectionate, some sensual, some playful, some erotic, and some include intercourse. Intimacy dates are a prime means to generalize gains and prevent relapse.

CHAPTER 13

The Ninth Step: Lusting for Life—The Erotic Marriage

Cᴀɴ ᴍᴀʀʀɪᴇᴅ ꜱᴇx be erotic? We hope we successfully answered that question in chapter 10, "Making It Special: Creating Erotic Scenarios." Can marriage remain erotic? Not only can it, but it is in your best interest to maintain an erotic marriage. Much of this book has focused on intimacy, nondemand pleasuring, and bridges to sexual desire. Intimacy, anticipation, touch, and pleasure are the bedrock for maintaining gains. However, they are not enough for arousal and orgasm. Eroticism is integral to sexual satisfaction and relapse prevention.

People associate "hot" or "passionate" sex with a new, intense, illicit relationship—a premarital or extramarital affair. These are powerful, but unstable and transitory, sexual experiences. "Hot" sex connotes the "fun but dirty" approach of X-rated movies, sex shops, and non–socially desirable exploits. Eroticism is associated with premarital sex, extramarital sex, and kinky sex. Is it naive to believe that married sex can remain erotic? We are convinced—theoretically, empirically, and in our lives—that sex in an intimate marriage can be creative, erotic, exciting, and satisfying. Keeping marital sex erotic is a powerful strategy for preventing relapse. Ideally, the basis is an emotionally intimate, secure marital bond with a solid foundation in nondemand pleasuring. Erotic scenarios and techniques are the crucial ingredients that promote desire, arousal, and orgasm.

It is not technique alone—or even primarily—that eroticizes sexuality. Eroticism is enhanced by spontaneity, playfulness, experimentation, but, above all, awareness of feelings and openness to creative expression.

An erotic marriage is based on three sources: awareness of feelings, thoughts, and fantasies; a dynamic process between you and your spouse that includes touching, teasing, and seductiveness; and openness to experimenting with erotic scenarios and techniques. Be aware of sexual feelings and desires and take the risk to play them out. Do not worry about performing to the standard of a Hollywood movie. Share and enjoy the pleasures of eroticism.

For marital sex to remain vital, you need to challenge routine, mechanical sex, which is the death knell of desire. Eroticism calls for creativity, energy, and expression. Eroticism cannot be taken for granted, nor can it rest on its laurels. Be aware of and communicate erotic feelings, thoughts, and fantasies. Eroticism elicits sexual desire and builds anticipation. Touching, teasing, and seductiveness are enticing, adding spice and adventure to marital sexuality. Romantic, seductive, or playful touch is not reserved for premarital or extramarital affairs, it is an integral component of marital sex. The core of erotic marriage is openness to a variety of sexual scenarios and techniques, which builds anticipation. Whether this occurs once a month or seven times a year, sharing creative, erotic scenarios allows you to feel like a vital sexual couple. This is a powerful antidote against regressing to a no-sex or low-sex marriage.

the myth behind extramarital affairs

Cultural attitudes toward extramarital affairs are schizophrenic—on one hand, affairs are viewed as immoral and a reason to terminate the marriage and, on the other hand, as seductive, erotic, and a way to break out of the doldrums of marriage. On daytime soap operas, marriage is the kiss of death. The couple is either written off the show or have an affair to generate excitement and drama. Affairs offer tension, conflict, and suspense to novels and movies. Without the torment of affairs, country music would lose its best-selling theme.

Often the crisis leading to a no-sex marriage is the discovery of an extramarital affair. The most common therapeutic strategy is to deal with the meaning of the affair and rebuild the trust bond. Couples make a firm commitment to not have another affair. If a potential high-risk situation arises, the partner agrees to discuss it beforehand with the spouse. This is a powerful technique for confronting a potential affair. People talk about a high-opportunity affair as being "swept away" by romantic or lustful feelings. With this technique, you make a planned decision in choosing to have or not have an affair. This means assuming responsibility for your sexual behavior. Discussing the meaning of an affair with the spouse raises consequences for you and the marriage. You do not just fall into a secretive affair.

Couples who value intimacy and sexual desire are strongly advised against extramarital affairs. Affairs have a high potential to subvert your marital bond.

Why are affairs erotic? Can you expect the same type of eroticism from the marriage? Extramarital affairs are erotic in the same way that premarital affairs are. Newness, illicitness, adventure, quest for acceptance, and excitement of the unknown drive an affair. By their nature, affairs are sexually fragile. When the partners move in together or marry, the sexual charge dissipates. Stability and security disrupt the eroticism. Erotic affairs have a high risk of turning into a no-sex or low-sex marriage.

Affairs and marriage are different experiences. There are three erotic strategies that married couples can learn from affairs (you do not have to have an affair to gain these insights): (1) the value of anticipation; (2) how to fantasize and plan a sexual encounter; and (3) that playfulness, creativity, and abandon enhance eroticism. A favorite example concerns people who meet at a hotel for an afternoon sexual tryst. Both partners have to set aside the time, have someone cover for them at work or for child emergencies, be assertive enough to ask for the day rate, and fantasize and anticipate the sexual encounter. This is not the "natural, spontaneous sex" of movies and soap operas. Yet it is very erotic. Why should this be the domain of nonmarried people? You do not have to pay for a hotel room—you could meet for an afternoon delight at home. On the other hand, why not meet the spouse at a hotel? A new setting can be erotic. Married couples can go to rustic inns, bed and breakfasts, or X-rated motels. One reason that sex is better on vacations or weekends away is that this allows you to be sexual in a new environment. Anticipating this getaway builds sexual desire. Some people (Barry is a good example) very much enjoy fantasizing and looking forward to intimate weekends. The setting and milieu facilitate special, erotic feelings. You feel playful and creative, free to let go. Creative, erotic sex can be maintained in a marriage—you do not need an affair.

EXERCISE—MAINTAINING AN EROTIC MARRIAGE

The best way to revitalize eroticism in marriage is to review the exercise from chapter 10, "Creating Erotic Scenarios." What did each spouse identify as special turn-ons? What were favorite erotic scenarios and techniques? Do these continue to elicit anticipation and desire? Be specific with your spouse about how to integrate eroticism into lovemaking so that it remains special. Are there erotic scenarios and techniques that previously elicited sexual desire, but no longer do? Do not be embarrassed; this is normal. Sexual techniques that felt erotic 5 years ago may now feel "worn out," even boring or mechanical. Not only can you drop these scenarios, we urge you to. Boring, routine, minimally involved sex subverts and destroys desire. Even if the sex is functional, it does not enhance desire or eroticism.

To maintain a creative, erotic marriage, put time and energy into sexuality. Each spouse suggests at least one and preferably three special turn-ons to experiment with during the next 6 months. Be clear and specific (writing it first makes it easier to discuss). Do not just say, "I want to try oral sex in the morning"; say, "I want us to shower the night before; wake me up by orally stimulating me." Do not say, "Be passive"; say, "Let me control this sexual scenario—put your hands behind your head or I can tie your hands with a silk scarf." Do not say, "Be natural"; say, "I want to try a sexual experience where we don't talk. Let's share erotic feelings through eye contact, movement, and touch."

Each spouse initiates at least one and up to three erotic scenarios. This could include a major external stimulus like planning a couple weekend, buying a VCR for the bedroom so that you can watch erotic videos, getting a hot tub, going on a camping trip and being sexual under the stars. More commonly, it is a nitty-gritty addition such as having a pillow with a message of "tonight" on one side and "sorry" on the other; a special light or scented candle in the bedroom; being sexual in the shower or bathtub; or using a vibrator, beads, or feathers for erotic stimulation.

The most common form of creative sexuality is a monthly sexual date, with freedom to play sensually and erotically, but with a prohibition on intercourse. Many couples find that this is their most fun time, sexually. You can experiment with alternative pleasuring positions, a new lotion, music, a different time of day, varying amounts of light, different types of clothing, one giving or mutual pleasuring to orgasm, or being turned on but not going to orgasm.

Sexual dates (whether planned or spontaneous) allow you to experiment with personal and external turn-ons to facilitate eroticism.

maintaining creative sexuality

The essence of creative sexuality is sharing yourself emotionally and sexually—sometimes warm, sometimes erotic, sometimes fun, sometimes lustful, a special intimacy. Sexuality is more than genitals, intercourse, and orgasm. Creative sexuality is usually mutual, with each partner contributing to the erotic scenario. Mutuality requires both verbal and nonverbal communication. When thoughts, feelings, and sexual expression flow, each spouse's arousal enhances the other's. This is an extension of the "give to get" pleasuring guideline—giving and sharing eroticism.

Couples have a favorite room (or rooms) for creative sexuality. For some, it is the bedroom; for others, it is the den, the living room, in front of the fireplace, or the guest room. Unlike with other exercises, we advise against a detailed scenario. Be open to your creative feelings. Let the sexual scenario be as free and playful as possible. Experiment with a multitude of positions—standing, lying, kneeling, and sitting. In creative sexuality, there are no artificial barriers between sex play and intercourse. Allow creative eroticism to flow into creative intercourse. Experiment with positions, multiple stimulation during intercourse, expressing feelings, and making requests. Intermix intercourse and nonintercourse sexuality. Creative sexuality does not end with orgasm. Enjoy afterplay. You can express affectionate, sensual, romantic, and playful feelings verbally and nonverbally.

JOHN AND JENNY

The fact that John and Jenny were married with a 2-year-old daughter and Jenny 5 months pregnant was a tribute to their love, commitment, and persistence. They met 15 years ago as sophomores at a state university, a typical romantic college couple. There was plenty of playfulness and romanticism. The quality of sex might not have been great, but it was frequent and exciting.

In the 5 years after college, John and Jenny were an on-again, off-again couple. The emotional turmoil of breaking up and getting back together provided drama and intrigue that allowed them to ignore intimacy issues. Jealousy and comparisons inherent in dating others provided an emotional and sexual charge. At 27 they began living together and, 3 years later, married. This dating and relationship pattern was common for their peer group. Another unfortunate commonality was that the best sex was while dating. Living together did not improve sexuality.

They married in spite of a poor sexual relationship. In the first 4 years of marriage, they had intercourse less than 25 times. Throughout living together and being married, they had been a no-sex couple. Jenny had an affair in the second year of the marriage (contrary to popular mythology, affairs are most likely to occur early, not late, in marriage). It was a brief affair with a married man from work. When John heard rumors of the affair, he was agitated, but not surprised. There was anger, but more angst with feelings of guilt and blaming. A side effect of the affair was to totally stop marital sex, which had been marginal anyway. For some couples, an affair is a wake-up call, an opportunity to revitalize intimacy and sexuality. For John and Jenny, it added to marital alienation and devitalization, serving as another reason to avoid sex.

They had tried individual, marital, and couples' group therapy before sex therapy. Individual therapy had been particularly valuable to John in challenging his depressive view of life and encouraging him to take career risks and switch to an organization that rewarded his innovative ideas. Marriage therapy and couples' group therapy served to normalize their struggles and reinforce that they were a viable couple. Unfortunately, it reinforced the mistaken view that sex would improve only when all the other emotional and marital issues had been dealt with. For the majority of couples, addressing sexual issues concurrently with emotional issues is the optimal strategy.

It is easier to conduct sex therapy with a committed couple than with a tenuous couple. John and Jenny entered sex therapy with a great deal of marital commitment, but with self-defeating sexual attitudes, feelings, and experiences. They were an affectionate couple, but not an erotic couple.

The structure of pleasuring exercises, followed by erotic exercises, was of great value. Jenny was responsive to the permission-giving aspects of sex therapy, especially to experimenting with erotic scenarios and techniques. She was turned on by playing out scenarios where she was the dominant partner. John was responsive and aroused by Jenny's arousal; her sexuality was an aphrodisiac for him. Jenny was afraid that to maintain erotic feelings, she would have to exaggerate the dominance scenarios, something she was not interested in. The therapist suggested that they continue to use erotic scenarios with a dominance theme, but to broaden them, not deepen them or make them extreme. Either spouse had a right to veto anything that was psychologically or sexually uncomfortable.

For John, the best way to maintain marital eroticism was by setting aside time for sexual dates. John enjoyed varied sexual experiences: sex in a hotel, sex at the in-laws' house (especially in the living room during the middle of the night), sex under the stars on a camping trip, sex in the middle of the day. Jenny could appreciate this, but for her eroticism was closer to home. Jenny felt that for sex to be an integral, vital part of the marriage, they had to be erotic at home with the reality of her pregnancy. Jenny would awaken early because of pressure on her bladder. If she could not go back to sleep, she would awaken John by sucking on his penis—she enjoyed seeing him in the combination of arousal and drowsiness. She liked the quickie intercourse of woman on top, where she did the thrusting. John was orgasmic and went back to sleep. Jenny cuddled against him, which allowed her to fall asleep.

People do not think of pregnancy as erotic, but maintaining emotional, affectionate, and sexual contact during pregnancy is important. The birth of a second child is a major transition for the marriage and family. Maintaining sexual vitality was a priority for Jenny and John. Jenny found the sitting-kneeling intercourse position particularly erotic and fulfilling. She looked forward to the third trimester to use this again. Jenny sits on a low slung chair with a pillow for back support and scoots to the end. There is no pressure on her stomach or on the fetus. John kneels in front of her with pillows under his knees for support; his penis is at the same height as her vulva. This position allows eye contact, both hands free for touching, and being able to kiss and caress and engage in genital stimulation. Jenny guides intromission. They enjoy additional erotic stimulation—John gives clitoral or breast stimulation, Jenny does testicle or buttock stimulation. They plan to continue using this position after the baby is born.

If Jenny does not feel like being sexual herself, she stimulates John to orgasm. Jenny enjoys one-way sex—feeling so much control over John's arousal and watching him just before orgasm is gratifying. John prefers mutual sex, but finds one-way sex erotic. John and Jenny feel more intimately connected than during the first pregnancy.

With two young children and two careers, they realize it will be a challenge to maintain a quality sexual relationship, but a challenge they are prepared to meet. Erotic scenarios and techniques are not the core of their intimate relationship, but an important component in keeping sexual desire vibrant. John and Jenny value intimacy, nondemand pleasuring, and eroticism.

special sexual experiences

Should every sexual experience be special? That is a self-defeating expectation. In truth, even for well-functioning couples, less than half of the time is there equal desire, arousal, and orgasm. Positive, realistic expectations promote sexual satisfaction. Forty to 50 percent of sexual experiences are very good for both spouses; of these, 5 to 10 percent are special. If you have one or two special sexual experiences a month, you can count yourselves lucky. Quite a different way of thinking from the way sex is portrayed in movies or soap operas, where it is always perfect and special. Our concepts will not sell songs or movies, but they fit the reality for married couples and enhance martial satisfaction.

What makes a sexual experience special? It is the feelings, not the technique or the orgasm. Sometimes feelings are intensely sexual— high arousal, letting go, experiencing sexual abandon, feeling free. Sometimes feelings are intensely intimate—loving, feeling desire, closeness, pride in overcoming inhibitions, self-validation, satisfaction with the spouse and marriage. Special sexual experiences energize your intimate bond—like a shot of adrenaline. If each encounter was highly erotic, it would feel less special.

Creative sexuality is sometimes a special experience, sometimes very good, sometimes satisfactory, and sometimes a bust. We encourage couples to take sexual risks, but there are no guarantees the risk will result in a special erotic experience or even a successful one. This is not to discourage sexual risks or creative sexuality. You will not have special erotic experiences unless you are willing to take risks and play sexually.

An advantage of intimate marriage is that you can risk failure without being embarrassed or frightened of the spouse's reaction. Trust in the spouse allows you to share feelings, your body, and eroticism. This results in intense feelings, creative experiences, and special sexual encounters. Other times it results in failure, we hope with the ability to laugh or shrug off stupid or silly experiences.

Intimacy and special feelings are more important than the sex itself. Couples feel closer and more open during pleasuring and afterplay than during intercourse. An insight from one of Barry's clients was, "Intercourse and orgasm are great, but they're only a small part of making love." For us, a special part of a sexual experience is taking a walk and talking afterward. Afterplay is a positive, integral component of lovemaking. Integration of erotic and intimate feelings facilitates special experiences that you remember for months and even years.

making requests for special turn-ons

How can you make clear, erotic requests without these becoming self-conscious demands? One technique is to separate verbal requests from the sexual interaction. One of the worst times to talk sex is in bed right after a sexual experience. You do not need an instant replay with a detailed critique. Some of the best places to talk sex are on walks, in the car during a long drive, sitting on the porch, and over the kitchen table. Some of the best times are the day before a sexual experience, an hour before a sexual date, the next morning, and on Thursday before going away for a couple weekend. Make requests for special turn-ons in a comfortable, anticipatory manner that invites your spouse to be open, experimental and playful.

The main miscommunication regarding sexual turn-ons is that the spouse feels pressure to perform and give you exactly what you want.

Rather than being a sexual sharing, it feels like a coerced performance. To stay away from that trap, be clear that your request is to engage with your spouse so that pleasure and eroticism are enhanced. Experience this together—be open to your spouse's feelings and desires. Direct or indirect coercion has no place in marital sexuality.

Special turn-ons keep your sexual relationship vital and exciting. Marital sexuality is different from premarital sex or extramarital affairs. Special turn-ons promote integration of intimacy with eroticism. Some turn-ons remain vital for 20 years or longer. More commonly, the couple adds or revises sexual scenarios and turn-ons so that these retain their erotic capacity. It is like cooking a special meal; over time you like to spice up the ingredients. Special turn-ons involve experimentation and playfulness; they cannot stand on past laurels.

Creative sexuality and special turn-ons are not the same, but are related. Both require openness to your own and your spouse's feelings. Both require taking risks and making requests. Because special turn-ons are specific and planned, there is potential for awkwardness, self-consciousness, and performance pressure. If you value an erotic marriage, experimenting with special turn-ons and encouraging the spouse to be an involved sexual friend are crucial. This is the best way to combat self-consciousness.

Creative sexuality is a team effort. It is normal for some experiences to be more erotic for one spouse than for the other. The main aphrodisiac is an aroused partner; your arousal is arousing for your spouse. This is another example of the "give to get" pleasuring guideline. Her arousal will increase his arousal. When he was 20, the man's arousal was autonomous, needing nothing from the woman. Beginning in the mid-30s and increasing with age, male arousal is enhanced by the woman's arousal. By the 50s, female arousal is easier and more predictable than male arousal. The wife's special turn-ons are good not only for her, but for the man and their marriage.

The prescription for healthy sexuality—integrating intimacy, non-demand pleasuring, and erotic scenarios and techniques—reaches fruition as the couple ages. The importance of creative sexuality and special turn-ons increases with both the age of the couple and the age of the marriage.

closing thoughts

Bridges to sexual desire, intimacy dates, and nondemand pleasuring are major strategies to maintain marital sexuality. Yet the importance of erotic scenarios and techniques cannot be underestimated. Seeing yourselves as an erotic couple and enjoying arousal and orgasm play integral roles in maintaining a sexually vital marriage. Erotic dates keep sex special and energize your intimate bond. Creative sexuality and special turn-ons ignite marital sex. Eroticism is not the core of sexual desire, but is an integral component. You owe it to yourself and your spouse to maintain an erotic marriage.

CHAPTER 14

The Tenth Step: Your Parents Were Wrong—Valuing Marital Sexuality

INHIBITED SEXUAL DESIRE and a no-sex or low-sex marriage pose a major threat to marital satisfaction and viability. When sexuality is pleasurable and functional, it is a positive, integral part of marriage, but not a dominant factor, contributing 15 to 20 percent to marital vitality and satisfaction. The main functions of marital sexuality are to create a shared pleasure, a means to deepen and reinforce intimacy, and a tension-reducer to cope with the stresses of life and marriage. Sexuality energizes and makes special your marital bond. Sexuality that is dysfunctional, inhibited, or nonexistent plays an inordinately powerful role. It becomes 50 to 70 percent of the marriage, draining intimacy and good feelings. Paradoxically, bad sex has a more powerful negative role in marriage than the positive role of good sex.

This book has presented concepts, strategies, techniques, guidelines, exercises, and case studies to help you understand and change inhibited sexual desire. Knowledge and awareness are necessary, but not sufficient, to address the complex problem of low-sex and no-sex marriages. Intimacy and sexuality are best understood as a couple issue. It is crucial to maintain motivation so that the problem is resolved and marital sexuality revitalized.

Once the self-defeating pattern of the no-sex or low-sex marriage is broken, do not be passive and expect sexuality to take care of itself. Your sexual relationship needs continual thought, communication, energy, and time. Sexuality cannot rest on its laurels. We have been married 36 years and still need to devote time and energy to maintain sexuality as a positive, integral part of our lives and relationship. A desirous, arousing, orgasmic, and emotionally satisfying sexuality energizes and makes special your marital bond. Intimacy and sexuality keep marriage vital and special.

Couples with a satisfying sexual relationship and no dysfunction still have to put time and energy into sexuality. The movie, media, love song, and fiction approach to sexuality sells products, but leads to self-defeating, unrealistic expectations. Acceptance of sexual variability and flexibility helps maintain positive, realistic expectations. Your comfort with, anticipation of, and feeling that you deserve sexual pleasure are the bedrock of marital sexuality.

You cannot wait for everything to be perfect before you are ready to be sexual. Do not expect every experience to be perfect. Mutual desire, arousal, orgasm, and satisfaction are ideal, but in truth, sex is not always equal and mutual. Quality of the sexual experience is more important than frequency of intercourse. Do not allow sex to fade away. Touching occurs both inside and outside of the bedroom. Sometimes it is affectionate touch to maintain contact, sometimes sensual touch, sometimes playful touch, sometimes erotic touch, and sometimes intercourse touch. Both spouses are committed to maintaining a vital sexual bond. Try to go no longer than 2 weeks without some kind of sexual contact. Marital sex cannot be taken for granted or treated with benign neglect. Sexuality requires time, communication, and energy.

If this is true for couples who have no sexual problems, it is crucial for couples with a history of inhibited sexual desire. Maintaining a vital sexual bond and preventing relapse are both individual and couple commitments. When sex functions as a shared pleasure, a means to reinforce intimacy, and a tension-reducer to deal with the stresses of life and the relationship, you have a powerful marital resource. When you maintain an intimate sexual connection through good and bad times, you can be confident (although do not become overconfident) that sexuality will continue to nurture and energize your marital bond.

how much intimacy?
how much sexuality?

At the beginning of this book we discussed couple styles (complementary, best friend, conflict-minimizing, emotionally expressive). Each couple develops and individualizes a couple style. A crucial dimension is finding a mutually comfortable level of intimacy. Lack of intimacy and not valuing the marriage are self-defeating. However, the opposite is not true. People who say the only thing that matters in life is marriage, give up individuality for coupleness, strive for intimacy at the cost of personal well-being, or believe that sex six times a week is more important than anything else are setting themselves up for failure. The key is finding a healthy balance between autonomy and intimacy—more intimacy is not necessarily better. This is even truer for sexuality; more is not necessarily better. Being sexual six times a week is not necessarily better than being sexual twice a week, and for many couples can be destructive.

How does a couple reach a comfortable understanding about intimacy? It is easier to say what not to do. Do not elevate intimacy into the test of marriage. Do not sacrifice individuality. Do not confuse intimacy and intercourse. Do not treat intimacy solely as a "feel good" concept. What to do? Each spouse honestly asks herself or himself what is a healthy balance between autonomy and coupleness. This is not a matter of being "politically correct" or giving the "socially desirable" response, but of what fits each individual and the marriage.

In our marriage we share almost all thoughts and feelings about emotional, psychological, and sexual issues. We have a female friend whose parents had a bitter divorce in which emotional secrets were exposed in a hostile divorce litigation. Although she trusted her husband and is committed to her marriage, she does not share emotionally sensitive issues with him (yet she does discuss these with female friends). We have as friends a couple that shares a great deal emotionally, relationally, and parentally. However, their financial lives, especially investments and retirement funds, are handled separately. Theirs is a strongly held philosophical position. They do not respect partners who are dependent on one another financially (which includes us). A last example is a couple in which the man travels extensively on business—he is out of town at least half the time. Their agreement is that when they are together, their relationship is a priority. When apart, they have separate lives, which includes not asking questions about what they do or how they spend their time. Many married couples (including us) would find this unacceptable, but it has worked well for this couple.

Each person needs to ascertain whether there are prerogatives and feelings he or she will keep separate from the marital bond. We advocate telling your spouse about this parameter, but many people prefer that it remain implicit. We suggest two guidelines. First, be sure that maintaining autonomy in this area(s) is in your best interest, not a defensive or avoidant reaction. Second, be sure that this parameter does not undermine couple intimacy and sexuality. You can integrate autonomy and intimacy in a manner that facilitates self-esteem and marital sexuality. Psychological well-being is enhanced by valuing both self-esteem and an intimate marriage. These are complementary, not antagonistic.

Autonomy involves individual needs, preferences, and desires. Intimacy involves couple understandings and agreements, thus establishing a comfortable, viable level of connection. Do you want a "best friend" level of intimacy? This is the cultural ideal and the model we adopt in our marriage, but is not the right model for the majority of couples. This is especially true for couples with a history of inhibited sexual desire. Often the sexual problem was compounded by unrealistically high expectations about intimacy, which resulted in hurt, anger, blaming, and devaluing the marriage.

Striving for the maximum amount of intimacy is the wrong strategy for most couples. A healthier strategy is to develop a comfortable level of intimacy that balances autonomy and coupleness. Be sure that this level of intimacy supports sexual desire. For many couples, intimacy is the main bridge for desire; for others, intimacy is a lesser factor. What is comfortable and healthy for you?

accepting and valuing

A common cultural myth is that women value marriage, men value sex. Marriages are healthier when the man and woman value both emotional and sexual intimacy. The culture and media emphasize gender differences (even gender wars). This is not scientifically true, nor does it promote marital or sexual satisfaction. Marriages where both spouses value intimacy and both value sexuality do not regress to a no-sex state.

Divorce is hard on both men and women, but, contrary to popular mythology, it is more difficult for men. Physical and mental health for never-married or divorced men is poorer than for married men. Men are more likely to remarry than are women. The data are clear. Men need marriage. If that is so, why is it that men do not put a high value on marriage? Valuing one's wife and marital sexuality is not part of the masculine image. Men in second marriages are more likely to value this marriage than are men in first marriages.

Valuing a marriage is not contingent on the spouse or marriage being perfect. Valuing means that you accept, respect, and care about the spouse and marriage, with its strengths and weaknesses, special characteristics, and vulnerabilities.

Contrary to cultural myths, women value sexuality as much as men. One reason that sex therapy is more acceptable to women is the emphasis on broad-based sensual and sexual expression, integrating intimacy and sexuality. Valuing touch—affectionate, sensual, playful, erotic, and intercourse—goes a long way toward building and maintaining sexual desire. A major barrier to valuing sexuality was the wife's belief that sex had to be on the husband's terms—"Real sex is intercourse and orgasm." We are strong advocates of intercourse and orgasm, but there is more to "real sex" than that. The core of sexuality is giving and receiving pleasure-oriented touching. Desire, intimacy, pleasure, and satisfaction are more important than intercourse and orgasm. Sexuality is not like money—there is not a competition where one wins, one loses, and there is one objective measure. Sexuality is not a zero-sum game. Individual sexuality is an integration of attitudes, behavior, and feelings. At its core, sexuality is a couple, rather than an individual, concept. Sexual satisfaction involves subjective feelings, not frequency of intercourse or number of orgasms. The more you accept the importance of broad-based sexuality, the stronger will be your bond. This inoculates you against sexual dysfunction and inhibited sexual desire as you and your marriage age.

the importance of being an intimate team

Valuing intimate sexuality, accepting broad-based sexuality and having a variable, flexible sexual repertoire that includes affectionate, sensual, playful, erotic, and intercourse touch are crucial. The intimate team concept is the core factor in maintaining a healthy sexual bond. A major roadblock is the traditional male–female double standard. The male is afraid that accepting the team approach is giving in to his wife, it makes him less of a man, and there will be less intercourse and fewer orgasms. He resentfully holds on to the narrow definition of sex as intercourse. Barry heard a man say, "We haven't had sex in 3 years, so she owes me 156 orgasms." What a self-defeating approach.

Sexuality is integral to who you are as a man, a woman, and a couple. The issue is how to express affection, sensuality, playfulness, eroticism, and intercourse so that these promote desire and satisfaction. When you both value touching and being an intimate team, you will have a viable, satisfying, secure marriage.

These concepts are of particular value for individuals with a history of negative or traumatic sexual experiences. Those include childhood sexual abuse, incest, rape, being sexually humiliated or rejected, a painful divorce, being sexually harassed, dealing with an unwanted pregnancy or sexually transmitted disease, and guilt over masturbation or fantasies. Feeling responsible for sexuality in the context of an intimate marriage is validating. You no longer feel victimized and controlled by past trauma. You are a survivor who deserves sexual pleasure. Sexuality enhances your life and your intimate relationship. One of the most healing and healthy cognitions is "Living well is the best revenge."

Negative sexual experiences or traumatic incidents can occur in childhood, adolescence, young adulthood, or adulthood. It happens to men as well as women. Inhibited sexual desire and a no-sex or low-sex marriage compound past negative sexual experiences. Take responsibility for your sexuality, take pride in being a survivor, trust that the spouse is your intimate friend, enjoy touching and pleasure, and see sexuality as something that enhances your life and marriage. Intimate sexuality is a personal victory and source of pride for the survivor and the marriage.

Negative experiences affect couples, not just individuals. Couples with a history of alienation, drug or alcohol abuse, affairs and distrust, separation and threats, physical or emotional abuse, or sexual coercion take special pride in overcoming these problems and becoming an intimate, secure couple. These painful experiences would have broken up less caring, committed people. Having survived and developed an intimate, satisfying marriage is a source of personal and couple pride.

Abusive or destructive marriages are not worth maintaining. A marriage that negates one or both people's psychological well-being should be ended, not saved.

You have worked as an intimate team to address, understand, and change destructive emotional and sexual patterns. You could not do this alone; you needed the support and involvement of the spouse. Together, you have revitalized your marriage. Reestablishing intimacy and sexuality is a couple task. This is even truer in maintaining an intimate, sexually satisfying marriage. Both spouses valuing intimacy and eroticism reinforces sexual desire and functioning.

accepting nonperfect sexuality

Barry's clinical work has convinced him that no couple has a perfect marriage or a perfect sex life. One of Emily's pet peeves with self-help books is that they overpromise a perfect solution for everyone. This is intimidating, making partners less accepting of their marriage and marital sexuality. Our joke is that because we do not have a perfect marriage or perfect sex, why should anyone else?

All marriages have strengths and weaknesses (as do all individuals). There are *no* couples who report equal desire, arousal, orgasm, and satisfaction *every* time. Human sexuality is inherently flexible and variable. Key to maintaining sexual desire is anticipating sexual pleasure and having positive, realistic expectations. Perfectionism is poison for sexual desire. Sexual competition or comparing yourselves to an ideal couple subverts desire. The myth that sex should compensate for past marital problems robs your relationship of intimacy and pleasure. Acknowledge changes, enjoy pleasure and eroticism, commit time and energy to maintain an intimate bond, enhance your couple style, do not strive to be perfect, do not make comparisons to other couples, and do not try to compensate for the past.

A common anxiety is that if you are not hypervigilant, you will regress to a dysfunctional or at least boring sexual relationship. How much is enough? How do you know when you are "accepting," as opposed to "settling" or "giving up"? What are positive, realistic expectations for intimacy and sexuality?

All couples need to establish a comfortable, satisfying style for themselves, not in comparison to a perfect ideal, a romantic love fantasy, or guidelines we propose. Broad-based sexuality facilitates enjoyment of affectionate, sensual, playful, erotic, and intercourse touching. Intimacy and sexuality help you accept and value the spouse and marriage, not be a drain or source of stress. Sexuality energizes and makes special your marital bond.

Couples with a history of inhibited sexual desire seldom consider sexuality the forté of their marriage. However, in happy marriages sexuality is a positive and integral part of your marital bond. Sexuality is now 15 to 20 percent of your marriage. Sexuality has become a shared pleasure, it reinforces intimacy, and it serves as a tension-reducer (rather than as a source of tension). No longer do inhibited desire and sexual conflict play a dominant role in your lives and marriage. Intimacy and sexuality reinforce marital vitality and satisfaction. If this is not true for you, we strongly suggest marital or sex therapy. Having read this material gives you better understanding and resources for change. Therapy provides the motivation to address complex problems and frustrations, deal with setbacks, and individualize the change process. Appendix 2 provides information about choosing a marital or sex therapist.

In rereading the book, Emily felt that we had done a good job describing the problem of low-sex and no-sex marriages. Inhibited sexual desire has been shadowed by embarrassment, shame, guilt, and stigma. What a paradox that a problem that affects 40 to 60 million Americans has been shrouded in secrecy and denial. Throughout, Emily has advocated respect for individual differences, values, and life situations. Barry has emphasized sexual strategies and techniques for changing and enhancing intimacy and sexuality. Emily revised by emphasizing complexity, individual differences, and resolutions that are not as complete or satisfying as hoped. Intimacy and sexuality have many causes and dimensions, with individual, cultural, and value differences. You are an individual and your marriage is unique—choose what fits you, not in comparison to anyone else or even to our models and guidelines.

You owe it to yourself and your marriage to use the resources necessary to feel good (not perfect) about intimacy and sexuality.

valuing marital sexuality, not just sexuality

In revitalizing marital sexuality, being an intimate team is crucial. A 43-year-old man who developed an erection problem and inhibited sexual desire after he stopped drinking said that if it were just having orgasms, he would not have cared about revitalizing marital sexuality. Since age 14, he had always associated sex with alcohol abuse. He did not know how to be sexual in a sober state and at 43 had little desire to learn. He was afraid that frustrations about erectile dysfunction and feelings of humiliation would lead him back to alcoholism. This viewpoint was reinforced by his AA sponsor and most group members. Sex is not a major topic at AA meetings because so many recovering alcoholics associate sex with drinking. They fear that sexual problems will destabilize their lives and recovery.

With the help of his wife and a couple therapist, he realized there was a whole world of intimacy and sexuality to be explored. He learned that sexuality is more than penis, intercourse, and orgasm. He felt better about himself, the spouse, and their marriage as he became more comfortable with intimate, flexible sexuality.

He could no longer depend on alcohol to lower inhibitions, which allowed him to feel sexually free. He was afraid he would be stuck at the opposite extreme—inhibited, self-conscious, obsessed with his penis, and failing at intercourse. He, with his wife's active involvement, learned a new style of pleasure-oriented touching. He became comfortable with affection, sensuality, and erotic stimulation. They enjoyed a broad, flexible couple sexual style that included intercourse and orgasm, but not as the sole means of being sexual. Intimacy and sharing pleasure were more important than intercourse. This involved major changes in the wife's view of sexuality. Although she enjoyed the intimate, erotic, and flexible aspects of their sexuality, she missed (as did he) easy, predictable intercourse.

If it were just sex—desire, easy arousal, intercourse, and predictable orgasms—most couples would give up on sex after a few years of marriage. If it were just orgasm, people would masturbate rather than have couple sex. Masturbation is easier, more controllable, predictable, and reliable than partner sex. Intimacy and sexuality have multiple dimensions and meanings. Sexuality is more about desire and satisfaction than are intercourse and orgasm. Quality is more important than frequency. Sexuality is to reinforce, energize, and make special your marital bond. At its core, marriage is a respectful, trusting friendship that requires emotional and sexual intimacy to thrive. A marriage can survive without orgasm; it cannot survive without touching and emotional connection.

What does this mean in terms of you valuing marital sexuality? Establishing an intimate connection that includes affectionate, sensual, playful, erotic, and intercourse touch is crucial; it is especially draining when this connection is absent. Ideally, you would have a vibrant sexual relationship, with easy arousal and orgasm. However, that is the exception, not the norm. There is not "one right way to be sexual." Couples develop their unique style of intimacy and eroticism. It is crucial to affirm that you are an intimate team. Pleasure-oriented touching is integral to your marital bond. Broad-based, flexible sexuality is valued by both spouses. Try to maintain erotic contact at least twice a month. Not all touching has to or should culminate in intercourse—touching is valued for itself, as affection, a way to connect, an erotic stimulus, and a bridge for sexual desire.

A major characteristic of couples who overcome a no-sex or low-sex marriage is increased self-acceptance. You no longer need to prove something to yourself or your spouse. You are committed to maintaining an intimate, sexual marriage. The focus is on sexual quality and connection more than on intercourse frequency. You do not compare yourselves to a romantic movie ideal or to the sexual high of a new couple. Value the quality of your intimate marriage. Enjoy what is happening at present; you do not need to compensate for the past.

closing thoughts

An intimate, satisfying marriage is highly valued by both people. You take pride in overcoming inhibited sexual desire and a no-sex or low-sex marriage. Marriage and sexuality need continued time and psychological energy. Sexuality plays a vital, integral role in marital satisfaction as a shared pleasure, a means to reinforce intimacy, and a tension-reducer when dealing with the stresses of life and marriage. Broad-based sexuality enhances special feelings and energizes your marital bond.

It takes courage to confront and change inhibited sexual desire and a no-sex or low-sex marriage. You deserve credit for facing this secret, stigmatizing problem. Easy solutions, total cures, and "happy ever after" stories are for novels and movies, not real-life couples. Maintaining intimacy and sexuality is a couple task. Enjoy pleasure-oriented sexuality that is flexible and broad-based. You owe it to yourself, your spouse, and your marital bond to maintain a vital sexual intimacy.

APPENDIX 1

Choosing a Marital or Sexual Therapist

As STATED IN THE first chapter, this is not a do-it-yourself therapy book. Couples are reluctant to consult a therapist, feeling that to do so is a sign of "craziness," a confession of inadequacy, or an admission that their relationship is in dire straits. In reality, seeking professional help is a sign of psychological strength. Entering marital or sex therapy means that you realize there is a problem and you have made a commitment to resolve the issues and promote marital and sexual growth.

The mental health field can be confusing. Marital and sex therapy are clinical subspecialties. They are offered by several groups of professionals, which include psychologists, social workers, marriage therapists, psychiatrists, and pastoral counselors. The professional background of the practitioner is of less importance than her or his competency in dealing with your specific problem.

Many people have health insurance that provides coverage for mental health and thus can afford the services of a private practitioner. Those who do not have either the financial resources or insurance could consider a city or county mental health clinic, a university or medical school mental health outpatient clinic, or a family services center. Clinics usually have a sliding fee scale (i.e., the fee is based on your ability to pay).

When choosing a therapist, be assertive in asking about credentials and areas of expertise. Ask the clinician what percentage of her or his patients remain married, how long therapy can be expected to last, and whether the focus is specifically on sexual problems or more generally on communication or relationship issues. A competent therapist will be open to discussing these issues. Be especially diligent in questioning credentials, such as university degrees and licensing. Be wary of people who call themselves personal counselors, marriage counselors, or sex counselors. There are poorly qualified persons—and some outright quacks—in any field.

One of the best resources for obtaining a referral is to call a local professional organization such as a psychological association, marriage and family therapy association, mental health association, or mental health clinic. You can ask for a referral from a family physician, minister, or friend. For a specific sex therapy referral, you can contact the American Association of Sex Educators, Counselors, and Therapists through the Internet at Aasect.org for its therapist referral network, or write or call for a list of certified sex therapists in your area—P.O. Box 5488, Richmond, VA 23220, 804–644–3288. You can also contact The American board of Sexology through the internet at sexologist.com to find a practitioner in your area. For a marriage therapist, you could check the Internet site for the American Association of Marriage and Family Therapy at Therapistlocator.net.

Feel free to talk with two or three therapists before deciding on one with whom to work. Be aware of comfort with the therapist, degree of rapport, and whether the therapist's assessment of the problem and approach to treatment make sense to you. Once you begin, give therapy a chance to be helpful. There are few miracle cures. Change requires commitment and is a gradual and often difficult process. Although some individuals benefit from short-term therapy (fewer than 10 sessions), most people find that the therapeutic process will take 4 months to a year or longer. The role of the therapist is that of a consultant, rather than of a decision maker. Therapy requires effort, both in the session and at home. Therapy helps to change attitudes, feelings, and behavior. Do not be afraid to seek professional help to revitalize your marital and sexual bond.

APPENDIX 2

Books for Further Reading

Butler, & Lewis, M. (2002). *The new love and sex after sixty*. New York: Ballantine.

Ellison, C. (2001). *Women's sexualities*. Oakland, CA: New Harbinger.

Foley, S., Kope, S., & Sugrue, D. (2002). *Sex matters for women*. New York: Guilford.

Goodwin, A., & Agronin, M. (1998). *A woman's guide to overcoming sexual fear and pain*. Oakland, CA: New Harbinger.

Gordon, S. (1990). *Why love is not enough*. Boston: Bob Adams.

Hafner, D. (2002). *From diapers to dating*. New York: Newmarket.

Heiman, J., & LoPiccolo, J. (1988). *Becoming orgasmic*. New York: Prentice-Hall.

Leiblum, S., & Sachs, J. (2002). *Getting the sex you want*. New York: Crown.

Maltz, W. (2001). *The sexual healing journey*. New York: HarperCollins.

McCarthy, B., & McCarthy, E. (1998). *Male sexual awareness*. New York: Carroll and Graf.

McCarthy, B., & McCarthy, E. (1998). *Couple sexual awareness*. New York: Carroll and Graf.

McCarthy, B., & McCarthy, E. (2002). *Sexual awareness: Couple sexuality for the twenty-first century*. New York: Carroll and Graf.

Michael, R., Gagnon, J., Laumann, E., & Kalota, G. (1994). *Sex in America*. Boston: Little, Brown.

Zilbergeld, B. (1997). *The new male sexuality*. New York: Bantam.

Zoldbrod, A. (1998). *Sex smart*. Oakland, CA: New Harbinger.